ENGLAND'S PRINCES OF WALES

England's Princes of Wales

by Annette Joelson

DORSET PRESS
New York

This edition published by Dorset Press,
a division of Marboro Books Corporation,
by arrangement with
John Francis Marion.
1991 Dorset Press

ISBN 0-88029-670-4

Printed in the United States of America

M 9 8 7 6 5 4 3 2 1

FOR PETER AND CHRISTINE

AUTHOR'S NOTE

This story of the Princes of Wales is based entirely on published material, on diaries, memoirs, letters, autobiographies, biographies, state papers, and the writings of scholars, historians, and chroniclers. I gratefully acknowledge my debt to all the authors, editors, and publishers mentioned in the Bibliography. I have, wherever possible, indicated in the body of the book the sources of long quotations and, in addition, I wish to express my thanks for the brief quotations and phrases culled from the following authoritative works: *Edward of Caernarvon* by Miss Hilda Johnstone; *The Black Prince* by Mr. John Cammidge; *Catherine of Aragon* by Mr. Garrett Mattingley; *Palace Extraordinary* by Mr. Charles Graves; *Jacobean Pageant* by Mr. G. P. V. Akrigg; *The Tragedy of Charles II* by Miss Hester W. Chapman; *Royal Dukes, George IV,* and *Hanover to Windsor* by Mr. Roger Fulford; *The House of Hanover* by Mr. Alvin Redman; *The Hanoverians* by Mr. V. H. H. Green; and *The Four Georges* by Sir Charles Petrie.

With sincere pleasure I also wish to record my gratitude to Mr. P. W. Hasler who read and corrected my manuscript and to whom I am indebted for invaluable advice.

CONTENTS

[History] hath triumphed over Time, which besides it nothing but Eternity hath triumphed over.

Sir Walter Raleigh
(From the Preface to his
History of the World)

श्री

PART ONE: PROUD PRINCES

PART ONE: PROUD PRINCES

Long before there was an English Prince of Wales there were princes *in* Wales and a century before England achieved national unity under one king, nearly all of Wales was ruled by a single man, by Rhodri Mawr, meaning Rhodri the Great.

King Rhodri had six sons. When he died in 878 his realm, because of the Welsh law of divided inheritance, had to be parceled out among them. So Wales then had six ruling princes but no king. Sixteen decades later, the number of princes having greatly increased, one more ambitious and able than the rest made himself master of the whole of Wales. A contemporary of Edward the Confessor, his name was Gruffydd ap Llywelyn and he died in 1063 fighting his great enemy Harold, the English king's right-hand man. This same Harold, after marrying Gruffydd's widow, succeeded Edward the Confessor in 1066 as the last native English king. In that fateful year, in the last-ditch English defence against the conquering Normans, he was killed at the Battle of Hastings. The legend that an arrow pierced his eye is open to doubt.

There were no more kings in Wales after Gruffydd ap Llywelyn. But there were still many princes. South Wales eventually substituted the word "lord" for "prince." The rulers of Gwynedd or Snowdonia—that is, North Wales—retained the title until the closing decades of the thirteenth century which saw the end of all Welsh independence. The most famous among the princes of the north were two Llywelyns, Llywelyn the Great and his grandson Llywelyn ap Gruffydd, the latter being the last of the native Welsh princes and the only one ever to assume the title "Prince of Wales." It is with the last Llywelyn that the story of England's Princes of Wales really begins.

II

The history of Wales in the Middle Ages, the time of the last Llywelyn ap Gruffydd, is starred with violence and bespattered with blood. The country was divided, more or less, into two parts: the larger, the southern and central areas of the land, was in the hands of English barons, the lords of the Welsh March, who had begun their acquisition of territory soon after the Norman Conquest; the north, of course, had its own native princes. But Welsh princes and Marcher lords alike were a constant source of irritation to the king of England, to whom they owed homage and fealty. Welsh turbulence reached its peak during the reign of Henry III of England and at no time more so than when England herself was torn by civil war. For Llywelyn ap Gruffydd, taking advantage of a split among the English, while at the same time keeping on friendly terms with Henry III, set about conquering some of the territory that belonged to the Marcher lords. Peace was restored in 1267 with the Treaty of Montgomery which Llywelyn made with Edward, the king's son. By its terms he was allowed to keep much of the territory he had taken from the barons on condition that he paid an indemnity and, of course, did the necessary homage to King Henry. In addition he was also permitted to keep what was known as the Four Cantreds, a district lying between the town of Conway and the river Dee which had, in fact, been granted to the Lord Edward by his father, the king. Furthermore, according to one of the clauses of the Treaty of Montgomery, it is chronicled that: ". . . . the Lord King of England, wishing to enhance the personal greatness of the said Llywelyn, and in him to honour others who shall succeed him by hereditary right, simply out of his kindness and generosity and with the free will and consent of the Lord Edward, his eldest son, grants to the aforesaid Llywelyn and his heirs the Principality of Wales, and that the same Llywelyn and his heirs shall be called 'Princes of Wales.' "

The treaty brought comparative peace to Wales for a while. But gradually Llywelyn, "Prince of Wales," allowed the indemnity to fall into arrears and, again and again, proudly refused to do the necessary homage. When the Lord Edward became King Edward I matters reached such a pass that, losing all patience, he again went to war against the Welsh prince. In the ensuing struggle Llywelyn was not so much fought to a standstill as starved into surrender. A new peace treaty not only compelled him to pay the indemnity and do the necessary homage, but lost him the Four Cantreds. It was these Cantreds, a few years later, which ignited the spark that brought about the final fire of warfare between Edward I of England and Llywelyn ap Gruffydd, "Prince of Wales."

For Llywelyn this last campaign was from the start a hopeless struggle against overwhelming odds, a struggle which ended with his brother David's capture and his own death in battle in 1282. A story, probably apocryphal, tells how his head was sent to the English king, then at Conway in Wales, who "received it with great joy, and caused it to be set upon one of the highest turrets of the Tower of London." Whether legend or fact, one thing is certain: Llywelyn was dead. The English king's victory over the last prince "of the blood of Cadwaladr the Blessed," seventh-century king of the ancient Britons and almost as fabled as Arthur of the Round Table, was complete.

III

Since Edward I was destined to father England's first Prince of Wales, it is as well to know something of his personal life apart from his victories over, and final vanquishment of, the last native "Prince of Wales." What, for instance, did he look like, this greatest of England's Plantagenet kings? He goes down in history as a splendidly handsome man. The droop of one eyelid, a peculiarity inherited from his father, did not in the least mar his fine looks, nor did a slight impediment, a mere lisp, detract from the forcefulness of his speech. Of magnificent stature, muscular and athletic, he was, because of his height and long legs, inevitably dubbed "Longshanks." A brilliant mind and wide vision matched his great size. In an era when even princes were not of necessity literate, he was well educated. He could read and write both Latin and French and spoke English well enough to pun when speaking it. To mention that an English king spoke English may sound strange, yet it is not at all so odd a fact, for French was the language of English kings until well into the fifteenth century.

Edward I, clever and just, was in every way and not least in courage, conduct, and religious ardor, a perfect medieval knight. Like his father, Henry III, but unlike his earlier Angevin predecessors, he was also a perfect husband. He was not quite sixteen when he married Eleanor, the pretty, passionate, levelheaded half-sister of King Alfonso X of Castile and a notable heiress. Primarily undertaken as a matter of policy, the marriage brought him not only the succession to the French counties of Ponthieu and Montreuil, Eleanor's possessions inherited through her mother, but great domestic happiness. As a wedding gift his father, King Henry III, presented him with the earldom of Chester and granted to him the administration of Gascony, Ireland, the Channel Islands, and Wales, that divided, virtually semi-independent land with its Marcher barons of the south and its princes of the north. Through the management of these various territories the Lord Edward, for so he was styled during his father's lifetime, came to learn the difficult craft of statesmanship at an early age. They also supplied him with an income, one doubly secured by the great generosity of the king who promised his son that, should the revenues from these sources not reach the sum of 15,000 marks, he himself would make up the difference.

Young Edward and his wife spent the first year of their marriage at Bordeaux. Then came a brief visit to England, followed by a return, once more, to Gascony. But in 1256, when their marriage was two years old, they were back in England again and Edward went off to fight the Welshmen of the north led by their prince, Llywelyn ap Gruffydd. Welsh troubles were scarcely, and only temporarily, settled when new violence broke out and England herself lay in the grip of civil strife. This period of weary turmoil ended in 1265 with Edward's victory over Simon de Montfort and the latter's death at the Battle of Evesham. For Edward it had been a time of double anxiety. His marriage had run into stormy waters and Eleanor actually left England to seek refuge in France for a while. Her return after Evesham, however, led to a happy reunion with her husband. For the next twenty-five years which they shared, their felicity in each other strengthened and became a model of conjugal bliss. So strong were the bonds of their affection that neither could bear separation for any length of time. Edward was flawlessly constant and devoted to his wife and like Ruth of the Bible, "whither thou goest, I will go; and where thou lodgest, I will lodge" became for her a tenet of faith. Small wonder that the life of the camp became as familiar to her as that of the Court.

In the course of the years Eleanor bore Edward a quiverful of children, nine daughters and four sons. Six survived to reach maturity. Like most medieval princes and princesses, kings and queens, Edward and his lady had little time to devote to their offspring. Yet they were fond parents. Old records frequently note how he showed his love for his children by presenting them with new toys or new furniture to give them pleasure. The claims of their children, for all that, took second place to the close bonds which existed between the parents. So, leaving a little girl and two tiny boys at home in England, and setting off together on a crusade to the Holy Land, a perilous journey from which, such were the hazards of the times, neither might have returned, held no serious qualms for the young couple.

When his son, the Lord Edward, accompanied by his wife Eleanor, undertook this journey in 1270, Henry III was still England's king. In Acre, which the royal crusaders eventually reached, after a long trek through Europe, a slow voyage across the Mediterranean, and the relief of the town itself from siege, Eleanor gave birth to a daughter, known in after years as Joan of Acre. At Acre, too, the legend was born of how the royal lady saved her husband's life by sucking the poison from a festering wound caused by an attempted assassination on his birthday in 1272. The truth of what actually happened probably lies in another account. This relates that a surgeon, in order to save Edward from death when his wound grew dangerously infected, insisted on "the whole of the darkened flesh" around it being cut away. The mere thought of this frightful excision plunged Eleanor into so terrible a paroxysm of grief and horror that, "weeping and wailing" uncontrollably, she had to be led from the room before the surgeon could set to work. Showing far greater distress for his wife than for his own plight, Edward bore the dreadful operation stoically—and survived.

In this year of his recovery came news of the death of one of the small sons whom the royal parents had left at home in England. It was followed almost immediately by the dire tidings that Henry III, too, had died. Edward's grief at the loss of his father was far greater than that for his son, a fact remarked upon by observers. Explaining the reason to them he said "this was because, though he might have other sons, he could never replace his father."

Urged to return home immediately, the new king and queen set off for England, but by a return journey so circuitous, involving so many visits en route—to Lombardy, where Edward was triumphantly received; to Eleanor's half-brother, King Alfonso of Castile; to the lands of Gascony, where she gave birth to another child, a son to replace the one so recently dead—that two years passed before they reached London again to be crowned together at Westminster. The measure of Edward's love for Eleanor may perhaps be gauged by his willingness to allow her to saddle the new baby, his third and second surviving son, with the alien name of Alfonso.

Hardly had the king and queen settled down in England when tragedy once again struck the royal nursery. Alfonso's elder brother Henry died, leaving the delicate little boy, born in Gascony and bearing his uncle of Castile's un-English name, heir-apparent to the crown of England. Though Eleanor had more babies in the years between Henry's death and the beginning of her husband's last campaign in Wales against Llywelyn ap Gruffydd, these were all girls and Alfonso was for the time a greatly cherished only son.

IV

When Llywelyn ap Gruffydd died in battle in 1282, King Edward immediately set about the annexation of North Wales to the crown of England. The reorganization of the territory proved no easy business to settle. English law and the English system of local government had to be set up and, to keep order and the peace, the king began the building of a string of strong and famous castles. For three years grave and urgent matters kept him nailed down in Wales and he never once set foot in London. Again and again Queen Eleanor journeyed to be with him; indeed in 1282, at Rhuddlan, she presented him with yet another daughter, Elizabeth, who ever afterwards was called "the Welshwoman."

When, at the end of the next year, the queen was again with child, it was decided that she should remain in London for a time. The decision was short-lived. Scarcely was the winter over before the king sent for her to come once more to the wild lands of north Wales. She arrived at Caernarvon towards the end of March, 1284, and there (whether in the castle or the town has never been satisfactorily established), was four weeks later delivered of her thirteenth and last baby, a son.

In Westminster Abbey an ancient chronicler recorded the news. "In the year 1284, on the day of St Mark the Evangelist, at Carnarvon in Snowdonia, there was born to the King a son, who was named Edward and at whose birth many rejoiced, especially the Londonders," he wrote. Why the Londoners especially? Of the king's rejoicing there is no doubt and ample evidence. Edward was a realist. Dearly as he loved Gascony-born Alfonso, now eleven years old, he was fully aware that this delicate little boy's life was balanced on a razor's edge. If death, which had already claimed his two elder sons, should lay its hand on this frail child so quietly playing with a toy fort and a little boat, his splendid heritage would go to a girl, to Eleanor his eldest daughter, whom he himself had named as his successor in the event of so great a calamity. But the spindle better becomes the distaff side than a scepter. So Edward had every reason to indulge in rapturous joy and thanksgiving when the blessing of a baby son was bestowed on him once more. He gave his own name to the infant. To this was added the place of its birth. The child was called Edward of Caernarvon.

On the day the baby was born King Edward was deeply engrossed in political problems at Rhuddlan Castle. There the news was brought to him. In overwhelming exultation he knighted the messenger on the spot, filled the man's pockets with gold, and there and then granted him a house and lands so that he might, from that day onward, live as befitted a knight. Then off the king went in great haste to Caernarvon, "conferred the first English charter of rights and privileges granted in Wales" on the town, in honor of his son born within its walls, and summoned the leaders of the Welsh to appear before him.

For some time the Welsh had been clamoring for a native prince, of "blameless life and free from prejudice," to act not only as the vice-regent of their English conqueror, but to take the place of their dead native princes, their Princeps Walliae and Dominus Snowdonia, of whom Llywelyn ap Gruffydd had been the last to hold the title. It was told that, after the Welsh chiefs had assembled to meet him, King Edward promised that, if they kept the peace, he would indeed give them a new prince, "one that was borne in Wales and could speake never a word of English." Upon receiving their willingness to accept his offer, he rushed into the queen's bedchamber, took his infant son in his arms, strode proudly before the assembled Welshmen and cried: "This is your man!" With those words, runs the legend, baby Edward of Caernarvon was created the first English Prince of Wales.

This charming story was brought to life with endearing sentimentality in a painting by P. R. Morris, A.R.A., which shows Edward I, magnificent in armor, his crusader's pennant fluttering from a staff, his right arm raised, holding a great sword aloft, the hilt upward to form a cross; his left, the shield arm, crooked to cradle a tiny naked baby whose nurse stands patiently at hand with a fur robe, awaiting the return of her charge. But twentieth-century historians have rubbed out the enchanting moment captured on this canvas by proving, conclusively, that the legend on which it is based only came into being some three hundred years after the event.

That Edward did show his baby son to the Welsh chiefs cannot be doubted. He had very sound political reasons for doing so. But that he named the royal infant "Prince of Wales" may be questioned on two grounds: Alfonso, his eldest son, was still alive and, secondly, the royal charter, which for the first time *styled* the boy Edward Prince of Wales, bears the date May 10, 1301. By then Edward of Caernarvon was just two months short of seventeen. Throughout nearly all his life he had certainly been the recognized heir to the throne of England, for sickly Alfonso had survived his Welsh-born brother's birth by only four months.

V

Like a gazebo raised on an eminence in time, the 1960's provide an admirable vantage point from which to view a seven-hundred-year-long avenue of British history. The seven centuries, from 1272, when Plantagenet Edward I came to the throne, to the present day, record a muster of twenty-six kings, five queens, a joint monarchy—when taciturn William of Orange shared the throne with his Stuart wife, Mary, after the 1688 Revolution (he remained England's Dutch king for a further eight solitary years after her death)—and, of course, a Commonwealth under Oliver Cromwell. Yet, despite the figure of thirty-one sovereigns, these centuries produced only twenty English Princes of Wales until 1958 when, on July 26, the present queen, Elizabeth II, created her eldest son, Charles, by Letters Patent, the twenty-first.

Prince Charles' great title rolls off the tongue with sonorous splendor: "His Royal Highness Prince Charles Philip Arthur George, Prince of Wales and Earl of Chester, Duke of Cornwall in the Peerage of England, Duke of Rothesay, Earl of Carrick, and Baron of Renfrew in the Peerage of Scotland, Lord of the Isles and the Great Steward of Scotland."

Edward of Caernarvon, the first Prince of Wales, could boast no title half so grand though he was, it is true, a count when six years old, "Principe Wallie" and Earl of Chester when not quite seventeen, and a duke before he was twenty-two. But countship and dukedom—he was Count of Ponthieu and Montreuil and Duke of Aquitaine—came to him from England's possessions across the Channel.

England's sovereigns held lands in France for five hundred years, from the time of William the Conqueror to that of sad Queen Mary I, Henry VIII's daughter, cruelly labeled with the epithet "bloody." In losing Calais in 1558, she lost the last of her realm's continental possessions. So, though he had foreign titles, neither that of Duke of Cornwall nor, it goes without saying, any of the Scottish titles, honored the first English Prince of Wales. Only in the reign of his son, Edward III, was a charter granted ordaining that the eldest son of a sovereign automatically became Duke of Cornwall from birth or from the time of his parent's accession. Titles in the peerage of Scotland only came to the eldest son of the king after James VI of Scotland was transmogrified also into James I of England.

A list giving the names of the Princes of Wales who followed Edward of Caernarvon, together with the names of the places where they were born, the years of their birth, the confirmation of their title, and the names of those from whom they descended, provides some useful, if cursory, information:

1. Edward of Caernarvon: b. 1284; created Prince of Wales 1301; son of Edward I. (Edward II)
2. Edward of Woodstock: b. 1330; created Prince of Wales 1343; son of Edward III.
3. Richard of Bordeaux: b. 1367; created Prince of Wales 1376; grandson of Edward III. (Richard II)
4. Henry of Monmouth: b. 1386; created Prince of Wales 1399; son of Henry IV. (Henry V)
5. Edward of Westminster: b. 1453; created Prince of Wales 1454; son of Henry VI.
6. Edward of the Sanctuary (or of York): b. 1471; created Prince of Wales 1472; son of Edward IV. (Edward V)
7. Edward of Middleham: b. 1473; created Prince of Wales 1483; son of Richard III.
8. Arthur of Winchester: b. 1486; created Prince of Wales 1489; son of Henry VII.
9. Henry of Greenwich: b. 1491; created Prince of Wales 1504; son of Henry VII. (Henry VIII)
10. Henry of Stirling: b. 1594; created Prince of Wales 1610; son of James I.
11. Charles of Dunfermline: b. 1600; created Prince of Wales 1616; son of James I. (Charles I)
12. Charles of St. James's: b. 1630; declared 1630 but

never formally created Prince of Wales; son of Charles I. (Charles II)

13. James Francis Edward of St. James's: b. 1688; styled Prince of Wales 1688; son of James II.

14. George Augustus of Hanover: b. 1683; created Prince of Wales 1714; son of George I. (George II)

15. Frederick Lewis of Hanover: b. 1707; created Prince of Wales 1729; son of George II.

16. George William Frederick of Norfolk House: b. 1738; created Prince of Wales 1751; grandson of George II. (George III)

17. George Augustus Frederick of St. James's: b. 1762; created Prince of Wales 1762; son of George III. (George IV)

18. Albert Edward of Buckingham Palace: b. 1841; created Prince of Wales 1841; son of Queen Victoria. (Edward VII)

19. George Frederick Ernest Albert of Marlborough House: b. 1865; created Prince of Wales 1901; son of Edward VII. (George V)

20. Edward Albert Christian George Andrew Patrick David of White Lodge, Richmond: b. 1894; created Prince of Wales 1910; son of George V. (Edward VIII)

21. Charles Philip Arthur George of Buckingham Palace: b. 1948; created Prince of Wales 1958; son of Elizabeth II.

A point made obvious by the above list is that the age at which a prince, whether the eldest or surviving son of a monarch or, as in two instances, the grandson, was created Prince of Wales, varied enormously throughout the centuries. Edward of Caernarvon was seventeen when he was first formally known by the title. Edward, the twentieth Prince of Wales (the present Duke of Windsor), was formally invested with the title at Caernarvon Castle at the same age, though the Letters Patent of his creation bear the date of the previous year. James I's two sons, Henry of Stirling and Charles of Dunfermline (afterwards Charles I), were both sixteen. Charles's son, who was to become Charles II in the course of time, was declared Prince of Wales soon after his birth, and named so but never formally created.

The majority of the princes, as the list shows, had the title bestowed on them when they were between the ages of nine and thirteen. Quite a number, however, were given the honor when infants. George Augustus Frederick of St. James's, the future First Gentleman of Europe and George IV, was, for instance, seven days old; Queen Victoria's baby, Albert Edward, was aged one month; James II's son, James Francis Edward, was described at his baptism, when four months old, as "His Royal Highness Prince of Wales"; and, finally, the infant son of Henry VI, Edward of Westminster, was five months old. In contrast to these baby Princes of Wales there are two conspicuously belated creations, those of George Augustus of Hanover, son of England's first Hanoverian king, and George Frederick Ernest Albert, son of Edward VII. The former became Prince of Wales when nearly thirty-two; the latter when thirty-six. There were, of course, specific reasons for these long delays.

Among the twenty Princes of Wales created before Prince Charles—who was nine-and-a-half when declared Prince of Wales in 1958—only two, the first and the twentieth, were actually presented to the Welsh people at Caernarvon. But whereas Edward I merely *showed* his baby son as a grand political gesture in 1284, George V actually invested his son at Caernarvon Castle in 1911. Oddly enough, too, during the intervening centuries it was not Caernarvon but the town of Ludlow, which was selected for setting up the little courts of the Princes of Wales when they visited their Welsh domains. Still more odd, perhaps, is the fact that a number of the Princes never went near their Welsh territories at all. Formal investiture through the ages, even that of the first English Prince of Wales, took place either in London or in some royal palace in England.

Another glance at the list of princes produces the curious fact that only fifteen kings and queens figure as those whose sons—or grandsons—became Princes of Wales. Yet, as stated earlier, there have been, excluding the joint monarchy of William and Mary, twenty-six kings and five queens on the English throne from 1272 to the present time. The discrepancy and the missing names can be accounted for quite simply. For instance, although the son of the first Prince of Wales was dubbed Earl of Chester and Duke of Aquitaine, he was never created Prince of Wales. No documents, at any rate, survive to show that he ever held the title. He was not quite fifteen when he ascended the throne as Edward III to begin a reign of half a century, one of the longest in English history. Then again, some monarchs left no son and heir to succeed them, as in the cases of Edward V, Edward VI, Mary I, Elizabeth I, George IV, William IV, and Edward VIII; some got the throne by force, as did Henry IV, Edward IV, Richard III, and Henry VII.

When Henry V died he left an infant son who was immediately proclaimed king without previously having been named Prince of Wales. And Henry VIII and Queen Anne both died without creating their sons Prince of Wales. Henry recognized his son by Jane Seymour—the boy who became Edward VI—as heir to the throne, but withheld the historic title; and indolent Queen Anne, last of the Stuart monarchs, never apparently got round to creating her son Prince of Wales. This little boy, the only one of the seventeen children she bore her husband, Prince George of Denmark, to survive infancy, lived to be twelve and predeceased his mother. He died plain William, Duke of Gloucester.

Fourteen of England's twenty-one Princes of Wales were born in England; only two, Edward of Caernarvon and Henry of Monmouth, the first and the fourth, in the Principality which gave them their name. Of the remaining five, Richard of Bordeaux was born in France; the two sons of James I in Scotland; and the son and grandson of George I in Hanover. The Scottish prince, Charles of Dunfermline, succeeded his brother, Henry of Stirling, as Prince of Wales; and brother also followed brother in the case of Arthur of Winchester and Henry of Greenwich, sons of the first Tudor king, Henry VII.

Ten Princes of Wales among the twenty predecessors of Prince Charles succeeded their fathers on the throne; two, Richard of Bordeaux and George William Frederick of Norfolk House, their grandfathers; and one, Albert Edward, his mother, Queen Victoria. Of the remaining seven princes, James Francis Edward, son of James II, lived in exile all his life, and six died before ascending the throne. The most distinguished of these last six was Edward III's son, Edward of Woodstock, the Black Prince, victor of Crécy and Poitiers; the one least regretted, Frederick Lewis of Hanover, son of George II. The Black Prince died at the age of forty-six, after a five year illness that devoured his strength but not his heroic spirit; Frederick Lewis, despised by his father and sisters and violently hated by his mother, left only his widow and a large brood of children to weep for him when his life ended at forty-four.

The four remaining princes who did not ascend the throne all died young. Edward of Westminster, son of Henry VI, was murdered at the age of seventeen, during his father's lifetime; the life of Edward of Middleham, "Crookback" Richard III's son, was brought to an end in his tenth year by an "unhappy death"; Arthur of Winchester, first Tudor Prince of Wales and first husband of Catherine of Aragon, died at sixteen, probably of a virulent variety of influenza known in early eras as "the sweating sickness"; and the eldest son of James I, Henry of Stirling, first Stuart Prince of Wales, fell a victim to typhoid fever when only eighteen.

Only five Princes of Wales were married and had children while holding the title, namely Edward of Woodstock; George Augustus of Hanover, first Hanoverian Prince of Wales; his son, Frederick Lewis; Queen Victoria's heir, Albert Edward; and his son, who became George V. Though many of the Princes of Wales were betrothed, some in their cradles and some several times over before they reached their teens, nine ascended the throne as bachelors.

Edward of Caernarvon married Isabella of France the year after he was crowned Edward II. Richard of Bordeaux was five years a king before his marriage to Anne of Bohemia, his first adored wife who in life brought him such great happiness and whose death crushed him with so bitter a grief that he ordered the destruction of the wing of the lovely palace of Sheen where she died.

Henry of Monmouth, son of the man to whom this King Richard with his own hands gave away his crown, was Henry V of England and victor of Agincourt before he became the husband of Catherine, the French king's daughter. Edward of the Sanctuary was thirteen and still only betrothed to Anne of Brittany when he came riding towards London with his uncle, Richard, Duke of Gloucester. His coronation as Edward V never took place for, once housed in the Tower of London, he was never to come out of it again.

Henry of Greenwich married his brother Arthur's widow, Catherine of Aragon, less than two months after being proclaimed King Henry VIII. Perhaps at this point it should be remembered that Catherine was Henry's wife for just one month short of twenty-four years before he divorced her and set off on that wayward path which led him to wed five times more in fifteen years.

Both the Stuart and the Hanoverian royal houses produced bachelor Princes of Wales who became kings. Charles of Dunfermline married Henrietta Maria of France only in the year of his accession as Charles I; their son, Charles of St. James's, was restored to the throne after the Cromwellian era as Charles II before Catherine of Braganza became his wife; and Hanoverian George William Frederick of Norfolk House did not marry Charlotte of Mecklenburg-Strelitz until after he was George III. Finally, Queen Victoria's great-grandson, Edward of the seven names who became Edward VIII, was a bachelor throughout his brief reign. He is known today as the Duke of Windsor.

Royal babies and, in particular, those who were heirs to the throne, have throughout the centuries been swaddled in praise for their beauty, their strength, and astonishing lustiness. Only one little Prince of Wales has gone on record as having been downright plain. "He is so ugly," Henrietta Maria wrote in a letter to a friend, describing her infant son, Charles of St. James's (afterwards Charles II), "that I am ashamed of him; but his size and fatness supply the want of beauty." So probably, did his precocity, for at four months old he not only looked as big as a yearling but he had begun to teethe. Still his mother complained. "He is so dark," she continues to moan in yet another letter. Charles never outgrew either his ugliness or his swarthiness but, as a man, to these two characteristics was added that unmeasurable Stuart charm which made him irresistibly attractive to women and the most amiable and cultivated of companions to men.

The Wars of the Roses, that political strife for power between Yorkist and Lancastrian Plantagenets which brought anarchy to England, began in 1455. It dragged on through the reigns of Henry VI, Edward IV, and Richard III, and only ended in 1485 when Henry, Duke of Richmond, picked the crown from a thorn bush on the battlefield of Bosworth and, as Henry VII, founded the Tudor dynasty. During the last fourteen years of these terrible wars there were no less than three Princes of Wales. All three were named Edward and all were tragic figures. Henry VI's son, Edward of Westminster was the first to die. He was, it is believed, murdered after the Lancastrian forces which supported him were defeated by the Yorkists at the Battle of Tewkesbury. Edward IV's son, Yorkist Edward of the Sanctuary, who should have been crowned Edward V, was also presumably murdered. He is one of the two little princes who so mysteriously vanished in the Tower of London. The last of the Wars of the Roses' Prince of Wales was ten-year-old Edward of Middleham, son of Richard III, whose mysterious death took place soon after his father's double coronation.

In contrast to these fourteen years during the fifteenth century which produced three Princes of Wales, there came two long periods, one of one-hundred-and-one, another of sixty-five years, when there was no prince *in* England bearing the title. The hundred-and-one years stretched from the accession to the throne of Henry of Greenwich as Henry VIII, to the creation of Henry of Stirling as first Stuart Prince of Wales; the sixty-five years, from the execution of Charles I to the creation of the first Hanoverian Prince of Wales in 1714.

Though "travelling Europe" during the Cromwellian era, Charles I's son, Charles of St. James's, was in fact king of England after his father's execution. He was restored to the throne as Charles II in 1660. Father of many natural sons, Charles II left no legitimate heir. At his death the succession went to his brother, James, Duke of York, who became James II. But James was bereft of his throne within a few years by the bloodless revolution of 1688 which brought his daughter and son-in-law, childless Mary and William, from the Netherlands to take his place. James II, having first sent his son, the infant Prince of Wales, James Francis Edward, and his wife, out of the country, eventually scuttled to France and joined them. There the little prince lived all his life, growing old as the "Old Pretender." In time this *ci-devant* Prince of Wales' half-sister Anne succeeded his half-sister Mary's husband (William of Orange) on England's throne and she in turn was followed by a string of Hanoverians.

There is a claim that James Francis Edward held the title of Prince of Wales during the whole of his life of seventy-eight years, but this is a controversial and much disparaged pretension. The prince who actually held the title for longer than any other before succeeding to the throne is Albert Edward, son of Queen Victoria. He was England's Prince of Wales for nearly sixty years. The "First Gentleman of Europe," George Augustus Frederick, runs him a close second with fifty-eight years, though these years were interrupted by the period of his Regency during the insanity of his father, George III. Nicknamed Prinney, this prince eventually became king as George IV. Edward, the Black Prince, thirty-three years England's Prince of Wales, died before his father.

Only thirteen among the first twenty Princes of Wales actually ascended the throne. Of these, four died violent deaths as kings. Three were murdered: Edward of Caernarvon (Edward II) most brutally at Berkeley Castle; Richard of Bordeaux (Richard II) at Pontefract; and Edward of the Sanctuary, who should have been Edward V, in the Tower of London. The fourth, Charles of Dunfermline (Charles I), met death with brave dignity on the scaffold.

PART TWO: PLANTAGENETS

PART TWO: PLANTAGENETS

For three hundred years, from Henry II to Richard III, the later Angevin kings, who are usually called Plantagenets, ruled England. Yorkists and Lancastrians alike belonged to this dynasty. The first seven Princes of Wales were, therefore, all Plantagenets, two among the last four belonging to the Lancastrian and two to the Yorkist branch of this great royal house.

When the Tudors ousted the Plantagenets from the throne Henry VII, first king of the new royal line, had the last male Plantagenet claimant executed. This was one of "several very unpleasant actions" forced upon him by Ferdinand and Isabella of Spain during protracted wranglings concerned with the marriage of their daughter, Catherine of Aragon, to Henry's eldest son and heir, Arthur, first Tudor Prince of Wales. All too vividly aware of the uncertainties that had beset the kings and princes of England during the recently ended era of anarchy caused by the Wars of the

24

Roses, Their Spanish Majesties were determined to insure that their daughter's future husband should tread a path cleared of all usurping thorns. Prudent, able, avaricious Henry VII, merciful in his own way when clemency in no way put his new-found dynasty in danger, a king with a businessman's understanding of money and intent, therefore, on receiving the noble dowry that Catherine would bring to his kingdom, acceded to their request. And so the young Earl of Warwick, last Plantagenet claimant to the English throne, lost his head.

This sanguinary settlement took place some two hundred years after Eleanor of Castile, consort to the great Edward I, gave birth at Caernarvon in Snowdonia to the Plantagenet baby who was to become England's first Prince of Wales.

II

Edward of Caernarvon was born on the feast of St. Mark, April 25, 1284. When he grew sturdy and strong, his father's custom of annually providing free meals to hundreds of his poor subjects in honor of the Saint's feast day, was further extended to include the distribution of still more free meals to as many hundreds of his poor people as the "year of age" of his son.

The royal baby, nurtured by a Welsh wet nurse named Mary Maunsel, was baptized when a week old, and four months later he and Mary, his nurse, together with other of the king's children, were transported from Caernarvon to Bristol while the royal parents set off on one of their usual lengthy "progresses," this time through Wales. Young Edward did not return to the land of his birth again until shortly before his seventeenth birthday when, having been granted "the royal lands of Wales" by his father, he came to receive the homage of his Welsh tenantry. In those intervening years his links with Wales were tenuous to say the least, depending on no more than the receipt of two gifts—four herons from a Caernarvon man and two greyhounds from the Constable of Conway—plus the fact that three Welshmen wore the livery of servants in his household. Mary Maunsel passed out of his life early, supplanted by a new nurse, "Alice wife of Reginald of Leygrave," an Englishwoman, who, to her own and her family's benefit, was to remain in his service until he was a grown man, king of England, and married.

At first Edward, the baby, shared with his sisters the royal household established for all the king's children and, naturally, was the center of this large and costly establishment run on the money from the king's own wardrobe. And a pretty penny it cost His Majesty. In the year 1289, when Edward was five, the housekeeping bill alone, excluding wines, amounted to £2140. On top of this, a sum of £400 was spent on shoes and gifts for the little boy and his sisters. This joint establishment for the royal children was abolished when Edward, about to be "brought into greater prominence and assume, at any rate in name, certain public responsibilities," was not quite thirteen. The boy was then given a household of his own, paid for out of the Exchequer.

Separation from his five sisters, from Eleanor, Joan, Mary, Margaret, and Elizabeth, profoundly affected the boy's life. Elizabeth, nearest to him in age, and dearest, he missed most. But it was Joan, born at Acre in the middle of a Crusade, a girl with a will and a mind of her own, resolute and unafraid even when face to face with a stern father whom the years transformed into a terrifying and formidable giant—it was Joan who might have helped to form her young brother's character and in so doing, have changed the course of his tragic destiny.

For any child to have survived and withstood the rigors of medieval upbringing postulates a more than usual healthiness. Little Edward appears to have taken in his stride the awesome combination of foods unsuitable for small children, the unsanitary conditions of the times prevalent even in the homes of kings, exposure to inclement weather and infection on long, wearisome and constant "progresses" which he had to undertake, and the dreadful remedies meted out to the young "to dryve away Deth." He probably did suffer the usual variety of childish ailments, but these in no way prevented him from growing into a handsome, sturdy little boy and later, into a youth of "notable strength and vigour." As the years went by it was, unfortunately, only in being "fair of body and of great strength" that he in any way resembled his splendid, knightly father, the king.

Edward, temperamentally a warm-hearted child in constant need of tenderness, cosseting and petting, was starved of these indulgences from his parents almost from the beginning of his life. Queen Eleanor possessed no strongly developed maternal feelings. Her consuming love for her husband left her, it would seem, with only small affection to give her children. In her own way she was fond of them and made much of them when they were near. But that was not often, since, inseparable from her husband, she was constantly on the move, traveling with him in England, through Wales, or to their possessions on the other side of the Channel.

When Edward was only two, his parents set off on one of these interminably long trips, this time to Gascony. They did not return to England until three years later. Those years, filled for the tiny boy with a cruel, hungry longing for their affection, bred in him a sense of insecurity from which he was never to escape. The companionship of his five sisters and the benevolent care and comfort of Alice, his nurse, were not enough to fill the vacuum of wistful yearning for his parents. Then at last they were home again and the world seemed golden. But the glow and the warmth was to prove transitory. It vanished fifteen months later when his mother died. Now

Edward, not yet seven, was left to confront a father suddenly and terrifyingly changed into a stranger. The torment of the king's grief at the death of his queen shook the very foundations of his character and a once genial and affable man became a being remote and unapproachable, either sunk in the depths of sullen sorrow or roused into frightening harshness and explosive irritability which kindled wild and uncontrollable rages—rages which were an idiosyncrasy of the Plantagenet temperament. And now, too, more than ever, the king was always on the move; incessantly setting off on royal progresses through the land, forever campaigning—in Scotland, in Wales, in Flanders.

Much of Edward's childhood was spent in traveling with the Court from place to place, never remaining anywhere for longer than a few days. These peregrinations were only interrupted with the arrival of winter. Then, for a few months, he became stationary, spending the time usually, and ecstatically, at (King's) Langley, a manor in Hertfordshire. At Langley there were all manner of things dear to a small boy's heart—water-meadows and watermills, one for grinding corn, another for fulling cloth; a small river dotted with minute islands; a park full of deer and stables full of horses. Once, on a visit when he was six, he was delighted to find a camel actually sharing these stables with the horses.

The manor of Langley had belonged to Queen Eleanor and after her death passed to Edmund, Earl of Cornwall. Years later, when the earl, too, was dead and Edward was eighteen, it came into his possession. It was the only real home he ever knew and the only one he truly loved. At Langley, when he grew older, he rowed, swam, and dived, rode horses and wrestled with stable-boys, learned to dig ditches, thatch roofs, sweated at blacksmith's work, and became skilled in a score more of country crafts. That the king's son actually enjoyed and loved pursuits no boy of his rank and time had any business with, shocked the young men of the Court. Many a knightly eyebrow was raised at the eccentric behavior of the heir to the throne, and very odd indeed his conduct became as time went on. For the emotionally insecure and unstable boy eschewing, for the most part, the intimacy of lords, knights, and ladies, found companionship in what for him was more agreeable good-fellowship, the camaraderie of household clerks, of servants, rustics, tumblers, and jugglers. On these he showered his immature and undiscriminating affection and loyalty.

The restless, roving existence to which Edward was subjected as a small boy was not conducive either to learning or discipline. His education, though in a general way very much that of all highborn boys of the age, was extremely perfunctory. He had, it is true, a *magister*, a tutor, in attendance, and was taught Latin as well as "the behaviour suitable to a knight and a gentleman, in Church, at Court and especially in warfare both mimic and real." Many historians hold grave doubts about his literacy and there certainly is little evidence to show that he was ever a lover of books. That he absorbed enough Latin to read, even if somewhat laboriously, is presumable, but it is unlikely that he ever mastered the art of writing it.

Undisputably, however, he was graceful in offering a gift at an altar and sat a horse superbly. But he never became that beau ideal of medieval times, a perfect knight of chivalry—which, of course, his father was in every way. Prince Edward had no stomach either for knightly exercises or for learning. What he most liked to do, the things which meant most to him, he learned to love at Langley. There, in his teens, the very thought of studying, of allowing himself to be enslaved by training for future kingship, bored him to distraction. There only was he truly happy in the enjoyment of what a chronicler described as "boorish doings" among grooms and gardeners, blacksmiths and watermen, and the people of the household whom he regarded as his true and cherished friends.

Langley which he loved, unfortunately for him, fostered tastes and fomented habits that not only shaped his character but chiseled and carved his destiny. "Had he devoted as much toil to arms as he gave to rustic arts," a chronicler wrote of him in after years, "England would have prospered and his name rung through the earth." The chronicler's lament against Edward's love of "rustic arts" is, however, sadly out of tune, for it was not this but weakness of will and character that, in the end, so tragically destroyed him.

Since Edward was his only surviving son the king was anxious to secure the succession to the throne. So, early in his life, plans for a diplomatically advantageous marriage for the royal heir began to take shape. The first of several such plans was devised in 1289 when Edward was five. Having conquered Wales by force of arms, the king now deemed the time ripe for uniting Scotland to England, by peaceful means. Nothing would be more satisfying than the simple expediency of marrying his only son to the heiress of the Scottish throne. The young lady in question, two years younger than her prospective bridegroom, was Margaret, daughter of Eric, king of Norway and granddaughter of Alexander III, the recently deceased king of Scotland.

Alexander had died as the result of an accident, leaving no male heir. But the Scots had magnanimously recognized his granddaughter, living in distant Norway with her father, as their future queen. The little Maid of Norway was still resident in her father's kingdom when the wheels of diplomacy began relentlessly to grind out her betrothal to Edward. Arrangements went on apace. First a convenient treaty was signed and then, since the children were related, for Alexander III had been the king of England's brother-in-law, a letter was addressed to the pope in the name of five-year-old Edward, stating his desire to marry Margaret and begging for a dispensation in order that all "scandals, rancours and hatred" might be avoided.

Pope Nicholas IV's permission having been granted, a final treaty concluded the arrangements, and the tiny Maid of Norway sailed out of her father's care to fulfil her duty. But fate had spun the threads of her life quite contrary to kingly design. On board the ship bringing her to her kingdom from the other side of the North Sea, the little queen-to-be died. With her perished one of Edward's most cherished dreams. Three hundred and thirteen years were to pass before James VI of Scotland peacefully became James I of England, thus uniting England and Scotland, at last, under one sovereign.

A second and equally diplomatic scheme for the marriage of young Prince Edward began four years later, in 1294. This time the king, anxious to secure allies against his enemy, Philip IV of France, settled on Philippa, daughter of the Count of Flanders, as an eminently suitable match. The count was the most formidable and defiant of the French king's feudal lords and, on the surface, a convenient friend in need. The plan had to be shelved for some three years, however, owing to the French king's strong, and natural, opposition.

At last a contract was actually drawn up, with the interesting proviso inserted that should Philippa, for some reason, be unobtainable or unavailable, one of her sisters would fill the gap. This pact was made when Edward I, expecting great things from his ally, the Count of Flanders, was ready to go to war against the French king. Just prior to his departure on this campaign, on a Sunday in July, 1297, he addressed a great crowd from a platform erected outside the Palace of Westminster. His thirteen-year-old son stood beside him on the dais as he raised his great voice in a stirring invocation to his audience.

"Behold, I am about to expose myself to danger on your account," a chronicler reports his speech. "I pray you, if I return, receive me as you have at present. But if I do not return, crown my son as your King." The oration over, so the report continues, "all the magnates there present did fealty to the

King's son at his father's bidding, and he was acclaimed by all the people, their right hands upraised, as heir, future lord, and successor to the kingdom."

This was the first time in his life that thirteen-year-old Edward, the king's son, had ever appeared on stage in the full glare of the limelight. But his regency of the kingdom during his father's absence abroad in the Flemish war was a purely nominal affair. The boy looked on while the real work of the State was directed by the king's councilors. In any case, his regency lasted no longer than seven months. The Count of Flanders proved so unsatisfactory an ally that Edward I, abandoning the Flemings, made peace with Philip of France. In fact he went several steps further. Not only did he scrap the proposed contract for his son to marry the Count of Flanders' daughter Philippa—or one of her sisters—but cemented his new and amiable relations with Philip IV by marrying that monarch's fifteen-year-old sister, Margaret. At the same time he began negotiating a third marriage plan for his son with Philip of France's five-year-old daughter, Isabella. Edward I's herculean labors in bringing about this union, which eventually took place only after his son had succeeded him as king, brought forth not a mouse but a "she-wolf." However, the agony of those years for young Prince Edward lay ahead in time.

Peace with France and his father home again, the boy-heir once more quitted the center of the stage and slipped into the wings. His father's return and his retreat into the background nevertheless brought compensations: a stepmother of nearly his own age, whom he grew to like, and the exciting friendship of a young man, some years his senior, named Piers Gaveston.

Piers was the younger son of a knight, Arnold de Gaveston, who, during the unsatisfactory Flemish expedition, had rendered good services to the English king. As part reward, the king took Arnold's son under his wing as a young squire in his household. Piers not only made great efforts to "win the King's favour" but succeeded, and so well, that Edward I brought him to England when the campaign came to an end. An intelligent, engaging young man, Piers pleased the King so much that, along with several other youthful squires of good family, he was soon established in young Prince Edward's household.

The nimble-witted Gascon, whose mother, so rumor shrilled in after years, had been burned as a witch, was not only older than young Edward, but infinitely more mature and far cleverer. Gay, brave, and impudent, he could tell the most exciting and romantic stories of his experiences both in the field of war and at Court. Though young, he had cut his eyeteeth in the former and sown large sackfuls of wild oats in the latter. Immature Edward soon came to regard his part-servant, part-companion, as a full man indeed, a nonpareil. For Piers to make himself cock of the walk in young Edward's household and leader among the boy's associates proved easy. In no time at all this self-seeking, dissolute, unprincipled, and fascinating worldling was living on terms of closest intimacy with the king's son, sharing everything with him, even his lessons—or, rather, it is chronicled "to such light studies as were in fashion then, they addressed themselves in company, and were united in learning or neglecting such lessons as each was expected to master." Piers was strong and Edward was weak; Piers led and Edward followed. For "Perot," as he was soon calling the Gascon affectionately, Edward developed a love and loyalty that was, in the end, to prove fatal for them both.

When Piers Gaveston arrived on the scene Edward was a tall, handsome, athletic, graceful boy. Grown in stature, he had unfortunately imbibed little of the training necessary for his high position. The insecurity of his early childhood had marked his character; he was a youth without purpose or ambition, irresponsible, vacillating, lacking in will power. Neither affairs of State nor the glories of knightly chivalry held any meaning for him. Fond of luxury and fine clothes, the "rustic arts" were still among his chief delights. These and play-acting, dogs, horses, riding, swimming, diving, having fun with his fellowship of "single people" as he called the least desirable of his young male companions, were the occupations that filled his days. Though irresolute, self-willed and, like all weak men, fickle and unreliable, he was constant in loyalty and extravagantly generous to those he loved.

In this coterie Piers Gaveston stood paramount. The ambitious Gascon and the king's son who, loving pleasure and disliking work, made no efforts and had no wish to learn the duties of kingship, lived together, inseparable companions. That their intimacy was an unnatural one is beyond question and, naturally, it was a scandal of the times. Probability suggests that they did not confine themselves to a homosexual relationship but, like Julius Caesar, were apparently "lovers of all sexual pleausures" since both eventually married and Edward fathered four children. Certainty lies only in the knowledge that the paths of waywardness along which Edward and Piers walked hand in hand led to the poisoning of Edward's relationship with his father and, years later, to the destruction of his adored favorite. It was Edward's tragedy that his passion for favorites and his weakness in allowing them to lead him, finally brought about his own downfall. But years still separated these events from the days when "Brother Gaveston" was Edward's favorite, the happy days of hunting and swimming, of training dogs and working in a smithy, of thatching and ditching and play-acting with Gascon Piers.

These pleasures were temporarily interrupted in 1300 when, supposedly to win his spurs, Edward set off on his first campaign with his father, who was waging war against the Scots. Though nominally he placed Edward in command of the rearguard, the King, unsure of his son, took the wise precaution of seeing that "close to his bridle rein rode a picked group of experienced soldiers." The boy, "newly bearing arms" and managing his steed "wonderfully well," according to a herald-poet, gave so good an account of himself during the expedition, "an occasion to make proof of his strength," that the king was overjoyed. In recognition of his pride and pleasure, he conferred the royal lands of Wales and the earldom of Chester on Edward when they returned to London. The charter making this gift is dated February 7, 1301. The word "prince" does not appear in it.

Two weeks later Edward went off to inspect his new domain and to receive, at certain specified places—Caernarvon, strangely enough, was not included—the homage and fealty of the Welsh people. The Welsh, "esteeming him their rightful lord, because he derived his origin from those parts," gave him a warm welcome. The young man, however, was not particularly moved by this, his first visit to the Principality since he left it as a baby. For one thing, being a connoisseur of such matters, he did not at all approve of Welsh dogs and Welsh palfreys. But being an expert, too, on music, plays, and playacting, he took interest and pleasure in the musicality of the Welsh and enjoyed listening to their singing and playing on their own and very distinctive musical instruments.

The visit lasted five weeks. When he returned to London still more of the territory of Wales was granted to him in a new charter dated May 10. It bore the heading "Pro Edward filio regis, principe Wallie etc." This was the first time that Edward was actually styled Prince of Wales. Now he was given not merely a household but a "Court"; and still more territorial perquisites. Wales was his as well as Ponthieu and Montreuil across the Channel, which he had inherited from his mother, Queen Eleanor, after her death in 1290. And in April, 1302, the manor of Langley, where he had so often resided and which he dearly loved, came into his possession, too, on the death of the Earl of Cornwall. There, during the first Christmas of his ownership, he lavishly entertained his father and stepmother, Margaret, throughout a week of amiable conviviality.

The relationship between Edward and his father was not always loving and congenial. This Christmas was but one of widely scattered interludes of contentment and pleasure in each other's company. The young Prince of Wales never felt completely at ease with his stern father, whose furious Plantagenet rages were so unpredictable and so terrifying. Though he was now a great landowner and the center of a splendid court, Edward, Prince of Wales, was still, as he had always been, at the mercy of his father's decisions and irascible moods. Emotionally unstable, frivolous, foppish, eccentric, and wildly extravagant, he desired only to be left to lead his life in his own way. That way was not the king's and, inevitably, vehement clashes occurred in which the king always got the better of the son who stood in such great dread of him.

One of the most violent of the quarrels between father and son took place some four years after Edward was named Prince of Wales. The Bishop of Chester, Walter Langton, treasurer of the Exchequer, a man on whom the king greatly depended for sound advice on domestic, foreign, and financial policy, complained to his sovereign that the Prince of Wales and his friends had broken into his woods and that, when reprimanded by him, the prince used the most unprincely and insulting language. The king, ever loyal and strictly honorable in his association with his ministers, considered an insult to them as a personal dishonor, and promptly flew into one of his tempestuous rages. He forbade Edward to come into his presence, forbade him to see certain of his friends, Piers Gaveston among them, and ordered that all support of the upkeep of the prince's court must be instantly stopped.

Young Edward was terrified, horrified, and alarmingly incommoded. There seemed only one way out of the impasse;

he would hang around at some distance from the royal presence in the hope of once again being taken into his father's favor. But waiting brought him no reward and, as the king was constantly on the move through the country, all the young man could do was to follow in his father's wake "at a distance of ten or twelve leagues." These peregrinations continued for a whole month and every day Edward's funds grew lower and lower, grew so low, indeed, that he had to borrow in order to continue the pursuit of the king.

The end of a month brought a slight cooling off of the king's fury, enough, anyway, to make him order that the prince should be given "a sufficiency of necessaries." It was not an elegant sufficiency and luxury-loving, extravagant Edward found it impossible to keep up the standard of living to which he was accustomed. At this point Margaret, his stepmother, who always made brave efforts on his behalf when trouble came between him and his father, again came to his aid. The young girl's influence over her old husband must have been great indeed, for she managed to persuade the king to give permission for Piers and other of Edward's disgraced friends, to be again in the prince's company "to alleviate the anguish which we have endured and still suffer daily through the ordinance and pleasure of our lord the King." But the king would not see his son and, aware of his way of life, kept him under strict supervision, forbade him to return to Langley, and commanded that he remain in or near Windsor Park until he, the king, wished otherwise. Edward was so terrified of his father that he obeyed each of these commands punctiliously, even going so far as to refuse invitations to visit his sisters, Joan and Mary.

After a little while matters further improved and Edward was at last admitted into the king's presence. He was called to a banquet at the Palace of Westminster though not allotted a royal seat. The old king had by no means either forgiven or regained confidence in his son. But it was expedient at this time that, in public at least, it should appear that he had taken him back into favor. The king was sixty-six and far from well. Trouble was brewing again in Scotland and he realized that, should the condition of his health worsen, Edward would have to act as his substitute. For these reasons, under pressure from his queen and his daughters, Elizabeth and Joan, who were deeply attached to Edward, he agreed to the reconciliation. At the same time important formalities concerned with Edward's marriage to Isabella of France were begun. Before they could be completed, however, unrest in Scotland and the king's health grew steadily worse.

Edward was now twenty-two. A month after his birthday he was "adorned with the belt of knighthood" and granted further honors and territories, the latter including the Duchy of Aquitaine and the island of Oléron. Edward was knighted in the chapel of the Palace of Westminster on May 22, 1306. His sick old father girded him with his swordbelt and the Constable of England and the elderly Earl of Lincoln fastened on his spurs. This ceremony over, the royal party repaired to the Abbey where, at the high altar, the Prince of Wales himself knighted some two or three hundred young men, all of whom "were bound in succession to their fathers to become knights, and had means whereby they could perform the duties of knights."

In celebration of the knighthood conferred on the Prince of Wales, a banquet, of a splendor and magnificence never before seen, was held in the Palace of Westminster. The proceedings were enlivened by eighty minstrels in bright and rich garments. Their hiring for the occasion cost the old king £130, a vast sum for those times. While the company sat at table, two swans were brought in. Upon these royal birds all present then took vows. The king swore that, once he had settled his account with Bruce of Scotland, he would never again draw his sword except in the cause of the Holy Land; and the

Prince of Wales swore that he would not sleep two consecutive nights in any place until he reached Scotland and there helped to discharge his father's vow.

Two weeks later, having gone to say farewell to his stepmother in Winchester, and taking his pet lion, chained and collared, and its keeper, in a cart, Edward set off on his mission to Scotland. The king, though now seriously ill and unable to ride, left London two days later. This new campaign against Scotland in which, not the king, but the Prince of Wales played the major role, was to prove one of great cruelty. Edward, whose army was ahead of his father's, showed no mercy to his enemies. A contemporary chronicler wrote that "He would spare neither sex nor age. Wherever he went, he set fire to villages and hamlets and laid them waste without mercy. This is said much to have displeased the King his father, the more so as the hapless populace were paying the penalty for their betters, as the rich had taken to flight," wrote an ancient historian.

It is nevertheless doubtful whether the king really disapproved of his son's mercilessness. What Edward did was strictly within the limits of the knightly code of the times, a code which rarely, if ever, was applied in dealings with or treatment of people belonging to the lower social strata. The old king was displeased for quite another reason, this being that, in the middle of the campaign, a number of well-known knights, mostly Edward's friends and members of his court, growing bored, left Scotland without leave, "deserting the King and his son in those parts, in contempt of the King and to the retarding of the King's business there." By command of the king "the lands, goods and persons" of twenty-two of the deserters were seized. Again young Queen Margaret was able to pacify her desperately sick and aged husband and secured pardon for sixteen of these undutiful and irresponsible young knights.

Edward suffered in no way from the king's wrath and, in

fact, despite his ruthlessness and the waywardness of his friends, was in better grace with his father than usual. Indeed, feeling himself more secure than ever before in his life, the foolish young prince took an unprecedented liberty. He who had publicly called Piers Gaveston "brother," who vowed that his affection for Piers was "above all mortals," went before his father and requested that the fief of Ponthieu, which he had inherited from his mother, be given to the Gascon.

The scene that followed this appeal surpassed in violence any that had ever before taken place between father and son. "Thou to give away lands!" shouted the dying, frenzied king. "Thou who never won any! God alive! Were it not that the kingdom might fall into anarchy, I would take care that you shouldst never come to thine inheritance!" Beyond himself with rage, the old man flung himself at his son, grabbed at his hair and began pulling it out by the handful.

After this monumental scene the king banished Piers from England for life. Edward was made to swear on his father's "holiest relics" never to have Piers Gaveston "near him or with him" and never to give lands or titles to this "certain Gascon knight." Since Piers went to France and was there well provided for financially, it might be assumed that the king may have regarded him as much sinned against as sinning, and that it was Edward whom he saw as the real culprit, the actual worker of iniquity in the scandalous intimacy that existed between the two young men.

Piers stayed in France only until the death of Edward I, for almost the first thing Prince Edward did on his accession was to recall his "idol," making him soon afterwards not only Earl of Cornwall but the husband of his niece Margaret, daughter of his sister Joan.

When King Edward I died in 1307 his undisciplined son, the first English Prince of Wales, became Edward II. Shortly after his coronation, at which Piers Gaveston appeared "so decked out that he more resembled the God of Mars than an ordinary mortal," the new king crossed to France for his bride, Philip of France's daughter, Isabella. Piers did not accompany him. The "idol" remained behind in England as regent of the kingdom.

From the start of his married life Edward neglected his girl-wife for his favorite and, according to the first Viscount Falkland, "she saw the King a stranger to her bed, and revelling in the embraces of his wanton unions, without so much as a glance or look on her deserving beauty." In fact, she did not bear Edward a child until after the murder of Piers, five years later. But after that, still other favorites claimed Edward's attention, and the gulf between him and his queen grew ever wider with the years. Isabella was to become for him "the she-wolf of France," his greatest enemy and the most powerful instrument in bringing about his final overthrow. Weak, incompetent Edward grew to hate her with so corroding a repugnance that, it is said, "the King carried a knife in his hose to kill Queen Isabella, and had said that if he had no other weapon he would crush her with his teeth."

This disastrous marriage lasted for almost twenty violent years. And so did Edward II's reign. When, in 1327, Parliament declared him unfit to rule, he was forced to resign his throne to his son, born at Windsor and also named Edward, eldest of his four children by Isabella of France. Eight months later Edward II was dead.

England's first Prince of Wales was the first English king to be deposed. He was also the first to be murdered.

III

However weak a king and perverted a man England's first Prince of Wales became, he did not merit the inhuman torture and brutal death which, planned and ordered by his wife's paramour, Roger Mortimer, in connivance with Queen Isabella, ended his life at Berkeley Castle in Gloucestershire one terrible night. The nearby villagers who heard his ghastly despairing screams when, at last, even his iron constitution could bear no further agony, crossed themselves and prayed for the passing of a soul in such pitiable torment.

The dead king was buried in Gloucester Cathedral, in a tomb so imposing and beautiful that it "obscured all his many faults" and men went to it from far and near on pilgrimage. His fifteen-year-old son, Edward, succeeded to the throne from which Edward II had been most ignominiously forced to resign and, within a few brief years, aided by powerful advisers, succeeded too, in avenging his father's murder. Roger Mortimer was overthrown and hanged and, freeing himself at last from his queen-mother's clutches, the new young king, Edward III, sent her into "Honourable retirement"—from which Isabella "looked looks of passion" for the rest of her life.

Edward III who, apparently, was never created Prince of Wales, ruled England for fifty years. He only resembled his eccentric, tragic father in fine looks and physical vigor. Like his grandfather, Edward I, he was a perfect knight and the very "mirror of chivalry." Soon after he became king, he married buxom, attractive Philippa of Hainault. Though still a mere child, her appearance already, it is reported, proclaimed her "fit to be truly the mother of men." This prognosis was to prove extraordinarily accurate, for nine of her thirteen children were sons. Three of her nine sons, Edward, future hero of Crécy and Poitiers; Lionel, who stood seven-foot-two out of his armor; and the almost equally tall and sinewy John of Gaunt, were destined to write their names large in history.

IV

When Queen Philippa gave birth to her eldest son at
Woodstock on a June morning in 1330, Edward III was
eighteen. The event threw him into such ecstasy that he immediately settled an annuity of £100 on Joan of Oxford and
another of £10 on Maud of Plumpton, nurse and "rocker" respectively to the newborn princeling.

According to chronicles, the infant Edward of Woodstock was a paragon. "Very fair, lusty and well-formed," all
who "beheld the beauty of his shape, the largeness of his size,
and the firm texture of his body" straightway were filled with
high and happy hopes for his future. Though Joan of Oxford
and Maud of Plumpton were always in attendance to nurse
and rock the royal baby, his mother, young Queen Philippa,
suckled him herself, a most unusual procedure for the times,
and a "fairer mother and more beautiful child were not to be
found in Christendom." Romantic enthusiasm, flavored with
flattery, inspired many an artist of the day to use the sixteen-
year-old mother and her bonny baby as models for their pictures of the Madonna and her Son.

The arrival of this baby made not only the artists but the
whole nation happy. After long years of perplexity, discord,
and disorder, his birth seemed to augur a more settled phase in
the life of the kingdom and "a new face of things began from
this time to appear." It was as well for the people that they
could not peer ahead into time, for eight years later war broke
out between England and France, that wearisome war which
was to fill almost the whole of Edward III's reign and, with
intervals of uneasy peace, go on for a hundred years. It should

not be forgotten that Edward III regarded the crown of France as his heritage, as passing to him through his mother, Isabella the "she-wolf." During his reign the arms of France were actually quartered with those of England, and so remained for the next four hundred years until Hanoverian George III had them removed.

The first seven years of the life of Edward of Woodstock, the boy who was to become England's second Prince of Wales, were passed tranquilly in growing into a strapping, handsome lad. Over the kingdom, after years of storm, lay a peaceful lull, broken only when Edward, the king, with his "knightly love of fighting," went campaigning against the Scots as his grandfather had done decades before. And with equally unsatisfactory results, for neither Edward I nor Edward III succeeded in making themselves overlords of Scotland.

Meantime the king's eldest son grew strong enough to bear the burden of great honors. In his third year little Edward of Woodstock was made Earl of Chester and in his seventh his father, girding him with a sword, made him duke of the newly created Duchy of Cornwall. So for the first time the title of "duke" appeared in English history.

The seven-year-old duke's earliest exploit was the dubbing of twenty young men as knights. He exhorted them to go forth "to do some deed of chivalrie for love of England," a command which they were able to obey soon enough during the interminable hostilities with France, called the Hundred Years War. At seven young Edward of Woodstock was also considered ripe for the start of expedient marriage negotiations. The king's initial choice for his eldest son was a French princess. Such a union would, he hoped, break up the alliance between Scotland and France. The plan, however, met with no success. Next followed subtle bargaining, first with Alfonso the Brave of Portugal, then with the Duke of Brabant, for the hands of their respective baby daughters. Nothing came of those hopes either. Young Edward of

Woodstock meanwhile went on playing happily with his companions, among whom was his nine-year-old cousin, Joan of Kent, like him a grandchild of Edward I, for whom he had a great fondness.

In his eighth and ninth years, after the war with France had begun and the king was campaigning across the Channel, the boy not only twice presided over Parliaments held in Westminster and Northampton but, as his father's representative, his "Locum tenens Regis or Warden of the Kingdom," actually occupied the throne. He probably understood little of what took place around him, yet he must, in some degree, have been impressed by the importance of being his father's alter ego, even though he played the part only at intervals and always briefly. But playing at king was no more than a respite from the daily training for his high position to which he was subjected almost from infancy.

The queen, sensible Philippa, had chosen her almoner, Dr. Walter Burleigh (or Burley), an erudite scholar of Merton College, Oxford, to be her son's tutor. A small group of boys shared young Edward's lessons so that "companionship might lend an increased interest in his studies." One of these little boys, Simon Burley, a kinsman of the tutor, became Edward's great friend and, years later, it was to this friend of long-standing that he entrusted the education of Richard of Bordeaux, his own son and heir.

The small boys who shared the royal pupil's early education sometimes got more than learning from these sessions. When he was naughty or rude or lazy, it was they who had to take the cuffs and whippings intended for him. The person of the king's son was, of course, sacred, so Edward could not himself be punished for boyish misdemeanors.

There were, it seems, no rebels against this absurd injustice, an unquestioned and accepted rule. Punishments, in any case, may have been meted out only infrequently. Edward was an exceptionally good boy, a true embryo knight.

His training in all knightly exercises, like his book-learning, had also begun early. From the age of six he was taught how to "sitte at mete seemly," how to behave in a courtly manner and "to danse and synge and speke of gentlenesse." For lessons in knightly behavior, a wide curriculum, the queen placed him in the hands of Sir Walter de Manny "who had performed so many gallant deeds in such various places that they were not to be counted." It was Sir Walter who taught him to sit well on a horse, to manage his arms, to "foreswear avarice and treason," to be liberal, just and modest, respectful and obedient to superiors, to acknowledge "as his only aim glory and virtue" and always to show the greatest courtesy to ladies: in short, the whole code of chivalry as well as the art of jousting.

Young Edward was an apt and enraptured pupil. Long before he was old enough to take part in tourneys he showed his prowess, eagerly watched by his mother, in "little tournaments"; in big ones he frequently appeared as page to his father, the king. As for the rules of court life, these he had at his fingertips long before he reached his teens. When only ten, during a visit paid to his father in Antwerp, this boy who could "sitte at mete" so well, could sing and dance and "speke of gentlenesse" with so much charm, was so handsome and graceful, so precociously mettlesome, so gallant and courteous to ladies, won the hearts of all the young Flemish girls invited to attend the king's Court. In years to come, of course, Edward was to be known far and wide as the "flower of all the chivalry in the world," the example par excellence of the nobleness and greatness of a perfect knight.

It should, perhaps be explained, in parenthesis, that the splendid code of knighthood had its limitations and that these were extraordinarily narrow. The perfect knight, as indeed Edward was, showed every possible sympathy, liberality, courtesy, justice, and consideration to friend and foe alike; but *only* if they were people of his own class. Of ordinary mortals knightly piety took no cognizance at all. They had no rights. For them there need be no parade of mercy, kindness, compassion, and humanity—a fact that must be remembered when making any sort of assessment of the life and character of Edward of Woodstock who became England's second Prince of Wales. To judge him by the standards of today would be both unreasonable and wrong. Loved and lauded by his contemporaries, he can only be sketched and evaluated within the cordon of his times.

When the war with France was four years old, shortage of money brought Edward III back home to England during a truce. One of the first things he did on his return, to "the Delight of the English Nation," and, so one historian surmises, to cheer himself up, was to create his thirteen-year-old son Edward, Prince of Wales. The boy was invested with a golden coronet, a gold ring, and a silver rod at the Palace of Westminster; he was granted lands, monies, and many privileges and in one swoop became a rich and powerful young prince. The great occasion was brilliantly celebrated. In some of the spectacular jousts that took place the newly created Prince of Wales showed his skill, much to the delight of his parents and the Court, who proudly watched as he went "everie daie his armour to essai in fete of armes."

But celebrations, tournaments and hunting the deer did not divert the king's anger against France. He still firmly upheld his claim to the French throne. At last he summoned Parliament. The young Prince of Wales, taking his seat for the first time as a peer of the realm, heard his father declare the truce with France untenable and that only "by battle or an honourable peace" could the situation be properly ended. And battle it was.

When the war started up again not Edward, the king's heir, but one of his brothers was made Warden of the Kingdom. This time the Prince of Wales sailed off across the Channel with his father to fight for the throne of France. On this, his first campaign, the prince was sixteen, his father thirty-four. They were more like brothers than father and son, two brothers who, steeped in the ideals of chivalry, regarded fighting as the only true vocation for gentlemen and war as a great adventure.

The English army landed at La Hogue and almost immediately the prince was in the thick of a battle. In this he acquitted himself so well that, the fighting over, the king knighted him on "that open field," an incentive that added further fuel to young Edward's burning desire for action. And action came his way quite soon.

On a day that began with a bright sun—"but the Frenchmen had it in their faces, and the English on their backs"—an August day at Crécy, he won his spurs. At Crécy, as was to be expected, the English knights fought gallantly, but in the struggle the English bowmen demonstrated, and much more positively than the refined spirit of knightly chivalry, how well-trained men, shooting off clouds of arrows, could rout an enemy.

The king, having complete confidence in his son's courage, entrusted the van of his army at Crécy to the sixteen-year-old boy. Nevertheless, he prudently placed two men of great military experience and judgment, the Earl of Warwick and Sir John Chandos, beside the young prince who, that day, was arrayed in a suit of dark armor.

The odds against the English were enormous. Thirty thousand of them waited to give battle to an enemy four times that number. But the dark-armored young prince had no doubt about the ultimate result of the struggle. There *could* only be victory for his cause. With Warwick and Chandos at his side, he led the attack. Three charges were made. All three failed to put the enemy to flight. The fighting raged with such violence around the prince at one stage of the battle that Warwick, far from happy about his responsibility for the safety of the heir-apparent to England's throne, sent a messenger asking help from the king who, at the head of reserves, was watching the grim struggle from a small hill.

"Is my son killed or wounded beyond help or to the earth felled?" Froissart chronicled the stern king demanding of Sir Thomas of Norwich who delivered Warwick's message.

"Not so, sir, but he is in rude shock of arms and does much need your aid," Sir Thomas answered.

"Go back to those who sent you hyther, Sir Thomas," the king ordered imperiously, "and say that they send no more to me for any adventure that falleth so long as my sonne is in life, and also say to them that they suffer him to win his spurs, for, God willing, this day shall be his and the honour thereof shall rest with him and those that be about him."

So, unaided by the king's reserves, the fierce fighting continued until the enemy forces began to crack. Banners wavered and sank, among them that of the old blind King of Bohemia with its "crest of an eagle's wing" and the motto *Ich Dien*. When at last Philip, the king of France, himself fled the field, the day belonged to the English, to Edward the prince, and to "those that be about him." Proudly then the king rode down from his hillock to embrace the "marvellous boy" crying, "Sweet sonne, God give you good perseverence, ye are my good sonne that ye have acquitted you nobly, ye are worthie to keep the realme."

A truce was called next day. While the French collected and buried their dead—the English casualties were incredibly small—the king and Edward, riding across the field of battle, came upon the body of the King of Bohemia. About him lay his dead knights, their dead steeds still joined together by bridles, for so the knights had striven to protect their sightless lord. Reverently the English king and his son had the body of Bohemia's sovereign carried to the nearest abbey and there, like true knights of chivalry, acted as chief mourners at the ceremonial funeral.

Prince Edward adopted the old blind sovereign's motto, *Ich Dien*, and from the dead sovereign's armorial bearings of an eagle's wing devised his own crest of ostrich feathers, the crest of England's Princes of Wales to this day. From this time onward, too, he always wore his suit of somber armor. One legend says that men called him the Black Prince after Crécy because of his dark armor; another that it was the French who gave him the name in awe of his "dread acts in battell" on that day. But there is still another which alleges that the name only came into use nearly two hundred years after Edward won his spurs at Crécy in 1346.

From Crécy the Prince of Wales led his men on to further victory, to besiege and, later, to capture Calais, which surrendered in August 1347 and remained an English port for the next two hundred and eleven years.

It was a proud moment for England when the king and his brave son came home again. They brought with them spoils so great that the whole nation was enriched. London acclaimed the prince with tumultuous hosannas. The whole nation lauded and idolized him. Everywhere splendid celebrations were held. There was jousting and feasting and great jubilation. To crown all these transports of rapture and ovations of triumph the king held a noble meeting in the Round Tower at Windsor. At this meeting he founded the peerless company of the "Knights of the Blew-Garter." It gave birth to that highest of all English honors, the Order of the Garter. Twenty-five men were the first to be honored that day in the Round Tower when chivalry was at its zenith in the reign of Edward III. Among them was the king's son, Edward, Prince of Wales. All the brave "Knights of the Blew-Garter" were young men: four not yet twenty years old; ten under thirty; the king himself only thirty-five.

Rejoicings were still at their height when the plague, the "Black Death," came sweeping across England. This dreadful scourge had scarcely begun to abate when, in 1350, the king of Castile out of friendship for the king of France, sent the first Spanish armada to attack the English coast and harass English shipping.

Edward III and the Prince of Wales, each in command of a flotilla of small ships, lay in wait for the enemy off the Sussex shore. From this vantage point they watched the approach of the Spanish fleet, ships "so handsome that it was a pleasure to look at them." As on a later occasion many of the proud Spanish vessels were soon at the bottom of the sea. The king and the Black Prince sank twenty-seven between them. The rest fled under cover of darkness. Dawn broke on an English naval victory, the "Batell of Espagnols sur mer," fought and won off Winchelsea.

After Crécy and the capture of Calais, the king stayed almost constantly in England, devoting himself to the home affairs of his kingdom. War and truces with France, ruled by a new king named John, continued, but from now on the Prince of Wales always led the armies that went to fight on the other side of the Channel.

One of these expeditions took place in 1355 when the Prince was twenty-five. It was an excursion primarily undertaken for the love of fighting for fighting's sake and the rewards of plunder, a wanton kind of adventuring that showed up the dark side of the moon of chivalry.

The Black Prince's small force which sailed from Plymouth to Bordeaux on this enterprise, found itself at Poitiers three months later. The time, after landing at Bordeaux and reaching Poitiers, had been spent in devastating a vast area of the French countryside and in bringing ruin, horror, and death to thousands of ordinary people. For them the prince's name became, as Napoleon's did centuries later, a synonym for terror. But the rich, the influential, and the aristocratic

French continued to see the Black Prince in a different light. They belonged to his "class spirit," understood the ideals of chivalry which he upheld and so for them he was still the courageous enemy worthy of their admiration and their prowess, in every way a "verray parfit gentil knight." After all, they could appreciate the true meaning of chivalry, for was it not in their land of France that the first seeds of chivalry germinated and burst into full bloom?

The English force that reached Poitiers numbered eight thousand; at its head the Black Prince and his knights, the rest simple archers. Facing them the French were in enormous strength, "for all the flower of French nobility was there: no knight nor squire, for fear of dishonour, dared to remain at home." Despite this huge disparity in numbers, the Black Prince was determined to give battle. God, this pious, uncomplicated prince believed with unquestioning conviction, would defend the right. Speaking words of cheer and encouragement, he went from group to group of his followers "so that they were all in high spirits." After which, drawing a little apart from them, he remained for a while in prayer, alone . . . And then the fighting began.

As at Crécy, it was the archers who made this day an English victory, though the lion-hearted Black Prince and his knights fought with superb dash and courage. All were brave men at Poitiers but bravest of the brave, it is said, was the prince. Yet, he was so modest a man that, in letters which he sent home to England he made no mention at all of his own achievements and took no credit to himself. Quite simply he told only the plain facts of that day's events.

The fighting ended when King John of France was taken prisoner together with his son and many of his nobles. To the conquered king the Prince, who had so recently ravaged towns and lands and allowed great violence to be done to thousands of ordinary people, bent his knee "in the best manner" and "spoke many comfortable words" of consolation.

As usual on the evening after a battle, the victor held a great banquet for the vanquished. Since the English had practically no provisions the repast was entirely composed of excellent foods captured from the French. Placing the prisoner king, his son, and nobles in the seats of honor, the Black Prince himself waited on them, speaking words of encouragement to each in turn, praising their courage and consoling them for their ill-luck in the battle, "ascribing all to the will of God." He was particularly attentive and compassionate to the captured king of France. "Dear Sir, do not make a poor meal because the Almight God has not gratified your wishes in the events of this day," he begged. "Be assured that my father will show you every honour and friendship in his power, and will arrange your ransom so reasonably that you will henceforward always remain friends."

When the prince returned to a London that once again rejoiced wildly in welcoming him home, he took his captives with him. With him they rode through the streets. The prince deliberately chose for himself a small, neat black horse, but mounted his august prisoner, the king of France, royally on a great white charger. At the Palace of Westminster the king of England received the noble prisoners and his beloved son, whose courage had enlarged England's possessions in France to an extent as great as in the days of the old Angevin empire of a hundred and fifty years before.

The royal captives were entertained right chivalrously by King Edward and the prince. In knightly fashion the French king's ransom was arranged; the amount, a sum of three hundred thousand crowns—equal to the English king's income for five years. It was further agreed that the king of England would renounce his claim to the throne of France. This renunciation, however, was never fully implemented and future English kings again and again resuscitated this right.

All the new territories which had been conquered the king ceded to the Black Prince. At the same time he also agreed to buy from him, for a sum of £20,000 a number of lesser prisoners captured at Poitiers! The prince needed money urgently and this was one way of getting it. Overgenerous and wildly extravagant, he was always in want of funds.

Edward the Black Prince—irrespective of his being known by that name in his lifetime or not—was now in his twenty-seventh year, a man renowned not only in his own country but throughout Continental lands for his bravery as a soldier and as the living personification of chivalric ideals. To the amazement of the world, he was still unmarried. When he was a little boy there had been, it will be recalled, a number of projects for marrying him suitably, all of which had failed. When he grew older there had been still others. These also had proved fruitless, though not, let it be understood, for diplomatic reasons. The ladies in question at these later dates had all been most willing to ally themselves to so handsome and splendid a prince. In each instance it had been the prince who held back at the crucial moment. For this there was a good and romantic reason. His heart was otherwise engaged.

Ever since childhood he had truly loved only one woman, the playmate of his stripling days, his cousin Joan of Kent. Not that he had not savored love affairs with attractive young women. On the contrary, he was a full man and manfully had fathered several natural children. But his heart belonged to Joan who had married and was engulfed in domestic duties when he was still a boy. Theirs is one of the great love stories of English history.

It is difficult to understand why the prince had not wed Joan of Kent before she embarked on the first of her marriages. True, they were both children, she his senior by a few years, but that was a matter of no consequence. She was a beautiful girl, a great heiress, and of royal blood. Yet despite love and beauty, wealth and royal blood, diplomatically she was no wife for Edward the prince. Instead, she married Sir

Thomas Holland, who later fought with the prince at Crécy.

It was while Sir Thomas was engaged in this campaign that William de Montagu, Earl of Salisbury, suddenly produced a prior claim to Joan and, in her husband's absence, married her! When Holland returned to England, very much alive and well, he immediately set machinery in motion to annul this in-between matrimonial venture, and succeeded. Very happily, he and Joan then resumed their former union and had children, to one (or more) of whom the Black Prince, Joan's "dear friend and cousin," was godfather. Holland eventually became Earl of Kent, having assumed the title which his wife inherited on the death of her brother. He died in 1360.

With Holland dead, the Black Prince, who had all his life hidden his love for his cousin, dreamed at last of asking for her hand. The widow was besieged by wooers and the prince, a modest man even in love, feared greatly that he stood but a poor chance of winning this battle. He made his first overtures tentatively by representing himself as the spokesman for a friend. Eloquently expressing the passionate desire of his supposed friend, he urged Joan to marry. No, said the lady, she was fully determined never to wed again.

The prince attacked again and yet again; talked, pleaded, cajoled, and put forward a crop of cogent reasons why she must take a husband. Still he spoke only on behalf of his alleged friend. When Joan could no longer defend herself against his constant cannonade of persuasion, she sought shelter in tears. The prince, gentle in comfort, kissed his cousin and begged to be told the reason for her distress. She told him, weeping, a half-truth of the matter. She loved only one man, "the most chivalrous knight under Heaven," and never, never, could she think of marrying another. Who was this incomparable man, Edward begged to be told. She dared not, she declared, ever mention his name. When he implored, entreated, supplicated, he secured for answer only more tears.

But at last she capitulated. "My dear and indomitable lord," she confessed, "It is you—and it is for love of you that I will never have any other knight by my side."

Prince Edward, it is chronicled, was "greatlie amazed" to hear these words. For a man of his caliber, a strangely naïve amazement. His astonishment could have been of brief duration only since he forthwith poured out his love in a gush of words. "My lady," he cried, "I also vow to God that as long as you live, never will I have any woman save you to wife."

Though at first Queen Philippa was not at all enamored of her future daughter-in-law, Edward married Joan in spectacular magnificence at Windsor on October 10, 1361. The groom was thirty-one; his lady two years older.

Never before in England had there been a marriage of a Prince of Wales. The unique occasion sent the nation into wild rapture. Even the poorest in the land agreed that, whatever the cost of the wedding, magnificence became such a prince.

For several months, through the old year and into the new, the prince and his bride lived in gaiety and glitter either at their grand house in London or their country house at Berkhampstead, in Hertfordshire, for the prince "was addicted, when serious duties did not prohibit it, to a joyous life and accessories of splendour." Edward, nonpareil of princes in knightly ardor and courage, generous to his friends and magnanimous to his enemies, was in fact the most extravagant of heroes. He loved dash and splendor and opulent living. Fortunately the people of England, who lauded and loved him, did not begrudge his surcharged lavishness. For them it was an extension of his image. How else should so noble and great a prince live if not extravagantly and magnificently?

In July, 1362, the year when a second and more severe wave of plague struck England, the king invested the Black Prince with the principality of Aquitaine and Gascony and gave him the title of Duke of Aquitaine.

During this terrible 1362 epidemic many people of high rank died, among these Edward III's cousin, the Duke of Lancaster. Lancaster left no male heir. He was survived only by two daughters. Blanche, the younger, married Edward III's and Queen Philippa's tall and sinewy son, John of Gaunt. Later, when Blanche on the death of her sister inherited all her father's wealth and her right to the title, her husband became Duke of Lancaster and, in time, "Time honoured Lancaster."

In this year of the devouring plague Edward the Black Prince and Joan left England to live and rule over Aquitaine and Gascony. At Bordeaux they set up a court so brilliant, so magnificent, so rich in entertainment and in the presentation of great feasts and jousts, that its renown spread throughout Europe. Every "travelling king and ruler" made it a port of call. All of which was, of course, tremendously exciting, but also a vast drain on Edward's finances. The citizens of Aquitaine, unlike the people of England, viewed the great prince's extravagance with far less kindly eyes.

For nine years Edward and Joan lived in the greatest imaginable splendor at their court in the duchy of Aquitaine. There the two sons of their marriage, Edward of Angoulême and Richard of Bordeaux, were born; there, at the age of five, Edward, the eldest boy, died—since it is chronicled that he "did not die too soon," it is usually presumed that he was mentally defective. From there the famed Black Prince set out on a gallant, generous, and foolish adventure in support of wily, unreliable Pedro and Cruel of Castile, a man he did not particularly like. But Pedro was a king and one, moreover, expelled from his throne with the help of England's old enemy, France. Chivalry demanded that he be succored.

Always short of money, the campaign on behalf of Pedro ate into the Black Prince's resources. When the shortage grew desperate, he melted down his plate to buy supplies in the hope of easing the sufferings of his men. But Spain took heavy toll of his followers, and of him. He became extremely ill, probably as the result of dysentery. Yet he continued with his crusade, won a great victory at Nájera and finally restored the tyrant Pedro to his throne, receiving in return not so much as a gesture of gratitude.

Though the opulent living at his court continued after the prince returned to Aquitaine, his coffers were now so depleted that he was forced to raise money by imposing a hearth tax on his French subjects. Not only did they protest vigorously against this measure but sent an urgent appeal for help to the king of France, Charles V, son of dead John captured by the Black Prince at Poitiers. Imperiously Charles summoned the Black Prince to Paris. "I will come," riposted Edward, "but with sixty thousand men at my back," a tocsin of an answer that set off yet another war with France.

This grim war proved so great a disaster that it cost England all her possessions in France excepting only the districts around Bordeaux and Bayonne and the port of Calais. When it started the Black Prince was not well. As it progressed, his condition grew steadily worse. At Limoges, the last battle in which he was able to take command, he had to be carried in a litter. He won a victory there, but paid dearly for it, sullying his great name by ordering the massacre of the people of the city.

When Edward at last returned to Bordeaux and to Joan, he was a bitter, broken man, wrecked in strength and desperately sick. His natural dash and cheerfulness wrung from him, he had become exacting, irritable, and morose. The death of his eldest son saddened him still further. So, leaving Aquitaine in the care of his ambitious brother, John of Gaunt, now Duke of Lancaster, he sailed to England with Joan and their only surviving child, Richard of Bordeaux.

For a short time after his return to England in 1371, the

Black Prince's health seemed to improve. But the state of the kingdom grieved him deeply. He had come home to find an England not only suffering from the effects of the disastrous war with France and faced again with the dire after-effects of another wave of the Black Death, but rotten with corruption and poor government. His splendid mother, Queen Philippa, was dead; his much-loved father the king, fast sinking into premature senility, was now ruled by Alice Perrers, his ambitious mistress.

Though his health soon began to worsen again, the prince gathered the last remains of his strength in an effort to right some of the domestic wrongs. In the last year of his life he played no small part in the deliberations of the "Good Parliament" which met in 1376.

Prince Edward's tortured body grew so weak that often, lying in a coma, his servants thought him dead. But again and again his great spirit rallied. On such occasions he would speak cheerfully to Joan and little Richard who were almost always at his bedside. During the last weeks of his life, though he knew that he was dying, he commanded that "hys doore sholde be shutt to none, nor to the leaste boy" (page). And he made his will. Neither in it nor on his deathbed did he forget to mention every one of his servants. He made little Richard promise, on his honor, never to dismiss "or cast off" any man who had served him long and faithfully. Kneeling beside his dying father Richard, small, thin, and very pale, listened to the once gay, manly voice now a mere trembling whisper. The child wanted to cry, to cry and run into the anteroom. He was desperately frightened. Not of his dying father, but of death.

On Trinity Sunday, 1376, in his forty-sixth year, Edward the Black Prince, Duke of Aquitaine, "Flower of all the Chivalry in the World at that time," the most romantic of all England's Princes of Wales, died at his father's Palace of Westminster. His body was embalmed and carried along the

Pilgrims Way to rest in Canterbury Cathedral. His helmet and gauntlets were placed above his tomb. Everywhere in English lands masses were sung for the repose of his soul. Even his enemies across the Channel held funeral services for him. And Joan, unconsolable, wept bitterly.

Joan, that once exquisite lady, survived Edward by ten years, by which time she had grown so stout "that motion was to her a rather troublesome process." She was buried not in Canterbury Cathedral where Edward, whom she had dearly loved, lay at peace, but in accordance with her own strange wish expressed in her last will and testament, in the Church of the Grey Friars at Stamford, close to her first husband, Thomas Holland, Earl of Kent.

V

Before he died the Black Prince begged his father to make his small son Richard, as soon as possible after his death, the next Prince of Wales. Even in the dark days of dying he was fully conscious of the desire for power, not only from behind the throne but on it, of his brother John of Gaunt, Duke of Lancaster. The sorrowing, suffering old king, whose own life was to flicker out a year and thirteen days after the passing of his eldest son, did as his loved son desired. So, for the last seven months of the fifty-year reign of Edward III, Richard of Bordeaux was England's third Prince of Wales.

Richard was born when his father was preparing to start from Bordeaux on that chivalrous expedition in support of Pedro the Cruel's restoration to the throne of Castile. It is in fact chronicled that he arrived prematurely, his birth brought on by Joan's distress at the prospect of parting from Edward.

"Alack!" she is said to have cried out in her grief, "what would I do if I lost the true flower of chivalry, the flower of most high nobility, he who in all the world has no peer for bravery? O Death, you would be near at hand! I have no heart, no blood, no veins, every limb fails me, when I think of his going. All the world agrees that never did man embark upon so perilous a journey. Most kind and glorious Father, comfort me with your pity."

Tenderly Edward tried to comfort her. "Lady, cease your weeping. Do not be cast down, for God is all-powerful."

But Joan could not, would not be comforted. And so, "from very sorrow," it is said, she was taken in labor. Her baby, soon to be named Richard, was born on Wednesday, January 6, 1367.

"Here is a right fine beginning," cried the Black Prince in happiness at the child's safe delivery, accepting it as a good omen for his forthcoming expedition.

One of the prince's officers, Sir Richard Punchardon, set off as soon as he was able to tell the good news to the chronicler Froissart. "Write," he cried to Froissart. "Write that it may be remembered, that my lady the Princess is brought to bed of a fine son. He is born on Twelfth Day, the son of a King's son, and shall be King himself!" Since the eldest son of the Black Prince, Edward of Angoulême, was still alive at the time, this was a remarkably odd thing for Punchardon to say. However, if poor little Edward was, as it is supposed, an imbecile, Punchardon's words might have expressed the widely held hope that the unfortunate child would soon die. Added to this, his emphasis of the fact that the Princess had given birth to a *fine* boy must surely have expressed the relief felt by the whole court that the new baby was apparently, unlike his elder brother, mentally normal.

Once, it appears, there were ancient chronicles, now unfortunately lost, which stated that Richard of Bordeaux was born "without skin and was nourished in the skins of goats."

For such a supposed deficiency the Middle Ages' treatment was singularly unpleasant. The skin-deficient infant had to be kept warm inside the bodies of newly slaughtered animals. An animal was brought into the room, its throat cut and belly slit wide open *in situ* and the baby immediately placed in "the cavity." When the carcass began to cool, another animal was brought in and the same procedure repeated indefinitely.

How long it took baby Richard to grow a "proper epidermal layer" no one knows. He was undoubtedly a tiny, frail slip of mortality, for he was baptized without delay—in the presence of many august guests, among them Don Pedro of Castile whom Joan actively disliked and the Black Prince was only befriending in conformity with the code of chivalry.

That Richard, yellow-haired and tiny, was delicate and, in consequence, much coddled, cosseted, and cuddled by his mother and her ladies, is beyond all doubt. Inevitably the fact of his premature birth, his fragility, his being confined too long to the care of women who indulged, petted, and pampered him, affected and determined his character.

Richard never knew his heroic father in the full vigor of his manhood in Aquitaine. The Black Prince, rejoicing in his son's birth on a Wednesday, proud at the baby's baptism at the holy font of St. Andrew's Church in Bordeaux on the following Friday—the King of Majorca and the Bishop of Agen, after whom Richard was named, were the godfathers—went off with his army to war on Sunday, the war from which he returned to Bordeaux broken in spirit and in health, a changed and stricken man. It was during the time that the Black Prince was campaigning in Spain on Don Pedro's behalf that his baby son took the first steps towards matrimony. Policy demanded that he be affianced to Leonora, the little daughter of the King of Aragon. The betrothal was short-lived.

In 1371, when the mortally sick Black Prince and his wife returned to England, Richard was not quite five. Sometimes the boy lived with his parents at their country house in Hertfordshire, at others in London, at their home in Kennington near the Thames. Still spindle-shanked and far from strong, the air of England agreed with him. Though soon "twice the boy he had been in Aquitaine," he was very thin and his blue eyes looked sad, dreamy and enormous in the small pinched, pale face crowned with its tumble of yellow hair.

When his illness increased in gravity, nothing gave the Black Prince greater ease of spirit, after a return to consciousness from long, dark intervals of coma, than to find the two most loved beings in his life, his wife and his son, seated at his bedside. That small, grave-eyed Richard shared his passion for fine horses was a source of deep joy to him. Long and earnestly they would talk together during these easier moments of the prince's dying weeks of this and that steed or charger, or gravely discuss the merits and demerits of the boy's newest pony. It was the Black Prince's dying hope that his son would one day be a fine horseman, a noble fighter, a great leader in war, and a most virtuous and gallant knight.

But Richard was not made of such clay. Neither his physique nor his mother's upbringing helped towards making him into the likeness of his dying father's visions. Intelligent and already thought by some "over-bookish" for his years, he was a strange child. Affectionate and gentle, his little, pale, aesthetic face was stamped with an almost feminine sensibility. Yet he was in no way effeminate, in no way unmanly, and never in all his life cowardly. Of exceptional sensitivity, easily affected and shocked by ugliness, by any form of cruelty and violence, he was a creature of dark moodiness that bred vehement passions. In consequence, for all his gentleness, he could, and did, often behave with extreme waywardness and obstinacy. Here was the spoiled boy who, when he did not get his way, flew into savage tantrums, unrestrained paroxysms of rage which set him tearing cushions to shreds, kicking at and breaking every object within his reach, even those precious to him because he found them beautiful. For Richard loved beauty. He loved flowers too. But not the flowers of chivalry. For these he had scarcely any liking at all.

This child was in every way father to the man he grew to be. As man and king his behavior was often as strange and contrary as that of the little boy. Idealist and pacifist at heart, he desired, and justly, during the first years of his reign, to make peace with France. His affectionate nature showed itself in his passionate devotion to his first wife, Anne of Bohemia, and in the warm-hearted regard and kindness he bestowed on Bolingbroke's son. Yet he savagely appropriated the estates of this same boy's father and, indeed, of many of his barons. He would give charters with one hand to his less fortunate subjects and take them away again immediately with the other. He was savage too in his attempts to make himself absolute, declaring that "the laws were in his mouth or in his breast" alone.

Some historians incline to the belief that Richard was perhaps a little tainted with the madness which made it best for his brother, Edward of Angoulême, to die in boyhood. The tragedy of Richard's life probably lies buried in the reality that fate forced a hollow crown of kingship upon the head of a child of strange passions who might have found happiness as a poet. But this is only conjecture.

There is, however, certainty in the fact that Richard's character was in almost every sense a complete contrast to that of his father. A love for horses and unrestrained extravagance were the only qualities he had in common with the Black Prince. When he became England's king, his court was renowned for opulent magnificence and, in particular, for the color, beauty, and pageantry of its clothes. The Black Prince loved fighting for fighting's sake: Richard at heart was a man of peace. The arts of peace, certainly, were dearer to him than the art of jousting. In his tragic reign, made dark with political strife, modern English literature was born. Chaucer lived and wrote. So did Wycliffe. And so did William Langland, author of the "Vision of Piers Plowman" which spoke of the wrongs of the era, the ills and injustices that led to the Peasants' Revolt fanned by fanatical John Ball demanding an answer to his insurrectional text:

When Adam delved and Eve span,
Who was then the gentleman?

Those days, however, were still far distant from the hour when Richard stood beside his dying father, far distant from the day, three weeks after his father's death, when he appeared in Parliament for the first time "that all might see and honour him as heir to the throne in his father's stead." For Edward III, though in his dotage and stricken with grief, kept the promise he had made to the dying Black Prince and raised Richard to his father's honors, privileges, revenues, and lands. The boy, not yet ten, was created Prince of Wales, Duke of Cornwall, and Earl of Chester at Havering-atte-Bower on November 20, 1376. On Christmas Day his grandfather held a grand banquet in his honor. "Great satisfaction," it is recorded, "was given to all who retained a Grateful Sense of the Merit of the Lamented Black Prince" when his son, the young Prince of Wales, was given precedence over his uncles and made to sit on the right hand of the old king, his grandfather.

In the spring of the new year—at the time when a treaty was being discussed for the boy prince's marriage with Mary, daughter of the king of France, for which, however, negotiations failed—Richard was made a Knight of the Order of the Garter. On the same day his cousin, Henry, Earl of Derby, a little boy his senior by just one year, was also invested with the Order. This boy, son of John of Gaunt, Duke of Lancaster, was later to be known as "warrior born" Bolingbroke. In years to come, by deposing his cousin Richard, Bolingbroke "mounted high to sit upon the throne." Already at the time of the Garter ceremony there were whispers that "it would have been more fitting" if Richard and Henry "could have exchanged sires." But as yet the whispering made no ripples on the surface of the kingdom's life.

Senile Edward III, all his knightly vigor decayed, died in June of this year (1377), seven months after creating his grandson Prince of Wales, and in July Richard was crowned king in Westminster. Since he was only ten years old the government of the realm was invested in a Council until such time as "the King was of an age to know good from evil."

So began the doomed reign of Richard II which was to last for twenty-two years and end in deposition and imprisonment in the Castle of Pontefract.

Some believe that Richard escaped from Pontefract, eventually reached Scotland, and there lived for the remainder of his life as a scullion. Others maintain that he died in his prison, either of cold or as the result of starving himself. It is, however, most likely that the poor, incompetent, brokenhearted king who had drunk so deep of griefs, was deliberately starved to death; in other words, conveniently murdered. He entered his longed-for "little, little grave" in February, 1400.

VI

The Black Prince was Edward III's eldest son and Richard, the king's grandson, was, therefore, the rightful heir to the throne. When Richard died (or was murdered) at the Castle of Pontefract, he left no children to claim his inheritance from his usurping cousin, Henry of Bolingbroke, once Earl of Derby. Bolingbroke was the son of Edward III's *third* (surviving) son, John of Gaunt, Duke of Lancaster—hence the establishment by Bolingbroke of the Lancastrian royal line of Plantagenets.

At the time of his ascending the throne Bolingbroke's guns might very well have been spiked by the descendants of John of Gaunt's older brother, Edward III's *second* son, long Lionel, Duke of Clarence. This, however, did not happen; that is to say, did not happen at the time. The eruption occurred fifty years later, after two Lancastrian kings had ruled and died and a third was on the throne—all of them named Henry. Only then did the descendants of Lionel, Duke of Clarence, join forces with the descendants of Edward III's *fourth* son, Edmund, Duke of York, and, calling themselves Yorkists, set about fighting the Lancastrians, the emblem of one side being a white rose; the other a red. The long, merciless, ferocious, and catastrophic struggle which followed, known by that fantastically euphemistic name "The Wars of the Roses," was instrumental in bringing about the destruction of the entire Plantagenet dynasty.

Back in 1399, however, with Richard in Pontefract and no one challenging Bolingbroke's usurpation of the throne made under cover of a somewhat bogus Act of Parliament, this son of John of Gaunt became Henry IV, first Lancastrian king of England. Two days after his coronation at Westminster he created his eldest son, Henry, England's first Lancastrian Prince of Wales.

Richard II was twenty and already ten years a king when Mary de Bohun, the sixteen-year-old wife of his twenty-one-year-old cousin Henry (still known then as the Earl of Derby) gave birth to her first child, a boy, at Monmouth Castle in Wales, in September, 1386. Neither prophecies nor portents heralded future greatness for the infant lordling. There was, after all, little significance to the realm in the birth of a son to the Earl and Countess of Derby. Yet, twelve years later, this baby was created England's fourth Prince of Wales and as King Henry V became in time "one of the greatest ornaments of the English throne."

Henry of Monmouth, the fourth Prince of Wales, had two things in common with Edward of Caernarvon, the first. They were the only two of England's twenty-one Princes of Wales to be born in the Principality which gave them their title and both remained grateful to the women who nursed them in babyhood. Delicate as an infant, Henry of Monmouth was cared for with so much tenderness by his nurse, Johanna Waring, that he never forgot her. When, in his twenty-sixth year, he ascended the throne, he showed his devoted affection by settling on her an annuity of £20 "in consideration of good services done to him in former days." At that moment in his life he had thoughts for another woman too, for Mary de Bohun, his mother, whose memory he cherished. One of the first acts of his reign was to have an effigy of her placed over her tomb in Leicester. She had died at the age of twenty-three, after bearing six children. Henry, her eldest son, was then only seven.

Nothing occurred during the first decade of Henry of Monmouth's life to indicate that within him, slowly but surely, the seeds of a great general and strategist lay germinating. Nothing in the boy's character suggested that "touch of Harry," that fire which was to make of him an able and ambitious man and a heroic king whose deeds for England were to match those of the Black Prince. Like all small boys he delighted in playing at soldiers, but books and music stood high among the pleasures of this lively, nimble-footed child. These facts are borne out by his father's household accounts. In the year 1397, for instance, there appear such contrasting entries as "8d paid by the hand of Adam Garston for harpstrings purchases for the harp of the young Lord Henry" and a sum of "4s" spent "for seven books of grammar," as well as "12d to Stephen Furbour for a new scabbard of a sword for young Lord Henry" and "1/6 for ¾ of an ounce of tissue of black silk bought at London of Margaret Stranson for a sword of young Lord Henry." Despite the scabbard and the sword, the young Lord Henry did not in his childhood receive the same exacting training in arms as Edward the Black Prince.

Henry's mother and Johanna Waring were the two women who most deeply held his affections until his seventh year. Then, his mother dying, his maternal grandmother, but in some small measure only, filled her place. Male influences in any case, had now come to bear on him, in particular those of his tutor. Of his father, engaged in wars and politics, he saw little. There is a tradition that he was sent, at the age of eleven, to study at Queen's College, Oxford, where his uncle, Henry Beaufort, was chancellor. Beaufort was certainly chancellor in 1398, but no records exist to prove that Henry of Monmouth was ever a scholar at the college. More than likely he was sent to live with Beaufort for a time and this uncle supervised his studies. His stay in Oxford could, as it happens, have been only brief, for by this time his father, once close to King Richard, had fallen foul of his unstable royal cousin.

Richard, more wayward now than in childhood and liable to unrestrained and destructive tempers of ruthless avengement, not only banished Bolingbroke (whom he had come to regard as a personal enemy) from his kingdom, but confiscated all his possessions. He also placed Bolingbroke's eldest son, the young Lord Henry, now aged twelve, under restraint. This, fortunately, proved so lenient and clement a captivity that the boy, though guarded to prevent his abduction, became devoted to his captor. And the king grew to love his little prisoner; loved him, yet gave evidence of his nature's ill-balance by allowing only a meager annuity of £500 for the maintenance of the boy whose father's entire properties he

had appropriated to himself. Apart from this strange mean-
ness, Richard never showed anything but affection and kindness to the twelve-year-old boy "of fine parts" whose intelligence, vivacity, and good manners pleased him greatly.

England was at this time rapidly moving towards revolt
against the king. Whether blind to the approaching storm or
ostrich-like burying his head in the sand, Richard at this moment chose to set off and restore peace in ever-troublesome
Ireland. Determined that his young semi-prisoner should
"learn the art of war," he took Henry of Monmouth with
him; and Henry's brother, Humphrey, as well. For this adventure he fitted out young Lord Henry with clothes and
light coat-armor paid for "from his own purse." Henry was
able to make use of his light coat-armor soon enough after
landing in Ireland, for he took a manly part in the campaign
against recalcitrant chiefs. So impressed was King Richard by
the boy's behavior that at "the first opportunity that occurred" he knighted Henry on the battlefield under the royal
standard.

Richard and his two young semi-captives were still in
Ireland when news came that Bolingbroke had not only
crossed the Channel and landed in England but, with ever-
growing support, had resolved to make a bid for the throne.
Then came a second report. This told the unhappy king that
the Archbishop of Canterbury had taken sides with his enemy
and was promising all who fought with Bolingbroke "remis-
sion of sins, in the Pope's name" and "a sure place in para-
dise."

Before setting off in haste for England in August, 1399,
King Richard had a talk with the young Lord Henry. Ac-
cording to a chronicler, the king began the interview with
"Henry, my child, see what your father has done to me."
Sadly then he continued to elaborate the theme. In answer the

boy spoke of his grief at the dire news and begged the king to be "fully assured of my innocence in this proceeding of my father." To this, it is reported, the king replied: "I know that the crime which your father has perpetrated does not attach to you, and therefore I hold you excused of it." Nevertheless, before leaving Ireland, he took the precaution of having Henry and his brother Humphrey escorted to Trim Castle and there kept under strict guard. They were virtually prisoners. But so was Richard, the king, when he set foot in England.

August had not yet run its course before Richard II was made to resign his crown to Bolingbroke. He was then taken from the glory of his court to cruel Pontefract. The young Lord Henry and his brother were by this time safely back in London.

On October 13, 1399, the boys attended their father's coronation at Westminster. In the procession young Henry was given the honor of carrying Edward the Confessor's famous Sword of Justice, the great sword called Curtana. Two days later the boy himself appeared at Westminster as chief actor. His father created him Earl of Chester, Duke of Cornwall, and Prince of Wales. At a splendid ceremony the new king adorned the new Prince of Wales with a pearl-encrusted golden coronet, placed a gold ring on his finger, the rod of office in his hand, and blessed and kissed him. It must be further added that, almost immediately afterwards, eager for allies and anxious to strengthen his tricky position, especially vis-à-vis France, King Henry IV of England offered his son Henry, Prince of Wales, in marriage to a French princess. Courteously but firmly the offer was rejected.

Henry of Monmouth was thirteen years and two months old when he became Prince of Wales and not much older when his father sent him off to continue his education in "the art of war," begun under the aegis of King Richard II, in Ireland. The new exercise was against the Scots. It was followed a year later by another, against Owen Glendower in the Welsh

Marches. This campaign, like many another war, was expected to last only a matter of weeks. It dragged on for nearly fourteen years.

During the early stages of the fighting the young prince was always accompanied by a tutor whose duty it was to fill his head with book learning, to which Henry was not at all averse. However, by being so much and for so long in the company of fighting men, the young Prince of Wales learned a great many other lessons besides and found time, too, to indulge in his favorite recreations of hawking, hunting, fishing, riding, and running. Not till he was sixteen did he receive his first wound in battle. In 1403, at Shrewsbury, an arrow struck him in the face. When his men began to carry him to the rear he commanded that they take him forward. "How will others fight if they see me, a prince, the king's son, leaving the field?" he demanded angrily.

On and on the Welsh war dragged. Shakespeare says that during this war Prince Henry killed his namesake, Henry Percy, known as Hotspur, the brave soldier who once had fought on the king's side and then went into rebellion against him. Like many another story associated with the early life of England's fourth Prince of Wales, this has never been authenticated.

Fighting, constantly begging for money from his father and the Council, or pawning "a little stock" of his own jewels in order to go on fighting, were far from being Prince Henry's sole duties or interests during the war years. Frequently he went to London, spent longer or shorter interludes at Court and found time too, on three different occasions, to comply, though with little enthusiasm, to proposed marriage treaties. The first concerned a princess of Denmark, the second one from Burgundy, a third one from Brittany. The failure of these matches-in-the-making caused him no distress. To a lively, high-spirited young prince not yet twenty, life offered pursuits and adventures far more exciting than marriage.

Willingly, it is said, he gave his assent to these proposals as they came along. That done, he put such matters completely out of his head and set about enjoying himself with a great variety of "levities," for "passing the bounds of modesty and burning with the fire of youth, he was as eager in the pursuit of Venus as of Mars."

There are countless legends about Henry's riotous youth, of his "living insolently," mixing with bad company, of how, "accompanied with some of his young lords and gentlemen, he would awaite in disguise aray for his own receavers and distress them of theire money," and how "for imprisonments of one of his wanton mates and unthriftie plaisiers he strake the chiefe Justice with his fist on the face." The last accusation refers to Henry's alleged offence against Chief Justice William Gascoigne. First circulated more than a century after his death, this tale bears a remarkable resemblance to that incident in the life of Edward of Caernarvon, the first Prince of Wales who, for insulting Walter Langton, Bishop of Chester and treasurer of the Exchequer, was banished for a while from his father's presence. Since there is no formal record of Henry, the fourth Prince of Wales, ever being sent to prison by Chief Justice Gascoigne, the story can now never be proved either true or false.

It is difficult to gauge how much truth lies buried in any or many of the countless legends of Henry's youthful excesses. Probably their foundation rests on fact, but might it not be more probable still that towering pillars of gross exaggeration have risen up from the initial groundwork? After all, many a man's life has been clouded by the often erroneous belief that every puff of smoke presages a conflagration. Furthermore, Shakespeare has not helped matters by showing Henry as an unrestrained, bawdy, dissolute, scheming young man in the Henry IV plays. Indeed he has added to the enigma of the character of the prince in the years before he ascended the throne.

But if Henry really was a gay and irresponsible profligate, if he really did follow an abandoned way of life and, as Prince of Wales, was much given to secret plottings, would he have been made Captain of Calais, given a command in Wales, and, as was a later illustrious subject of the realm, Winston Churchill, made Warden of the Cinque Ports and Constable of Dover, as well as being given a seat in his father's Council? With so much work on his hands including the clearing of pirates from the Channel ports, taking a wide interest in politics, and carrying on lengthy correspondence with many rulers of the period, where did he find the time to indulge in all the great variety of excesses of which he is accused? Questions like these can reach pyramidal dimensions until one final query crowns the edifice. Was Henry, in fact, in any way more "riotous" than many a young man of his age and time?

As Prince of Wales he had his own Court and also exerted a certain amount of influence and authority at the Court of the king. At the latter he had enemies, some of whom sought desperately to destroy him in his father's eyes by maligning his character and belittling his merits. Was it these men who spread the rumors that he had taken money meant for the troops at Calais and used it for his own pleasures; that it was he, above all, who desired to force his father, an ailing king, to abdicate? That the king who, as Bolingbroke, had once been a master-plotter himself, should grow jealous and suspicious of his son, is not surprising. Nor is it surprising that sick, jealous, and suspicious, he should dismiss the prince from his Council.

The prince at this stage took strong action. First of all he sent letters to all parts of the kingdom refuting the "slanderous devises." Then, a band of followers at his heels and dressed in "blewe sattin full of small oilet holes, with at every hole a needle hanging by a silk thread," he went to Court. Leaving his friends "at a good distance," he approached his father and, kneeling before the king, told him humbly that he came before him as his liege man and obedient son, ready to die if his death would forever destroy the doubts and anger which dwelled in the king's mind. He had, he continued, made confession, taken the sacrament, and was ready to meet his fate. Whereupon, dramatically drawing forth his dagger, he proffered it to his father. Deeply moved, the king waved the weapon aside, clasped Henry in his arms, kissed him, and swore that never again would he doubt the loyalty of his brave son. It appears very clear that the king never wavered in his affection for his son and that the quarrels between them were at all times only political.

When the scene described above took place, Henry was in his mid-twenties, a young man of attractive appearance with thick, brown hair and bright hazel eyes which, it is said, glinted when he was angry. His face was oval in shape, his ears small and well-set, his nose straight, his chin deeply indented. An anonymous writer known as Titus Livius says that he "exceaded the meane stature of men: he was beawtious of visage, his neck was longe, his body slender and leane, his boanes smale. Nevertheless he was of maruelous greate strength: he was passing swift in runninge, in so much that he with two other of his Lords by force of runninge, with out any manner of hounds or greyhounds, or without bowe or other engine, would take a wilde bucke or doe at large in a parke"—a description that scarcely fits a man who allegedly gave up most of his time to wine, women, and the pursuit of vice in various forms.

At this period, too, as in the days of his boyhood, he "delighted in songe and musicale Instruments." He was also, according to the standards of his century, sincerely religious, though religious fanaticism never froze pity in his heart. The story is told of his attitude towards a poor Lollard doomed to be burned for heresy. The prince, it is related, spoke to the man for some time, in an effort to convince him of the error of his ways, but the Lollard refused to recant. Then followed the usual awesome execution: the unfortunate man was placed in a cask and committed to the flames. So terrible were his screams that Henry ordered him to be taken from the fire and again fell to pleading with the Lollard, promising that if he would but recant he, the prince himself, would provide for him for the rest of his life. Though by now more dead than alive, the poor victim remained adamant in his own beliefs and had to die in the consuming fire from which Henry, showing a compassion singularly alien to a fifteenth-century prince, had tried to save him.

Dick Whittington was Lord Mayor of London for the third time when Henry IV lay on his deathbed. The king had long been ill—he suffered from epileptic fits—and was so worn out in strength that to "bear the burden of the crown upon his head" had become too much for him. In *The Second Part of King Henry IV,* Shakespeare places the crown on the pillow beside the dying king's head, from where he makes Henry, the Prince of Wales, believing his sleeping father dead, lift it up and take it from the chamber. This crown-bearing episode has been proved no more than an invention. It passed from one chronicler to another and so from Holinshed to Hall, the sources on which Shakespeare drew when writing his great historical plays.

The king, who had so often quarreled with his heir on matters political, never, despite his bouts of jealousy and suspicion, ceased to love the prince and "died blessing him."

After his father's death Henry, it is recorded by Livius, "called to him a vertuous Monke of holie conuersacion, to whome he confessed himselfe of all his offences, trespasses and insolencies of times past. And at all things at that time he reformed and amended his life and manners. So after the decease of his father was neuer no youth nor wildnes, that might have anie place in him, but all his acts were sodenlie changed into grauitie and discretion . . . . wch is to saye he was sodenlie changed into a newe man."

On an April day in 1413 the son born to the Earl and Countess of Derby at Monmouth in Wales twenty-six years before, was crowned King Henry V of England. It was a day torn by a wind so wild and with snow falling so heavily that the people of London were frightened. Some, however, regarded the storm's convulsion as an omen that the "sodenlie changed" man had, in truth, "put off the winter of his riotous youth."

Among Henry's first acts as king was to honor his mother's memory and arrange for the comfort of his old nurse, Johanna Waring. He also paid a tribute of remembrance to the man whose throne his father had usurped and who, long ago, had shown him affection and kindness. He had Richard II's body taken from its little grave and laid in the tomb of Anne of Bohemia, the young wife Richard had deeply cherished. With this generous action he gave "due funeral honours to the remains of the King who had been buried without them."

The stirring reign of Henry V, greatest interpreter of "medieval English nationalism," lasted for nine years and four months. It was the reign of a happy warrior, a consummate general. Did the hero of Agincourt on that Saint Crispin's day think of Crécy lying less than thirty miles away? For his times he was a humane and generous man. If once, like many a gallant overcharged with youth's vitality, he may upon occasions have done foolish things, found fun and excitement in rash and reckless escapades, and taken no whip in hand against "the old offending Adam," the crown securely on his head made of him a king irreproachably decorous and exemplary in his private life.

During the little more than nine years of his reign, Henry conquered and occupied most of France, became heir to the French throne, and married the French king's daughter, Catherine of Valois. The baby she bore him was less than a year old when Henry died at Vincennes, in France, in August, 1422, mainly as the result, it is supposed, of the bungling quackery of his doctors.

VII

One of Henry V's dearest hopes, a hope often expressed, was of "begetting a son who should go to Constantinople and take the Turk by the beard." Instead, his and Catherine's only child, who as Henry VI inherited the English throne and was heir to that of France when only nine months old, grew into quite a different kind of man. Good he certainly was and also honorable, well-intentioned, and deeply religious. Learning and the whole republic of letters meant more to him than soldiers and soldiering. John Stow described him as "a comely prince." But he was, unfortunately, tainted with his French grandfather's madness. The fits of insanity to which he was frequently liable made it impossible during long periods for him to govern, a tragedy that proved disastrous not only to his country throughout one of its most turbulent eras, but also to the royal House of Lancaster.

Because Henry VI was so young a baby at his father's death, a regency had to be established and the boy was not crowned king of England until he was eight. Two years later he was also crowned France's anointed king at Notre Dame in Paris.

Though never created Prince of Wales, Henry VI is the only English king ever to be crowned king of France. He has one further distinction. He was the last *English first-born* son of a king to succeed his father for the next four hundred years. Such an event did not occur again until the seventeenth

Prince of Wales came to the throne in 1820 as George IV. The explanation for this is of interest.

To begin with, Henry VI's only son and the two Princes of Wales who came after him, form that trio of tragic princes, all named Edward, whose brief lives began and ended during the period of the Wars of the Roses that culminated with the advent of the Tudor dynasty. The first Tudor king's eldest son did not become England's sovereign; the second son did, as Henry VIII. This Henry was, it is true, succeeded by his son Edward. Edward was the child of Jane Seymour, third of Henry VIII's wives, but his first wife, Catherine of Aragon, had previously borne him two sons, premature babies who survived only long enough to be, in turn, christened Henry. The remaining Tudor monarchs, Edward IV and his half-sisters, Mary I and Elizabeth I, all died childless. Then, from Scotland, came the Stuarts. They also were not survived by *first-born* sons to succeed them and it took the Hanoverians, who followed the Stuarts, three reigns to produce an English first-born successor in the person of George IV.

Since it became clear early in his life that Henry VI, singularly shy and irresolute, was also mentally unstable, a strong-minded, vigorous girl was chosen as a suitable match for him. He was in his twenty-second year when he married attractive, talented Margaret of Anjou, the sixteen-year-old daughter of the titular king of Sicily and Jerusalem. Not till nine years later was their first, and only, child born at Westminster, coincidentally, on St. Edward's Day, 1453. According to the queen's wish, the baby was named Edward after three of Henry's great predecessors: pious Edward the Confessor, knightly Edward III, and the famed Black Prince. Since all of France won by Henry V had been lost again in the thirty years since his death at Vincennes, the name was an omen of hope to ambitious Queen Margaret. Passionately, she determined that her son would one day restore England's power over France.

King Henry VI was at Windsor, plunged deep in one of his "strange states of mental absence," when his son was born. Unfit to attend the christening, he did not see the infant until several months later. Even then he stared at it in blank silence, "uncurious and unconscious." Not until Christmastime did he become fully aware of the child's existence. Then, it is reported of this poor, often mad man, "he said he never knew, till that time, nor wist not what was said to him, nor wist not where he had been, whiles he had been sick till now."

For the Yorkist branch of the royal family the birth of baby Edward was no happy event. To Richard, Duke of York, heir-presumptive to the throne before the child's arrival and Protector and Defender of the king during his recent bout of insanity, it was especially unpalatable. The king might now be in slightly better health, but neither the Duke of York nor any of his noble supporters was prepared to knuckle down to the rule of an "enfeebled" Lancastrian. Though discontent was rising rapidly, baby Edward was created the fifth Prince of Wales in the first year of his life. Before his second birthday the Wars of the Roses had begun. Not so sweetly named at the time, this bloody and terrible struggle for power between the houses of York and Lancaster, each supported by their own magnates and servants, was to last, on and off, for nearly thirty years.

History records only the merest glimpses of Edward, the little Lancastrian Prince of Wales, during the early stages of the war, fought by his stout-hearted mother, sword in hand, and not his weak-minded father, against Richard, Duke of York. There is news of him in 1455 (he was then two years old) during a temporary truce, when, Henry VI being once again insane, the Duke of York was Protector of the kingdom. Parliament at this time agreed that ten thousand marks should be settled on the small prince until he reached the age of eight and that the sum be increased to sixteen thousand marks from his eighth to his fourteenth year. However, he was barely six when hostilities started up once more. During this period of fighting the victorious Yorkists captured Henry VI, took him to London and there forced him not only to accept the Duke of York as Protector of England, but to acknowledge the duke as heir to the throne, to the exclusion of his own son. Richard, Duke of York, was then, by ordinance of Parliament, actually styled Prince of Wales, Duke of Cornwall, and Earl of Chester.

So, for the first time in England's history there were two Princes of Wales at the same time; though the "true" Prince of Wales, that is little Edward the king's son, had been taken out of the kingdom. Evading the Yorkist clutches, his brave and adoring mother had fled with him across the border to seek refuge in Scotland. The fearful journey gained them their liberty, but during its many vicissitudes they were robbed of all their money and jewels.

In 1460, aided by the queen-regent of Scotland and with the help of Scottish troops, intrepid Queen Margaret, her small son always at her side, once more crossed the border, invaded England, and at Wakefield defeated the Yorkists. Richard, Duke of York, her bitter enemy, was killed in the battle. But now she had a new adversary, for York's son, Edward, Earl of March, took up his father's leadership and in turn claimed the throne.

With the help of the powerful Earl of Warwick, soon to be known as Warwick the Kingmaker, the Earl of March defeated the queen's forces soon after poor, mad King Henry had been reunited with his courageous wife and their small son. Together the trio fled into Scotland again, driven across the border by the Earl of March. March then returned to London and was there crowned King Edward IV. So, as a result of what Stow calls "all that heaving in and hurling out," England, which so recently had had two Princes of Wales, now had two kings!

Still the war continued. Finally, in 1465, King Henry VI

was taken prisoner for a second time and Edward IV had him "lodged" in the Tower of London. Again Queen Margaret and her little son, literally hand-in-hand, managed to evade capture. After perilous wanderings and great hardships they succeeded in returning to Scotland for a third time, helped, legend says, by a forest robber who happened to be a Lancastrian supporter.

From Scotland the queen and her son eventually made their way to the court of the Duke of Burgundy. Burgundy treated them gallantly, indeed royally, as if Margaret were still queen of England and little Edward heir to England's throne. In due course he sent them, suitably escorted, to the home of Margaret's father. There, for the first time in his life of less than ten years, and for nine more peaceful years, Edward of Westminster, England's fifth Prince of Wales, tasted the sweet comfort of security.

Edward's education had, of necessity been sadly neglected. Now in tranquillity he was able to begin his studies in earnest. His mother, Queen Margaret, procured the best masters she could find to prepare him for his future greatness as king of England. For that he would be England's king one day, she was fully determined. One of the small prince's best known teachers, a member of Queen Margaret's refugee court, was Lancastrian Sir John Fortescue who, for his pupil's special and thorough study, wrote a treatise on the laws of England.

Besides book-learning, the exiled Prince of Wales also received military training. Little else, unfortunately, is known about the boy's life during the years he spent away from England. Except for a vague description which portrays him as "possessing excellent natural qualities, which only need cultivation, and that the latter was assiduously furnished by the anxious care of the Queen," there is not much that throws a light on his personality. That life, and his indomitable mother, had taught him to be courageous was to be proved by later events.

When not engaged in training her son for future greatness, Queen Margaret busied herself by every means possible to further the cause of her pitiable husband, the often mad and still Tower-imprisoned Henry VI. So the years went by. Then suddenly the whole meaning of life for the queen and her son took on a new complexion. The glow was infused by none other than the Lancastrians' most powerful enemy, Warwick the Kingmaker, who had unmade Henry VI to make Edward IV England's king.

Warwick had come to realise that Edward was no easy bedfellow, that his protégé was a clever, able man unwilling to play the puppet and leave the control of State policy in Warwick's Svengalian hands. He found himself quite unable to control King Edward IV, even on the matter of a suitable marriage. For only when he had already begun negotiations for Edward's marriage to the sister of the king of France did he discover that his king was, in fact, actually and rashly married—and to a Lancastrian lady at that—Elizabeth Woodville. Furious at this turn of events, Warwick was specially incensed at having been made to look a fool in the eyes of the king of France. Straightway there followed a series of plottings and counter-plottings which finally caught Edward in Warwick's net. The Kingmaker imprisoned the king he had made. Edward, however, not only managed to escape, but succeeded in raising an army against the man to whom he owed his throne. In the ensuing struggle it was, this time, Warwick himself who was driven to flight.

Once across the Channel Warwick, violent in his passion against Edward IV, resolved to make his peace with Queen Margaret. The king of France, chagrined by Edward's spurning of his sister, engineered this reconciliation which brought the queen and Warwick in alliance. Almost in the same breath, as it were, they became family connections. The queen's son, Edward Prince of Wales, became betrothed to Warwick's daughter Anne, whom he soon afterwards married.

In September, 1470, Queen Margaret, the Prince of Wales, and their new ally Warwick landed in England and the Wars of the Roses recommenced. With powerful Warwick's help the Lancastrian forces set the Yorkists on the run. Edward IV was driven to seek refuge in Flanders and poor, sick-minded Henry VI was put back on the throne once more, to sit there, it is said, like "a sack of wool."

Six months later Edward IV was again back in England. Fully equipped, thanks to the help of Charles the Bold of Burgundy, he took up his fight against Queen Margaret and the Kingmaker. In the first battle of this phase of the war Warwick was killed; in the final encounter, at Tewkesbury, the Lancastrians were utterly defeated, Queen Margaret captured, and Edward, the Prince of Wales, slain.

There are several versions of how the eighteen-year-old Prince of Wales met his death. One says that he fell fighting; another, the one usually accepted, that he was captured and brought before Edward IV. At first the king treated the prince with courtesy, but suddenly flared into anger when, demanding to know why the boy had taken up arms against him, he received the answer, "to recover his father miserably oppressed, and the crown violently usurped." Disdainfully then, "with a look of indignation," the king pushed the prince aside with his gauntlet. Upon this, the account continues, King Edward's brothers, George, Duke of Clarence, and Richard, Duke of Gloucester, and two other lords, seized the prince and stabbed him to death with their poignards.

A month after the battle of Tewkesbury and the death of the Prince of Wales, a report was put out that Henry VI had died in the Tower "out of pure displeasure and melancholy." But rumor whispered that he had been murdered, and that Richard, Duke of Gloucester, was not entirely innocent of the sudden end of the life of the sad, mad "royal saint," founder of Eton College and King's College, Cambridge.

Queen Margaret was, for a time, held captive by Edward IV. Finally ransomed by the French king, Louis XI, she was allowed to go to France. There she died in 1481. Warwick's daughter Anne, the dead Prince of Wales's young widow, went into hiding. From this she was eventually flushed like a startled bird by Edward IV's brother, Richard of Gloucester. Richard of the withered arm and one shoulder higher than the other, married her, some say by force, a little more than a year after her husband's burial, "with maimed rites," in Tewkesbury Abbey.

VIII

When Edward IV fled to Flanders after his defeat by the Earl of Warwick, his wife, Elizabeth Woodville, took refuge with her three little daughters in the sanctuary of Westminster. At that time she had not, as yet, borne her husband a male heir. However, not long after seeking asylum in the sanctuary, attended by her doctor and a kindly woman who has gone down in history as "old mother Cobb," she gave birth to a son. The baby was baptized and given the name of Edward, after his father. According to Sir Thomas More, "the whole ceremony of the christening" was "as mean as a poor man's child."

The Queen certainly was poor at this time. While living in sanctuary she had to rely on the kindness and generosity of the world outside even for the food she and her family needed. The "beeves and muttons," gallantly sent as a gift to her by a Yorkist butcher, were a welcome weekly ration gratefully accepted.

The self-embarred life of Elizabeth Woodville, queen of England, changed dramatically two weeks after the battle of Tewkesbury. Edward IV returned in triumph to London, embraced his queen, gazed for the first time on the face of his baby son and instantly had his family removed from their "ignominious surroundings" to the comforts of Baynard's Castle. Almost at once he also appointed Sir Thomas Vaughan chamberlain to baby Edward of the Sanctuary and, so the story goes, ever afterward where the king went Sir Thomas had to go, carrying the infant in his arms.

No child could have been more cherished by his family than this little Edward. Soon, too, he became the adored baby prince of the people of London. He was created Prince of Wales in his second year and given a household of his own at the age of three. Sir Thomas Vaughan, ever in attendance, continued to hold the post of chamberlain, the Bishop of Rochester was appointed his tutor, and Earl Rivers, his maternal uncle, held the all-important position as governor of the little baby-court. When Prince Edward was not quite seven, William Caxton, who had set up his printing press in the precincts of Westminster Abbey, dedicated one of his earliest books to "my redoubted young lord, my lord Prynce of Wales whom I pray God save and increase in vertue . . . . . that he may come into his perfect age."

Big, burly, bluff, and hearty Edward IV, an immensely able but intrinsically and constitutionally lazy man, sometimes cruel, often reckless, debauched, and dissolute, oddly enough desired, above all things, that his adored son should develop into a prince of unparalleled perfection. It is to his credit that he did everything possible to make his hopes come true and that so licentious a man gave so much thought to the drawing up of a most remarkable set of rules "for the vertuous guyding of the person of our deereste first-begotten

Sonne." To Earl Rivers, his son's governor and his wife Elizabeth's brother, fell the lot of supervising the enforcement in every detail of the regimen the king had drawn up. It was strict and exact.

The young Prince of Wales must be made to rise early, at a time suitable to his age; no one was to enter his chamber after this until he was "ready to receive," except Rivers, Vaughan, ar d his chaplain; matins must then be said, after which the boy must go to his chapel or closet to hear Mass there "and in no wise in his chamber without good reason." Then came breakfast and "betweene that and his meate," the child must be occupied with such "vertuous learning as his age shall suffer him to receive." The prince's dinner must be "honourablie served" and during it only "noble stories" should be read to him, or he must be allowed such conversation only as would incline him to "vertue, honour and wisdom; he must hear nothing that shall incline him to vice." After his "meate," in "eschewment of idleness," he must be set to his lessons again. Only when these were done might there be shown "all such convenient disports and exercises as behoveth his estate to have experience," pleasures which had to be broken off so that the prince might then attend evensong. Evensong was followed by supper and this meal by "such disports" as could be devised "to make him merry and joyous towards his bed." Bedtime came at eight o'clock, after which no one except those who were to keep him "under sure and good watch" were allowed to enter his chamber.

The king also drew up a number of decrees relating to the actual manner in which the Prince of Wales's household had to be run and the behavior of those who staffed it. One of these emphasized that "we will that no person, man or woman . . . . be an customable swearer, brawler, backbiter, common hazarder, adulterer, and use words of ribawdery, and especially in the presence of our son"—this from a man noted for every one of these offences! Yet another order strictly forbade any man to "mistreat another, or his wife, daughter, or maid servant under payne of losing service." Furthermore, for companions in his household, the little prince must have only the sons of noblemen and gentlemen. These, too, had to be strictly disciplined with regard to virtuous occupations, hearing Masses, the learning of "grammar, musick, and other cunning," and the "exercises of humanitie according to their ages and births."

When he was eleven the young Prince was betrothed to little Anne of Brittany and not long afterwards a court was set up for him at Ludlow, a political move by which, it was hoped, "the authoritie of his presence there (as Prince of Wales) will refrain evil-disposed persons from the boldness of their former outrages." Earl Rivers, still the boy-prince's governor, accompanied him to Ludlow on every occasion and there apparently spent such leisure hours as came his way in making translations from the philosophers for the further education of his young charge, being ever careful to omit any "evil stories and epigrams in disparagement of Ladies."

The Prince of Wales was at his little court at Ludlow when Rivers received a message from his sister, the queen, announcing the death of her husband. Edward IV was only forty-one when he died, a martyr to libertinism, say some. On the other hand, the cause of death might have been typhoid "bred in a green salad that had been washed in dirty Thames water."

In her message to her brother the queen, instructing him to bring the now nearly thirteen-year-old Prince of Wales to London immediately for his crowning as Edward V, begged Rivers to make the journey with a strong escort. But shortly after her first command, Rivers received a second message from her. In this, while still urging him to bring the prince to London, she canceled the strong guard. This action had been forced upon her after a heated scene with the Council which had angrily demanded to know her reason for expecting treachery and whom she believed were the young king's enemies. Her intuitive fears, based on her awareness of the bitter resentment felt by the Dukes of Gloucester and Buckingham against her brother's governorship of her eldest son (fears which were to prove tragically justified), were in every way increased when she was made to send her second message to Ludlow.

So the boy-king set out for London accompanied only by his uncle Rivers, his beloved Sir Thomas Vaughan, and a handful of other gentlemen. The small cavalcade had gone no further than Northampton when Rivers was arrested. Upon reaching Stony Stratford, where the young king was met by the Dukes of Gloucester and Buckingham, he was informed by them that, with treason and treachery all about him, it was necessary to deprive him of the rest of his familiar companions. This meant that Sir Thomas Vaughan was taken from him too. The boy raged and wept, but all to no avail. Under the withered but allegedly guarding arm of his paternal uncle, Richard, Duke of Gloucester, he was swept onward. At last London was reached and entered, "the kyng ridyng in blew velvet and the Duke of Glowceter in black cloth, like a mourner." The duke, it is reported, "bore himself with such reverence before his nephew that it was seen none other could be so meete a Protector." The boy-king was then conveyed to the Tower where, ostensibly, he was to await the completion of the final arrangements for his coronation.

Meanwhile, the queen-mother, notified of what had happened and fearing the worst, once again sought refuge in the sanctuary of Westminster. Except for the young king, she had all her children with her, her daughters and her second son, Richard, Duke of York, not yet ten but already a widower. The story of little Prince Richard's marriage is of special interest in the 1960's, because of an exciting and touching discovery of great archaeological importance.

This boy, it is known, was four-and-a-half when, in 1478, his father, Edward IV, married him to Anne Mowbray, then just over five years old, the only child and sole heiress of deceased John Mowbray, the immensely wealthy fourth Duke of Norfolk and premier duke of England. Among the great "presse" of distinguished guests at the splendid wedding celebrations were the boy-bridegroom's uncle, Richard, Duke of Gloucester (afterwards Richard III) and the Earl of Richmond, who was later to become the first Tudor king, Henry VII. To Gloucester a pleasant duty fell that day in honor of the happy occasion. It was he who plunged hands into golden basins filled with gold and silver coins for distribution as largess to the vast concourse of spectators.

In 1481, when not yet nine, the little Duchess of York died and was buried in the Chapel of Erasmus in Westminster Abbey. There she lay at peace until 1502, when the chapel was demolished. Her remains were then reinterred in the choir of the Abbey of the Minoresses, or Minories, a convent situated in Stepney. In time the convent disappeared and with it the memory of the little girl who was once Anne Mowbray. Then, suddenly, the historically rich earth of London gave up, as it continually does, yet another of its vast store of secrets. This one had lain safely buried for nearly five hundred years.

In December, 1964, during excavations on a new building site in Stepney, two workmen dug up a small lead coffin. Attached to it was a sheet of lead bearing a blurred inscription in Latin. Careful scientific investigations proved that the coffin contained all that remained of Anne Mowbray who had married Edward IV's second son, Richard, Duke of York, nearly five centuries ago in St. Stephen's Chapel, Westminster, on January 15, 1478.

But now back to the year 1483 and to Edward IV's widowed queen huddled in the sanctuary. This unhappy woman knew full well that the forces of her brother-in-law, the Duke of Gloucester, though out of her sight, were keeping silent watch all around her quiet place of safety. One day, while the preparations for her eldest son's coronation were still allegedly in progress, the Archbishop of York came there to bring her a message from Gloucester. Would she, Gloucester requested, allow the little Duke of York to come and "be playmate to his brother" Edward, who, still in the Tower, would soon be crowned king? Stricken with grief and complaining bitterly, the queen-mother parted with her second "sweet sonne." The boy was taken to his uncle of Gloucester, at Council in the Star Chamber.

"Dear nephew, welcome with all my heart," cried Richard of Gloucester, taking the child from the Archbishop. A warm, avuncular greeting, but soon after it had been uttered the little boy was on his way to join his brother in the Tower.

By this time ambition had begun "to boil within the Duke of Gloucester." Now "untoward developments occurred" and young Edward's coronation was postponed. Among the "untoward developments" was the association of the queen's name with that of Jane Shore, one of Edward IV's many mistresses, on a charge of witchcraft. Next, a sermon was preached on the text "Bastard slips shall not take deep root," which drew attention to the illicit manner in which Edward IV had married Lancastrian Elizabeth Woodville. A case proving the illegitimacy of Edward IV's children was carefully and meticulously built up and in due course a well-rehearsed deputation waited on Richard, Duke of Gloucester, and offered him the crown. "Since I perceive the whole nation is resolved by no means to admit my dear nephews (being children) to reign, and feeling that the succession justly belongs to me as the indisputable heir of Richard Plantagenet, Duke of York, my illustrious father, we are contented to condescend to your importunities, and accept the royal government of the Kingdom," clever, self-contained Richard, Duke of Gloucester, grandly answered. On July 6, 1483, the crown was placed upon his head and he became King Richard III.

Did the cries of "Long live Richard III" reach the ears of the deposed boy-king and his brother, or were the sounds deadened by the thick walls of the Tower of London? After that day they were never again seen in the Tower precincts. Did they ever leave the Tower? Did they die natural deaths in that cold place or were they murdered? All Tudor historians, even including good Sir Thomas More, represent Richard III as a base and brutal tyrant. All accuse him of having engineered the murder of the two little boys. Since, undoubtedly, the death of these children would have been to Richard's advantage, truth may lie in this accusation. On the other hand, to have these princes irrevocably out of the way was a matter of equal importance to the first Tudor king who was soon, by force, to take the throne from Plantagenet Richard.

After five hundred years no convincing evidence has come to lighten the darkness of the mysterious disappearance of the two small princes in the Tower. The key to the riddle of their death, whether from natural causes or as the result of murder, remains buttoned up in the pocket of the past. During demolition work near the White Tower in 1674, two small skeletons were found. Such bones as had not in the meantime been lost, were, four years later, placed in a marble urn in Westminster Abbey, "mixed with a curious collection of bones of rabbits, pigs, chickens, fish and other creatures." Two-and-a-half centuries went by before further interest was taken in the contents of the urn. In 1933 it was opened. Medical evidence then testified that some of the bones were those of two male children, one aged about thirteen, the other about ten. England's sixth Prince of Wales, the uncrowned Edward V, born in 1470, disappeared into the maw of the Tower in 1483 along with his brother Richard of York, born in 1473. The ages therefore seemed to tally with those of the two unhappy boys. But since 1933 further investigations appear to have brought only further doubts. The mystery of the pitiful relics in the marble urn in Westminster Abbey still remains unsolved.

IX

At the time of the battle of Tewkesbury which brought about the death of England's fifth Prince of Wales, son of Henry VI and Margaret of Anjou, Richard, Duke of Gloucester was only nineteen. When he married the widow of that unfortunate boy, Anne, Princess of Wales—bitterly "unconsenting," it is frequently stated—he was twenty-one. He had loved her, so legend tells, ever since childhood, but had always met "with small return of affection" from her. However, in 1472, she became his wife. As part of her marriage portion she brought him the estate of Middleham, in Yorkshire, which she had inherited from her father Warwick the Kingmaker. At Middleham, in the following year, their son and only child, was born. They named him Edward.

Very little indeed is known of this boy who spent the first nine years of his life at Middleham with his mother. At the age of four he comes into momentary notice as the result of being given the title of Earl of Salisbury. Then he fades away again into the obscurity and tranquillity of happy years spent with his devoted mother in the country. Only in a single charming vignette of those blissful days is he seen riding about the castle grounds "in cloth of green, a feather in his cap, and whip in hand, upon a northern pony."

Suddenly, in 1483, his whole life changed. A messenger brought news to the Lady Anne that her husband, Richard, Duke of Gloucester, had been transformed into King Richard III. She was summoned to go at once to London to be crowned queen at Richard's side. So, from Middleham, Anne and her son set out on a brilliant progress, resting in castles and convents on the way, offering alms at shrines. It was to be the only royal progress the little Lord Edward ever undertook. They reached London early in July. On the Sunday after their arrival Edward of Middleham was proclaimed Prince of Wales. That night he and his parents spent in the "Palace of the Tower." A macabre legend relates that the new little Prince of Wales was given the state-apartments from which the two imprisoned princes had been evacuated and that he was actually put to sleep in the very bed recently occupied by his predecessor, unhappy, uncrowned Edward V.

The first coronation—for there was to be another—of Richard and Anne took place next day. At this splendid ceremony, to which the new king and queen walked barefoot, hand-in-hand, from Westminster Hall to the Abbey, the new Prince of Wales was for the first time seen by the people. Did he watch his parents "put off their robes for the anointing, standing before the High Altar all naked from the middle up"?

After the ceremony in London, the royal family left for a short stay at Windsor. There the Spanish ambassador came to call on them on urgent business; briefly, to propose a future marriage for Edward, the newly created Prince of Wales, to Isabella, eldest daughter of Ferdinand and Isabella of Spain, the same Spanish Majesties who later had another daughter called Catherine of Aragon.

Windsor became the starting point of a royal progress through the kingdom for King Richard and his queen. Little Edward was not of their company. He was sent back to Middleham, to riding his northern pony among the peaceful Yorkshire dales. The royal progress was scheduled to end at York, where a second coronation was to take place. There the little prince was reunited with his parents. First he was knighted with great pomp, then recreated Prince of Wales and for a second time invested with the "garland, ring and sovereign rod" by his father, who spoke of the son he idolized as a child of "singular wit wherewith (his young age considered) he is remarkably well furnished," a wit, furthermore, which did "portent that, by the favour of God, he will make an honest man."

Richard III's popularity ran high in Yorkshire regions and clamorously the people of York hailed the nine-year-old, small and delicate-looking twice-created Prince of Wales. Weighed down by his heavy jewel-encrusted robes and the demi-crown on his head, he walked through the city's streets, holding his mother's hand.

After the excitement at York little Edward was once again sent back to the tranquillity of Middleham, this time nobly escorted as befitted the son of a king and the heir to the throne. The people of England never saw him again. Nor, it is believed, did his parents. For in April of the next year (1484) the "Ryght hygh and mightie Prince Edward of Wales," aged ten, suddenly fell ill of a mysterious disease and "died an unhappy death" alone at Middleham Castle with only the members of his household about him.

The king and queen were at Nottingham when they received the fearful tidings. Both fell into "a state almost bordering on madness, by reason of their sudden grief." It was this grief that very probably killed Anne. By March of the following year she was dead and entombed in Westminster Abbey. In August of the same year (1485) King Richard III was dead too. At the battle of Bosworth, fighting a combined force of disaffected Lancastrians and Yorkists led by Henry Tudor, Earl of Richmond, he was defeated and killed. Slung across a horse, his corpse was taken from the battlefield to Leicester with a halter round its neck, head hanging down and the long hair sweeping the ground. He was the first English king to die fighting since Harold was killed at Hastings in 1066. The man who destroyed him was Henry Tudor, posthumous son of Edmund, Earl of Richmond, and the Lady Margaret Beaufort, great-grandaughter of John of Gaunt. Edmund, son of the Welsh squire, Owen Tudor, and Catherine of Valois, widow of Henry V, was Henry VI's half-brother.

Henry of Richmond, finding "the crown of England hanging in a thornbush on Bosworth field," picked it up and became Henry VII. With his accession a new dynasty took possession of England's throne—the Tudors.

PART THREE: TUDORS

PART THREE: TUDORS

Henry VII was twenty-eight and a bachelor when he was crowned king of England in October, 1485. A few months later he married Elizabeth of York, the tall, beautiful, blue-eyed eldest daughter of Edward IV. None of her many amiable qualities made Henry choose her for his wife. He married her for purely diplomatic reasons, in discharge of an oath taken in exile in Brittany two years earlier. There he had sworn that he, descended from John of Gaunt and a Lancastrian hating the House of York, would marry Elizabeth, heiress of York (because of the mysterious disappearance of her two little brothers) and by this union of the two rival dynasties restore order and tranquillity in England. An emotionally cold man, the peace of the realm meant more to him than personal happiness.

What he had sworn and what he had hoped for came to pass. When the Red Rose of Lancaster and the White Rose of York shared the royal bed that long period of anarchy called the Wars of the Roses, which had taken toll of one hundred thousand lives, was brought to an end. England became a united kingdom under its first Tudor king.

Henry was a highly competent ruler and the founder of a powerful and galvanic dynasty. In many other of its aspects his reign was one of great significance to England. It was the era that heralded the dawn of modern history. Into the kingdom of this first Tudor the Renaissance began shooting out branches from Italy. Everywhere windows were being opened on new worlds—by Christopher Columbus and Amerigo Vespucci, by Giovanni Cabot and Bartolomew Díaz, by Vasco Da Gama who, rounding the Cape of Good Hope, unlatched the sea-route to India. Prudent, clever, influential in continental politics and far-sighted in his understanding of trade and commerce, Henry was a cautious patron of some of these stupendous ventures. They smelled of riches and he was a man greedy to the point of avarice.

Though brilliant in statecraft, diplomacy, and business, Henry was no "indulgent husband" in the privacy of his hearth and home. Soon after he had placed the queenly crown on the head of Elizabeth of York, she faded into the background of his life. From these quiet shadows she emerged only for brief periods, those "moments of prominence" when she gave birth to his children. There were to be seven such occasions, for she had three sons and four daughters. Of all these only three lived to have children of their own—a son, the boy who was in time to succeed his father as Henry VIII; and two daughters, Margaret and Mary. Margaret married the King of Scotland and became the grandmother of Mary Queen of Scots; Mary, for a brief period queen of France, as the result of a second marriage to the Duke of Suffolk, became the grandmother of the Lady Jane Grey. Elizabeth lost her life at the birth of her seventh child. Her husband made no pretense of mourning her demise. But he gave her a funeral fit for a queen.

Elizabeth's confinements were handled with great ceremony and according to strict and implicit royal regulations laid down for the "deliverance of a queen." There were, for example, precise instructions prescribing the appearance of the birth-chamber. The walls and ceilings of the room had to be hung with "rich arras," the floors covered with carpets, the bed "arrayed with sheets of fine lawne or fine raynes, great pillows with a head sheete and . . . . a pane of ermines embroidered with rich cloth of gold."

Whether her first child, a son, entered the world in quite the same splendor as that prepared for his later brothers and sisters seems unlikely, since he arrived unexpectedly. He was born at Winchester, early in September, 1486, just eight months after his parents' marriage. The king himself chose the name for his first-born child. The baby would be called Arthur after the famous legendary Welsh hero-king, Arthur of the Round Table. King Arthur, so it is fabled, once held his Court at Winchester and in Winchester Cathedral the Tudor king's prematurely born son was christened. The ceremony, one of great and rich pomp, took place at the close of a day of cold and wearisome delay caused by the non-arrival of one of the baby's godfathers, the unpunctual Earl of Oxford. As darkness set in, after six hours of waiting had been endured with still no sign of the earl's approach, the king commanded that the proceedings should begin.

The first royal Tudor baby was not merely sprinkled with baptismal water. He was actually plunged bodily into a new and magnificent silver font. Wet and understandably vociferous, he was laid on the high altar, dried, swathed, swaddled, and arrayed in a sumptuous robe of crimson and gold. Preceded by torchbearers and loud-sounding trumpets, he was then carried in procession back to his nursery. This progress was greatly impeded by the immensely long and heavy train of the infant's christening-robe. The advance continued without hazard only after a knight gallantly came to the rescue and supported the train "in the middle."

Three days of celebrations followed the christening. The citizens of Winchester, as guests of the king, quaffed uncountable toasts to the health of the infant prince. Not Winchester alone, but the entire kingdom wildly rejoiced at the birth of this prince in whose veins ran the mingled blood of Lancaster and York. The realm acclaimed him "Rosebush of England, Rose in One."

In foreign lands across the Channel Arthur's birth was recognized as an event of paramount importance, too. Indeed, matrimonial schemes to make a husband of the baby prince soon began to evolve. Several overtures came under consideration, but few were to Henry VII's liking. He looked with biased favor only on the offer that came from Ferdinand of Aragon and his wife, Isabella of Castile. Their Majesties of Spain were equally anxious for a marriage alliance with England. Through it they hoped to strengthen their position vis-à-vis France.

Arthur was not quite a year old when the first Spanish ambassadors arrived in London with power to arrange a marriage between the baby English prince and Their Catholic Majesties' youngest daughter, Catherine of Aragon. Nine months older than the the still encradled Arthur, Catherine was a direct descendant of that very unpleasant Pedro the Cruel who had, long, long ago, behaved so badly to the Black Prince. Talks were conducted, ponderously and at great length, with the visiting ambassadors. They were enchanted when the king showed them his baby son "stark naked . . . . when they discerned such excellent qualities as seemed scarcely credible." All this they reported back to their sovereigns. Diplomatic cordiality dropped several degrees, however, when King Henry, ever the astute businessman, mentioned the size of the dowry which he would expect from the future bride of his little son. As wife for Arthur, said Henry, Catherine must bring with her two hundred thousand golden crowns. Though amazed by the size of this demand, the Spaniards nevertheless politely continued a bargaining discussion. The king remained adamant. Nothing less than two hundred thousand golden crowns would satisfy him. In face of such determination the ambassadors eventually took their leave, their mission unfulfilled. However, protracted, delayed, but unremitting negotiations continued from a distance.

Henry VII, neither affectionate by nature nor demonstrative in showing his feelings, held deep within him the greatest tenderness for his eldest son, the "jewel of his household." When the little boy was ill, a frequent occurrence, for prematurely born Arthur was always delicate and constantly ailing, the king became distraught with anxiety. At such times he spent hours on his knees in prayer to Our Lady of Walsingham in supplication for his son's recovery. Her first-born child was also the apple of his mother's eye. She loved him with greater passion than any of her other children. He was the one who most resembled her in looks though not in physique, for she was very tall. He had her beauty, her finely chiseled features, the same exquisitely shaped face, the same soft, bright hair, though hers was spun-gold in color and his of a yellow fairness. Living in an environment of cushioning adulation, adored by his parents, spoiled by the Court, the little boy not surprisingly developed a singular precocity from an early age.

Arthur was knighted by his father and created England's eighth Prince of Wales soon after his third birthday. Unusually intelligent, his first lessons, with a tutor named Friar Bernard André, began not long afterwards. Shy by nature and physically frail, Arthur cared little for games and sport. All his energy went into the lessons which he loved. During the next years the boy-prince showed so devouring a hunger for learning that the king engaged a second tutor for his son, the famous scholar and man of science and medicine, Thomas Linacre. To Linacre, primarily, Henry entrusted "the task of making the mind and body of Prince Arthur grow in wholesome vigour." At the age of ten the young Prince of Wales twice spent brief periods at Magdalen College, Oxford, where, it is reported, he appeared "rather in the grave than in the gay aspect of youth." Quiet, retiring, extremely handsome in his pink-and-white fragility, probably effeminate and rather precocious, he was unquestionably a very studious child. When he entered his teens, he was, it is said, "learned beyond his years and beyond the custom of princes." Arthur, in fact, was being given the broad education of a true Renaissance prince.

Long hours devoted to lessons must greatly have undermined his already brittle health. He appears to have taken little exercise. He danced only "modestly" and cared not at all for tennis, riding, or jousting, occupations which delighted his young brother Henry, his junior by nearly five years. When only four, little Henry "might have been seen trotting through the City, on his pony, to Mile End, to attend the tourney there, and figure at the butts." Arthur, too, "figured at the butts" set up for the practice of archery. At this exercise, at least, he outshone his little brother. Archery was the only sporting activity he really enjoyed. So expert a toxophilite did he become that the most noted archers of the day were always hailed as "true Prince Arthurs."

Year after year went by and still the negotiations for the union of the young Prince of Wales and Catherine of Aragon continued. The discussions had not been fruitless. They brought about a crop of proxy marriages. The first of these took place soon after Arthur's second birthday. The English ambassadors who had been sent to Spain to "inspect" the now three-year-old Catherine, were presented to the little princess as she sat on her mother's lap watching a bullfight. Finding her lively, though not "remarkable for beauty," they none the less sent home satisfactory reports and once again the vexed dowry question was hammered out.

To seal the bond of a compromise that was reached, the first proxy marriage took place. A second was celebrated when the little Prince of Wales began to speak properly; a third when King Henry had the last Plantagenet claimant executed at the insistence of Their Spanish Majesties who, it will be recalled, were determined to ensure the removal of every obstacle to Arthur's ascending the throne after his father's demise, thus making their daughter Queen of England. After each proxy marriage Henry VII asked that Catherine be sent to England. Always Ferdinand and Isabella found some excuse for delaying the "delivery" of their daughter. And so time went by.

The thrice proxy-married little Prince of Wales meanwhile diligently continued his long hours of study. Latin was a cardinal subject in his education since, in addition to its fundamental importance to a prince, it was the only medium through which he could communicate with his Spanish princess. During the long years of matrimonial negotiations frequent letters passed between the two children, all written in "choice Latin." Whether Arthur wrote his stilted and pedantic epistles spontaneously, or whether he copied them out in the manner of a schoolroom exercise under the eye of his tutor, will never be known. In illustration, here, "done into English" and quoted by Dr. Doran, is the translation of a letter that he wrote when he was thirteen and Catherine two months short of her fourteenth birthday. Ever since their first proxy marriage she had been known as the Princess of Wales. The letter is therefore addressed "To the Most Illustrious and Excellent Princess, the Lady Catherine, Princess of Wales, Duchess of Cornwall, etc., my most entirely beloved spouse."

"Most illustrious and most excellent lady, my dearest spouse" Arthur began this letter, "I wish you very much health, with my hearty commendation. I have read the most sweet letters of your Highness, lately given to me, from which I have easily perceived your most entire love for me. Truly, then, your letters, traced by your own hand, have so delighted me, and have rendered me so cheerful and jocund, that I fancied I beheld your Highness, and conversed with and embraced my dearest wife. I cannot tell you what earnest desire I feel to see your Highness, and how vexatious to me is this procrastination about your coming. I owe eternal thanks to your Excellency, that you so lovingly correspond to this my so ardent love. Let it continue, I entreat, as it has begun, and like as I cherish your sweet remembrance, night and day, so do you preserve my name ever fond in your breast, and let your coming to me be hastened, that instead of being absent we may be present with each other, and the love conceived between us, and the wished-for joys may reap their proper fruit.

"Moreover, I have done as your illustrious Highness enjoins me, that is to say, in commending you to the most serene Lord and Lady, the King and Queen, my parents, and in declaring your filial regard towards them, which to them was most pleasing to hear, especially from my lips. I also beseech you to exercise a similar good office for me, and to commend me with hearty goodwill to my most serene Lord and Lady, your parents, for I greatly venerate, value, and esteem them, even as though they were my own; and wish them all happiness and prosperity.

"May your Highness be ever fortunate and happy, and be kept safe and joyful, and let me know it often and speedily by your letters, which will be to me most joyous. From our Castle at Ludlow, 3rd nones of October (15), 1499. Your Highness' most loving spouse, Arthur, Prince of Wales, Duke of Cornwall, etc., eldest son of the King."

At last, and after an exchange of many such letters, Henry VII, by threatening to break off the marriage alliance if Catherine was not immediately despatched to England, forced Ferdinand and Isabella to end their years of procrastination. Accompanied by her suite, Catherine now fifteen-and-a-half years old, sailed from Corunna in August, 1501. Never before had she been separated from her mother.

Though Catherine was not beautiful, not even particularly pretty, her oval face, full of character, was far from unattractive. Her complexion was good, her grey eyes large and tranquil. She had russet-gold hair, small hands and feet, walked erect and with exquisite Spanish dignity and was graceful in all her movements. But poise and grace must have deserted the poor girl on the voyage from Corunna. The ship bringing her to England to fulfil her destiny was tormented by terrible storms. The waves were enormous, wild squalls carried away several of the vessel's spars, thunder roared and lightning split the heavens. So furious were the elements that "it was impossible not to be afraid."

After days of anxiety the dreadful storm abated. The sun was out and shining brightly on the Saturday afternoon in October when the ship dropped anchor off Plymouth Hoe.

Because of some mismanagement of arrangements, no royal official had arrived on time at Plymouth to welcome Catherine to England. Unwelcomed, she went ashore and then, attended by her whole suite, walked to the quayside church to offer up thanks for her safe arrival. Soon afterwards she began the long journey across the West country towards London, a slow progress that took three weeks so that she might be spared further fatigue after a voyage that had been fraught with so much danger. All along the route she was given a tumultuous welcome by the people. "The Princess could not have been received with greater joy had she been the Saviour of the World," a member of her suite reported in writing to Queen Isabella.

King Henry had intended to receive his son's bride in London, at Lambeth, on the south side of the Thames. Suddenly he changed his plans and, instead, set out with a splendid company to meet her at Easthampstead. Arthur, who had been in the Welsh Marches, arrived at this rendezvous half-an-hour after the king. Soon they received news that Catherine's cavalcade was approaching. The first of its members to arrive was the Spanish ambassador, Don Pedro de Ayala. He had come hurrying ahead, the bearer of a delicate message from Queen Isabella. She had commanded him to inform King Henry that, in strict conformity to the custom of high-born Castilian brides, it was her wish that Catherine should remain veiled until after the formal marriage ceremony had been performed. Her daughter was not to show her face even to her future husband.

Since, by this time, a number of proxy marriages uniting Catherine and Arthur had already taken place, Henry worked himself into a towering rage. With an angry tug at the bridle, he swung his horse round and rode off into a nearby field. There he held council with his attendant lords. Who did they think they were, these Spanish Majesties? He had had enough of their shilly-shallying and vacillations. Did they imagine for one instant that he would be browbeaten, induced to "buy a pig in a poke"? At last, still angry, he swung his horse round again and rode back to face the clamor of Catherine's formidable duenna, Doña Elvira Manuel, and the dignified Archbishop of Santiago.

Henry stood his ground firmly, would not give one inch, and the victory was his. That evening, her veil lifted, he met his daughter-in-law face to face. Arthur also was vouchsafed this honor. It is reported, that he said (or perhaps was made to say) he "had never felt so much joy in his life as when he beheld the sweet face of his bride, and no woman in the world could be more agreeable to him." For a shy, introverted boy of fifteen this expression of breathless ardor must have been a painful ordeal.

A great many fine speeches were made that evening. The king spoke in English. What he said was then turned into Latin by an English bishop. Catherine could already speak a little English, but Castilian good breeding decreed that she should not show herself to be a better linguist than her father-in-law. So she spoke in Spanish. The Spanish bishop translated her speech into Latin and then, for the king's benefit, the English bishop translated it into English!

Once again the Prince of Wales, small, fair, slim, diffident, and in appearance much younger than his years, plighted his troth to the poised and graceful infanta of Spain, his senior by nearly a year and half a head taller than he was. The company then retired, the king and his son to "freshen" their clothes. Later that evening they were both conducted to Catherine's apartments where she and some of her ladies entertained them with a performance of stately Spanish dances. Catherine loved dancing and danced beautifully; poor Arthur had neither liking for, nor skill in the art. On this occasion, however, urged on and encouraged by his father, he eventually took the floor with a lady who was a member of the English entourage, and modestly performed an English dance.

A fourth marriage between the young Prince of Wales and the Spanish infanta was now concluded and the journey to London continued. The king and his son rode swiftly ahead, Catherine's cavalcade following at a more leisurely pace.

London, agog with excitement at the prospect of playing so great a part in the official marriage of their Prince of Wales, acclaimed Catherine with loudly expressed affection and at Baynard's Castle, on the Thames, Arthur's mother welcomed her daughter-in-law with tender kindness. The queen had done everything possible to make the cold, grey dwelling warm and comfortable for the girl from Spain unused to the rigors of an English November.

King Henry was determined to make the wedding of his beloved eldest son an occasion of memorable brilliance and pageantry. The years of dowry-wrangling and procrastination had ended satisfactorily. Arthur was at last to have Catherine for his officially wedded wife and he, the king, would have control of the two hundred thousand golden crowns of the agreed *dot*, of which one hundred thousand were to be paid on the day of the wedding, fifty thousand more six months later and a further fifty thousand within a year. In addition, there were fifteen thousand crowns in cash that Catherine had brought with her, as well as her plate and jewels valued at thirty-five thousand crowns. For the king there lay an added relish in the fact that the City of London and the nobility were bearing the greater part of the cost of the celebrations.

It was Arthur's ten-year-old brother, rosy-cheeked, cherub-faced, robust Henry, Duke of York, who escorted the Spanish infanta, Catherine of Aragon, to the Palace of the Bishop of London, there to await the day of her marriage to the young Prince of Wales. On the morning of November 14, 1501, it was Henry again who conducted her through streets garlanded, festooned, and bridged with triumphal arches, to the west door of St. Paul's. The bells rang out over London and were answered by fanfares of trumpets as he entered the great church at her side and led her to waiting Arthur.

Hand in hand the Prince of Wales and his bride walked slowly to the high altar, to their final marriage conducted by the Archbishop of Canterbury. The groom and bride were both dressed in white. His very fair skin pink with nervousness, Arthur, boyishly slender, looked very young, very vulnerable, and exquisitely elegant. At his side tall Catherine had never appeared more handsome and "lustie." All through the ceremony, it is said, the big, strong, tall-for-ten lad, Henry, Duke of York, "stared at her unblinkingly."

When the wedding service was over and the bridegroom had hurried off ahead to await his bride at the Palace of the Bishop of London, it was again his brother Henry who led Catherine down the long nave, out of the church and onward to the Bishop's Palace. There a great feast was held. Catherine was given the seat of honor at the right hand of the king. Arthur, oddly enough, was placed at the head of a separate table, a sort of children's table, at which were also seated his cherub-faced brother Henry and Margaret, the gay, rompish sister whom both boys adored.

Later that evening when London's bells were still clanging and people made merry in the streets as a conduit, specially constructed, spouted forth "diverse sortes of good wine," Arthur and Catherine were conducted to Baynard's Castle and there boisterously and publicly "bedded" in accordance with the custom of the times. What happened later this night, or indeed, later during the married life of Arthur and Catherine, there is no way of knowing, but whatever it was, was destined to bring about vicious issues in after years. The shy, immature young Prince of Wales, according to one story, indulged in swaggering, indelicate boasting next morning. He said, it is alleged, that he was thirsty because "he had been in Spain where it was hot, and that to have a wife was a fine thing." Another version makes him declare that "he has been six miles into Spain." In contradiction of both these out-of-character bravadoes there is a simple statement that a "grave matron lay between the young couple on their first night." But, above all, there is the assertion Catherine was to make many years later when denying the consummation of the marriage. She had only, she said then, slept seven nights with Arthur during their entire marriage and swore that she had remained "intacta e incorrupta da lui, comme venne dal ventre di sua madre." To disbelieve Catherine, a woman of noble spirit, virtue and integrity, is almost impossible.

For more than a week the marriage of Arthur and Catherine was celebrated in London with all manner of displays, tournaments, and pageants. At a great feast in Westminster Hall she again performed Spanish dances with her ladies, while young Prince Henry of York, ever the extrovert, danced English dances partnered by his jolly sister Margaret, taking off his doublet so that he might put greater dash and agility into his performance. Arthur also danced; as usual, "modestly," with a widowed aunt. For a quite unexplainable reason this small incident seems to give added credence to the story of the "grave matron" and to make it even more difficult to believe in his taking pleasure in indecent boasting.

Despite all the royal jollity and junketings, the king was far from happy. Catherine's dowry was besieging his mind with anxieties. Only half of the first instalment had so far been paid. In gold, certainly; but only half, nevertheless. Her jewels and plate were another subject of concern to him. And then, because it was politic that Arthur should soon return to his Court at Ludlow, a new and vexing problem arose. Should Catherine accompany her young husband to the still rather wild land of Wales? Would it not be best if she remained behind for a while with the queen and Margaret? The king was not anxious for Catherine. Arthur was his main concern, Arthur so immature for his years and not at all robust. Was the boy not too young after all to begin "the duties of a husband"? Would it not be best perhaps if the young couple lived apart for a year or two?

The King could not make up his mind. But Doña Elvira, Catherine's duenna, could—and did. She strongly advised against her young princess going to Ludlow and supported the suggestion of the young couple's separation for a while.

Arthur, it seems, voiced no opinion. Catherine modestly declared that she left the matter entirely in the king's hands. But with this Father Alessandro Geraldini, her confessor and chief chaplain, strongly disagreed. He announced firmly that it was the emphatic wish of Their Most Catholic Majesties, Ferdinand and Isabella, that Arthur and Catherine should not be parted and that they should live together as man and wife —and at once. Whether this actually was their command or

Geraldini's own strong protests, will never be known. The result was the same. When the young Prince of Wales set off for Ludlow, Catherine went with him. The king, forced to agree to this arrangement, dug in his heels when it came to Catherine's taking all her jewels and plate with her. He also washed his hands of the expenses of the move. Arthur was Catherine's husband and must, from now on, be responsible for her.

These unfortunate squabbles took place during the five weeks that separated the pageantry of the marriage of the Prince of Wales and the infanta of Spain and their departure for Ludlow. Whether the boy-husband and his wife were aware of the full story of the wranglings no one knows. Before Christmas, which they might so happily have spent at the king's Court in London, they had left the metropolis. A small army of retainers accompanied the prince; Doña Elvira Manuel headed the princess's train of eleven ladies. Catherine rode pillion on horseback behind her master-of-the-horse for most of the journey, though a horse litter was included in the equipment for the expedition in case she tired and needed rest. After spending Christmas at Oxford the cavalcade moved on and eventually crossed the Severn. At Bewdley in Worcestershire, where Arthur had frequently stayed, there was another brief time for rest before the progress continued along the road which led to its final destination, the bleak, cold keep of Ludlow Castle among the Welsh mountains.

Few records survive to tell the story of the freezing months that Arthur and Catherine spent together at Ludlow. Thomas Linacre had accompanied them as director of their studies and the youthful couple shared daily lessons. In addition, Arthur also spent hours alone with his personal tutor, absorbing still more knowledge. He seems to have devoted the greater part of each day to work of one kind or another, to studying or listening to the debates of his council, frail shoulders hunched against the cold. Sometimes he had to receive Welsh lords who came riding to Ludlow to pay him their homage; on rare fine days he went out hunting; occasionally feasts were held in the great hall. These were enlivened by the songs of Welsh singers, the playing of Welsh harpists, by Catherine and her ladies executing Spanish dances, or the telling of stories about that other Arthur, the great legendary king, and his Kinghts of the Round Table. All these events could only have temporarily lifted the dreary gloom of Ludlow Castle.

Whether Catherine, hating the cold and often homesick for her mother and the sun of Spain, found happiness in the companionship of the boy-husband whom, contemporary chroniclers say, she loved dearly, it is not possible to know. Was their short life together a sweetly innocent childlike idyll or a patient submission to boredom in that bleak little Court besieged by a fierce winter's icy anger? With the arrival of March, 1502, there should have been warming dreams of beneficent, approaching spring. Instead there came a new frightening apprehension, an epidemic of the "sweating sickness"—probably a particularly virulent type of influenza. It took toll of many a strong man's life within a matter of twenty-four hours. Arthur and Catherine both contracted the dread disease. She managed to fight it and survive; he died on April 2, 1502. Married formally to Catherine for only four-and-a-half months, the Prince of Wales was five months short of his sixteenth birthday.

Arthur's body lay in state in Ludlow Castle. Through bitter weather and across rough and quagmired roads, great nobles came from every corner of the realm to view the remains of England's eighth Prince of Wales. King Henry and his queen did not come. Overwhelmed by grief Elizabeth was completely prostrate; the king, who never found it easy to show his feelings, was like a man struck by a thunderbolt.

For three weeks, pending instructions from the king for

its burial, the body of Arthur, Prince of Wales, remained on view in Ludlow Castle. It was taken to the parish church when at last the king's directions came. There, in the presence of the Earl of Surrey, as chief mourner representing the king, and of three bishops, many gentlemen of the Royal Household and great lords from all the chief families in the kingdom, the requiem was sung. The next day the funeral procession set out for Worcester where, by the king's wish, his son was to be buried in the cathedral.

That day, April 24, 1502, was one of fearful wind and rain. Mercilessly the elements battered and doused the long, slowly moving cortège, all in deepest black. On a carriage drawn by six horses the coffin lay under "common hangings" which hid its beautiful and priceless trappings and protected them from the ceaseless, drenching rain. On the way to Bewdley, where the coffin rested for one night, the lights of the great flaming torches were frequently extinguished by the strong wind.

At last Worcester was reached. The body of the first Tudor Prince of Wales lay guarded for one night in the cathedral and was buried next day "with weeping and sore lamentation." Contrary to usual custom, it was not embalmed but merely enclosed in the coffin with spices. At the burial, when the coffin was lowered and the Bishop of Lincoln, "also sore weeping," said the orisons, the dead Prince of Wales's two chamberlains stepped forward and, breaking their staffs, threw them into the grave, "and likewise did all the gentlemen ushers with their rods. This was a piteous sight to all that beheld it."

Catherine was not present at this melancholy scene. She still lay gravely ill at Ludlow. Not until weeks later, the weather having turned mild, could arrangements be made for her departure. Carried in a litter she was taken by slow stages towards London where, at Richmond, she was received into the tender embrace of Arthur's grieving mother, gentle Elizabeth of York, who ever showed the greatest kindness to the young Spanish girl so tragically widowed at sixteen after less than five months of marriage.

Bereaved and debilitated by a grave illness and desperately unhappy, Catherine wrote pitiful letters to her parents begging them to allow her to return to Spain. But this was not to be. The fates that had spun her destiny had entwined its threads into the history of England.

Though deeply afflicted by the death of his eldest son, Henry VII gradually again began to take a grip on the reins of authority and kingship once Arthur lay buried in Worcester Cathedral. Like palliative leeches his thought fastened themselves firmer than ever on Catherine's dowry, that dowry which was to be the source of so much anguish and misery to the life of the youngest daughter of Ferdinand and Isabella of Spain.

II

Unless Catherine had a posthumous son by Arthur, Henry VII's only surviving son, Henry, the eleven-year-old Duke of York, was next in line to the throne. The fear that the widowed Princess of Wales might be pregnant was soon dispelled and Prince Henry became the heir-apparent. During his elder brother's lifetime, as a younger son, he had been on equal footing with the king's other children. Like them he was pillowed by luxury and surrounded by elaborate ceremony, this despite the fact that, except at times of great occasions, they never stayed long in any of the great royal palaces in London. The king deemed country air infinitely more favorable to their health and, in consequence, they lived mostly in country houses belonging to their father. In one of these, a moated manor in Kent called Eltham, the young prince spent his childhood.

Arthur was not quite five when Henry was born at the royal manor of Greenwich on a summer's day in June, 1491. Unlike his elder brother, the new baby entered the world on time, large, lusty, and pump as a dumpling. Straightway he was put in the care of his nurse, Ann Luke. While still an infant he was appointed Warden of the Cinque Ports and Constable of Dover; aged two he was an Earl Marshal. In October, 1494, four months after his third birthday, came a still greater moment in his life. With Ann Luke in proud, inflexible attendance, he was brought from Eltham to Westminster for his father to dub him "Knyght of Bath, and after to creat hym duc of York," an honor that brought him a handsome annual gift of a thousand pounds. Ever since the day of Henry's creation as Duke of York the title has been borne by the second sons of English kings.

How delighted the little boy was that October day in 1494 by the brilliant scene, the dazzling robes, the blaring trumpets, the sonorous proclamation tongued by the heralds, and, later, how fascinated by the great celebrations that followed. These were kept up for several days and included the pageantry of tournaments held outside Westminster Hall. What ecstatic rapture shone in the eyes of the newly created little Duke of York as, with transports of excitement, he watched knights in extravagantly picturesque suits of armor, mounted on horses caparisoned with black velvet and cloth of gold or "trapped with green velvet and white damasc, enramplished with red roses," break many a goodly spear or be flung suddenly to the ground, unsaddled. The memory of that day remained with him all his life.

From the glory and glitter of this celebration Ann Luke carried him back to the elm-studded park and quiet country peace of Eltham. But she was not to have him in her charge much longer. Soon his education began. He was put in charge of hand-picked tutors, men of great distinction and erudition in various branches of scholarship. One of these was his brother Arthur's tutor, Friar Bernard André; another, Henry VII's poet laureate, John Skelton, was boastfully to write in after years: "The honour of England I learned (taught) to spell." The story that the king, having carefully selected the boy's tutors, "bade them ground the babe well in theology, languages and all such learning as would fit him to become Archbishop of Canterbury," though often told and retold by historians, is now viewed with considerable doubt.

The "hard mental labour" to which Henry was subjected almost from babyhood in no way affected his astonishing vigor and robustness. He remained always the very picture of good health. We have already caught a glimpse of this amazingly energetic child riding through the city on his pony at the age of four, eager to attend the tourney and to show off his prowess at the butts at Mile End. He thrived on learning and yearly grew stronger not only in knowledge but in physical well-being. On the rare occasions when long hours of study had tired him out he, like Luther, "used to amuse himself by playing on the flute." He was fond of music and possessed considerable musical talent. He learned to play not only the flute but also the organ and the recorder. He composed a song for the lute and "at ten he had his part assigned in the choir of the Chapel Royal, and at twelve composed masses" (now lost). He loved religious services and the study of theology. The latter certainly stood him in good stead years later when he was to show great brilliance in theological debate.

A natural linguist, he could speak Italian, Spanish, and French extremely well. To Latin he took like a duckling to water. In 1499, when Erasmus visited England, Sir Thomas More escorted the great man to Eltham to present him to the young Duke of York, then eight years old. Writing of his meeting Erasmus described the boy-prince, standing among his attendants, as "having already something of royalty in his demeanour." The little prince begged to be allowed to correspond with the great scholar and philosopher, a correspondence conducted in "elegant Latin" which so much delighted Erasmus that he often carried the boy's letters in his pocket and showed them to favored friends. In his early teens Henry was also corresponding, in "remarkable Latin," with Pope Leo X, communications that met fulsome praise, for "there cometh no letters from any other prince unto his Holiness to be exhibited in the Consistory, that he judged more elegantly written than they be."

As the tide of time bore young Prince Henry through the first decade of his life, it was obvious to all who knew or saw him that here was no ordinary prince; here was a boy wondrously endowed with a clever brain and splendid physique, inherited from his very tall and beautiful mother. Big for his years, strongly built and athletic, flatterers praised his countenance and dubbed it fair. But the face, even in so young a boy, was large and square; the ears, set too high, looked absurdly small in comparison; the eyes, always alert and watchful, resembled tiny flinty pebbles; the mouth was exceptionally small, tight and buttoned up. He was a pink and white cherub but not, one feels, a particularly likeable child. The precocity, tireless energy, and exhibitionism of this juvenile extrovert must have been exhausting to many who were constantly about him.

Unlike delicate Arthur, Henry took part with enthusiasm in almost every kind of physical accomplishment. He was good at archery, though not quite such an expert as Arthur; he loved wearing armor; practiced tilting and shone in tournaments; adored riding and hunting; played hard games of tennis, not merely with energy but skill; danced gracefully and with great abandon—as he did at Arthur's wedding to Catherine at which he played, it will be recalled, a leading role.

The life of strong, energetic, lively, talented and acutely intelligent Prince Henry changed course completely when, in April, 1502, his brother Arthur, Prince of Wales, died at Ludlow. Now at the age of eleven he became heir-apparent to the throne of the new Tudor dynasty. He was made Duke of Cornwall and, in February, 1504, became Prince of Wales and Earl of Chester. His lovable and beautiful mother had died and the king was in very poor health at the time—a malaise brought on not by the demise of his queen, but from bronchitis, which was the bane of his life and his destroyer when he was fifty-two.

The people were enchanted with their new tall, virile ninth Prince of Wales and gathered in crowds to gaze at him whenever he appeared in public. The young prince, on these occasions, was always charming, courteous, and bland, a blandness defined as "oiliness" by those who were not particularly enamored of the Tudor dynasty. They disliked certain of his habits, particularly his irritating practice of "rapidly blinking his eyes," and the freezing expression of "high royal rank" which he sometimes adopted, when rapid blinking gave way to an unblinking stare. Generally speaking, he was "not addicted to look in the face of people to whom he spoke." His sudden changes from courteous blandness to curt waspishness were also sources of annoyance to those close to him at Court who were often stung by his sharp, tart replies. Already, it would seem, this boy was a mirror fleetingly reflecting the man he was to become, the man transformed by the years into the enormous, imperious-willed Henry VIII, a king adored by the ordinary people of his realm, learned, brilliant, tremendously able, bursting with energy, kind when in the mood for kindness, bellowing forth loud laughter when in high good spirits, but in most other humors egotistical, cunning, cruel, an autocrat, and a tyrant. But that time was not yet. Henry was still twelve, the newly created Prince of Wales and, dynastically, immensely important, a fact seized upon by Ferdinand and Isabella of Spain.

Soon after Arthur's death Their Spanish Majesties began scheming for a marriage between their widowed daughter Catherine and the new heir-apparent to the English throne. They took but slight notice of the sad, pleading letters she wrote, telling them of the neglect she was suffering and the near penury in which she was living. For though she had been granted one third of the revenues of Wales, Cornwall, and Chester after her young husband's death, the apparently handsome income helped her not at all, since it was never paid. While the queen was alive, negotiations for a marriage between Catherine and Prince Henry went along quietly. But no sooner was the queen dead when King Henry VII declared that he was prepared to marry Catherine himself. The Spaniards countered by sending ambassadors to London to demand Catherine's return, along with that portion of her dowry which had already been paid, both "in the best manner," a proceeding that did not at all suit parsimonious Henry VII. After fluctuating negotiations, a bargain was struck and the king agreed to his second son's betrothal to Arthur's widow. This engagement was formally sanctioned by a dispensation from the pope in the following year when Henry was thirteen and Catherine six years older.

Catherine was deeply distressed by this pillar-to-post arrangement. She openly expressed her distaste for the policy that sent her from brother to brother. But Prince Henry, much attracted by her "mature beauty," was eager for the marriage. So, of course, were Catherine's parents. Had they not schemed ardently for this union with "so noble a Prince," a union that would after all, one day make Catherine queen of England?

In spite of the dispensation from Rome, the betrothal ran into stormy weather during the next years, chiefly as the result of Henry VII's efforts to lay hands on Castile after the death of Queen Isabella. To gain his ends he was even prepared to marry Ferdinand of Spain's mad, widowed daughter, Juana. These machinations very naturally enraged Ferdinand and added to Catherine's sad plight in England. Neglected and without resources, she lived in misery and poverty. She complained bitterly that "she lacked means to procure linen under-garments" and that from the day she left Spain with her Spanish wardrobe, she had only "purchased 2 new dresses." When she needed a black velvet robe—"I was all but naked," she wrote to her father—she had first to sell her bracelets. Her servants, too, went "unseemly clad" and she lacked money to pay their wages. The plight of her ladies was no better than that of her servants. But how could it be otherwise since she herself was in such great distress, kept short by her father-in-law not only of money but often, too, of food. "Each day my troubles increase," runs a letter to her father. "Since I came to England I have not had a single maravedi (a Spanish gold coin), except a certain sum that was given me for food; and *that* such a sum that it did not suffice, without my having many debts in London."

Catherine was often ill. She was cold, suffered bouts of ague, was desperately homesick and terribly lonely. In her letters she never mentioned her late husband nor yet the "so noble" Prince of Wales to whom she was betrothed. They seldom met. Much too busy with the business of living his own, vigorous life of study and sport, "his comings and goings supervised," Henry gave little or no thought to hers.

So the years went by, sadly for Catherine, richly for Henry, Prince of Wales, "precocious in wit and dignity" and bursting with robust health. In his middle teens he had already grown "above the usual height, with an extremely fine calf to his leg." It was "the prettiest thing in the world to see him play tennis with his fair skin glowing through a shirt of fine texture." When describing the young Prince of Wales, Sir Thomas Chaloner, later to become England's ambassador to the Netherlands, piles rapture upon lyrical rapture. Virtue, Sir Thomas declares, "breathed through his pores" and the mind of this prince of princes was as "fair as his body." Bursting the banks of his homage, the knight declaims, "young Hercules had not such arms as his to bend a bow, or such strength to wield a club. Polux could not wrestle, nor Castor tame wild horses like the Prince of Wales. In his armour he looked more resplendent than Hector; and in the chase, Hippolytus was a fool to him!"

On April 25, 1509, Henry, Prince of Wales, Hercules, Polux, Castor, Hector, Hippolytus all in one, became King Henry VIII of England. He was eighteen. "I do not for a moment doubt, beloved Erasmus," wrote Lord Mountjoy to the old scholar, "that your sorrow will be suddenly changed into joy on hearing that Henry Octavus, or rather Octavius, has succeeded his father. Oh! if you could but witness the happiness of the people, you would weep for joy. Heaven smiles, the earth leaps with gladness, everything seems redolent with milk, honey and nectar."

When Henry VII died, Ferdinand of Spain was quick off the mark in sending a not-so-gentle warning to the new king. He hoped, Ferdinand stated, that King Henry VIII would immediately marry his beloved daughter Catherine, to whom he was betrothed. Should any difficulties arise he, Ferdinand of Spain, would come in person to see the union sealed accompanied by an army, ships, artillery, and other "engines of war."

Neither the threat nor the journey proved necessary. Henry married Catherine two months after his father's death. The ceremony took place at the palace of Richmond, once called the palace of Sheen, part of which King Richard II demolished after the death of his much loved first wife, Anne of Bohemia. Though, later, the Lancastrians repaired the building, it was Henry VII—to whom England owes a noble chapel in Westminster Abbey and the glory of King's College Chapel at Cambridge—who completely transformed Sheen into a Renaissance palace of great beauty and distinguished it by the name of Richmond, thus honoring the title he had borne before he became England's first Tudor king.

PART FOUR: STUARTS

Part Four: Stuarts

Though the Tudors ruled England for a hundred and eighteen years, Arthur and Henry, sons of the founder of the dynasty, were the only Tudor Princes of Wales. After 1509, when the younger of these princes became Henry VIII, the title was not again borne by a prince for one hundred and one years. Henry VIII did not make his only son, the brilliant boy who succeeded him as Edward VI at the age of ten, Prince of Wales. The boy-king died aged sixteen and unmarried, though his father had once toyed with the idea of negotiating a match for him with Mary, the young queen of Scots.

Edward's death led to the tragic interlude in English history caused by the attempt to set aside the rightful claims to the throne of his two half-sisters, Mary, daughter of Catherine of Aragon, and Elizabeth, daughter of Anne Boleyn. Instead, the crown was to be placed on the gentle head of the Lady Jane Grey, granddaughter of Henry VII's daughter, Mary (first married to Louis XII of France), and her second husband, Charles Brandon, Duke of Suffolk. Doomed from the start, the venture failed utterly. Poor little Jane lost the crown and her head, and Edward's half-sister Mary became queen after all. She was the first woman to occupy the throne of England as queen in her own right.

The unhappy reign of Catherine of Aragon's pathetic, childless daughter lasted no more than five years. The news of her death was brought to her half-sister Elizabeth, resident at that time at Hatfield in Hertfordshire, whereupon Elizabeth, it is reported, accepted her accession by quoting from Psalm 118: "This is the Lord's doing; it is marvellous in our eyes."

Throughout her forty-five years' reign this great woman implemented every promise which she made to the Commons when she told that assembly, "Though you have had, and may have, many princes, more mighty and more wise, sitting in this seat, yet you never had, or ever shall have, any that will be more careful and loving." Fortunate in the genius of great men about her, Elizabeth made England a first-class power, supreme at sea and powerful in commerce. Her "nest of singing birds" produced the golden age of English literature.

In splendor the near half-century of the Elizabethan era passed on its way. At sixty-nine the great queen lay dying on a heap of cushions on the floor. There, for several days, her red wig askew, her body weak, worn, and old, scarcely able to speak or move, imagining herself "ringed by flames," she fought death indomitably.

It was, of course, unthinkable that the queen should die lying on the floor. Repeated efforts were made to get her to her bed; repeatedly she rejected them. Finally she yielded. A shrivelled mummy with death "visible in her eyes," she was laid on her majestic crested bed. Even in those last hours of her life it was not known for certain who was to succeed her. Again and again the question was asked. She made no reply. With more insistence, there came the probing demand: Was it to be the King of Scots? The dying queen gave, it seemed, an answer at last. One of her hands moved slightly towards her head, the now almost-bald head that had for so long borne the burdens of the crown. Tremulous, indeed barely a movement at all, it was taken as a signal of assent. To her it was perhaps a last supreme effort in extremis to purge herself of "yon unhappy fact" (the execution of Mary Queen of Scots), that had taken place in the great hall of Fotheringay sixteen years before. For Mary Queen of Scots was the mother of the man whom, with a weak lift of her hand from the entrance to death's door, she beckoned to the throne of England. At three o'clock in the morning of March 24, 1603, Elizabeth I slipped quietly out of life.

Immediately Sir Robert Carey, as bearer of this portentous tiding, dashed off on a wild ride to Scotland. In the middle of the night of March 27, the son of Mary Queen of Scots, James VI of Scotland, suddenly awakened, sat up in bed and looked down on the man covered with mud and half-dead with fatigue kneeling at his bedside. Kissing James's hand, Sir Robert, still on tired knees, proclaimed him "by the Grace of God King of England, Ireland, Scotland and France, Defender of the Faith!" For a moment of two James looked stunned, scarcely able to believe that his dream of years had become reality. Ten days later, in great spirits, he was on his way across the border, heading toward London, his ears eager to hear the proclamation that was to name him England's first Stuart king.

For various reasons the new "Queen's Grace of England" and her children did not make the journey with him. Instead he had for company that passionate belief in the doctrine of the divine right of kings that was to prove so base a bedfellow to the Stuart dynasty.

II

King James VI of Scotland's marriage with Anne, princess of Denmark, was not an unqualified success. Pretty, peevish, petulant Anne, a shallow, waspish lady—though she could be charming when it suited her—loved clothes, dancing, and theatricals, but not the king. James had no particular love for her either. To be fair, let it be added that women in general never touched his passionate emotions. He much preferred the company of handsome young men. Since a king must have an heir, he must first, of necessity, have a wife. Thus James acquired Anne of Denmark. Almost from the start Anne treated him with thinly veiled indifference. Yet, for all her not caring much for James and he, anyway, preferring his favorites to her wifely company, she bore him children. She was, in fact, almost constantly awaiting the birth of a child. In 1603, after "a disappointing number of the Queen's pregnancies which had ended in miscarriages," the royal couple had three surviving children: Henry Frederick, born at Stirling in February, 1594; a daughter, called Elizabeth, two years younger; and "Babie Charles," born at Dunfermline in November, 1600. And the queen was on the verge of yet another accouchement. This was one reason for her not making the journey to England with James. But there was another: the quarrel that broke out between her and the Earl of Mar.

Because of the uneasiness of the times in Scotland, King James had assigned to the Earl of Mar the duty of keeping little Prince Henry, heir to the Scottish throne, in literal safe custody in Stirling Castle and so out of the way of political machinations. When Henry became heir not only to the Scottish but also to the English throne, Queen Anne determined that she would take him with her when she went to London. Mar by now was out of the country with James, but he had left the little prince at Stirling in the secure charge of a body of "governors." From them Anne demanded her son. They replied that they could do nothing without the king's permission. Anne then began bombarding her husband with violent letters. As if further to uphold her case she "took a fever" which brought about another miscarriage. This concentrated congeries of crises forced James's hand and he sent the Earl of Mar back to Scotland with the necessary warrant for the handing over of Henry to his mother. So, in triumph, accompanied by her "rescued" son and her daughter Elizabeth, Queen Anne set off for England. Her third surviving child, three-year-old "Babie Charles," frail, delicate, and with but "a reluctant possession of life," she left sadly behind at Dunfermline.

Avoiding London which was in the grip of plague, the Queen and her entourage reached Windsor in June, 1603. Prince Henry Frederick, heir to the thrones of England and Scotland, had just entered his tenth year.

Henry made an instant and edifying impression on his father's new subjects. Even Ben Jonson was charmed into prediction, prophesying that the boy would grow into a hero equal in stature to Edward of Woodstock and Henry of Monmouth. Handsome, healthy, auburn-haired Henry was "generally conceded to be one of the finest boys of his age that Englishmen had ever clapped eyes on." The favor and popularity meted out to his little son delighted King James. Perhaps Anne's rages and the fever that had brought on her latest miscarriage had, after all, been for the best.

Henry was a sort of Wunderkind. His dazzling good looks were matched with a quite extraordinarily bright and original mind. When the boy was only six, James declared him perfectly able to understand the pedantically expressed ideas of the *Basilikon Doron,* a book the king himself had written for the specific guidance and education in kingship of his "dearest Son, and Natural Successor." Corpulent with precepts and principles, the treatise is divided into three parts. The first is a discourse "Anent the King's Christian Duty Towards God"; the second concerns "A King's Duty in His Office"; and the third, "Anent a King's Behaviour in Indifferent Things," covers such subjects as manners at table, food ("Let all your foods be of simples without composition of sauces, which are more like medicine than meat"), rest, clothes ("be also modest in your raiment, neither over superfluous, like a debauched waster; nor yet over base like a miserable peddler"), speaking and the use of words, hunting, and so forth. If only space allowed, it would be a delight to quote much of this amazing mass of instruction that little Henry apparently took in his stride.

In Scotland—and later in England—the prince's studies were supervised by Adam Newton who, at frequent intervals, sent reports of the boy's progress to his learned father. James may have been a fool in some matters but, let it not be forgotten, he was "the wisest fool in Christendom." Macaulay describes him as being "made up of two men—a witty, well-read scholar, who wrote, disputed, and harangued, and a nervous, drivelling idiot who acted." Henry himself regularly wrote to his father. Having studied and presumably digested the *Basilikon Doron* at six, it is not surprising to learn that on his ninth birthday he was able to inform James, in a letter written as usual in Latin, that he had completed the reading of Terence's comedies, the fables of Phaedrus, and the epistles of Cicero. Once in England, the boy's education swept relentlessly on and he was sent to Oxford, where, at the age of eleven, he matriculated at Magdalen College.

The waking hours of this remarkable child's daily life were not, however, solely devoted to gaining scholarship.

There were a great many other accomplishments to acquire. He was taught the use of arms, of which he was inordinately fond, and quickly became skillful in the handling of swords, guns, bows, and pikes. He developed into an excellent horseman, was good at games, loved music, sang well, and danced with elegance and grace. At a banquet in London, the year after his arrival he "danced for the company, exhibiting much sprightliness and modesty as he took the floor with the lady whom the King and Queen designated for his partner."

It is not, of course, unusual for small boys to love soldiers and soldiering or to dream of military glory. But from his earliest years Henry's interest was almost adult. He showed "a Noble and Heroic Spirit, no music being so pleasant to his eares, as the sounding of the Trumpet, the beating of the Drums, the roaring of Canon, no sight so acceptable as that of Pieces, pistols, or any sort of Armour." His enthusiasm for the arts of war led to a minor international incident in 1607. After a visit to England in that year, during which he had been much feted, the Prince de Joinville returned to France, taking with him in his company one of thirteen-year-old Henry's servants. The man, a military engineer, had, it would seem, been purposely selected by the boy-prince, for soon after arriving in France he was caught red-handed while investigating the fortifications of Calais! The French not unnaturally were perturbed and angered by this highly irregular action and the matter was heatedly debated. Finally it was explained away as "the vanities of a young Prince." The fiasco did not dampen Henry's ardor. He continued to delight in the companionship of military men to whom he could talk of "Wars, Battailes, Furniture, Armes by Sea and Land, Disciplines, Orders, Marches, Alarmes, Watches, Stratagems, Ambuscades, Scalings, Fortifications, Incampings." Ben Jonson's prediction that he would become a great heroic prince in the tradition of Edward the Black Prince and Henry V appeared to be well on the way to fulfillment.

Henry's fascination for military men was matched with an equal enthusiasm for ships and men of the sea. He had been in England for less than a year when the lord admiral instructed Phineas Pett, the famous shipwright, to build a twenty-five-foot pinnace specially for the young prince. The boy himself named his craft *Disdain* and sailed her on her maiden voyage down the Thames from opposite Whitehall to Paul Wharf. There the anchor was dropped, and in the tiny cabin of his ship, he swore the celebrated Pett, whom he loved and honored, "into his personal service." The French ambassador in London, writing of Henry less than two years later, remarked on the fact that "none of his pleasures . . . . savour the least of a child," that "he is never idle," and that he had already attained "a reasonable insight and judgement, in State-affaires." But, let it be added, the spying episode at Calais was still lurking round the corner.

When first they came to England Henry and his sister Elizabeth, to whom he was deeply devoted, shared a country establishment at the royal manor of Oatlands. There they were attended by fifty-six servants above stairs and eighty-five below. Later the prince was given his own residences, both in the country and at St. James's Palace, London, and his households increased in number with each passing year. At fourteen no less than three hundred and seventy-four people cared for and waited on him, above and below stairs. King James, ever concerned about his son's education, insisted that the boy's establishments "should rather imitate a Collegd than a Court." But others besides his father took a keen interest in his cultural development. The Archbishop of Canterbury, for instance, himself opened a subscription list for the purchase of a library for the young prince, and the eccentric and aged Lord Lumley bequeathed to him the celebrated Lumley Library, rich in manuscripts once owned by monasteries that Henry VIII had suppressed, and in books, some of which had belonged to Thomas Cranmer, Archbishop of Canterbury, whose life burned out at the stake in the reign of Mary I.

As a New Year's gift for 1609, the prince gave his father a long Latin composition based on the theme that "learning is more needful to kings and princes than to men of lesser station." Since it titillated his mania for monarchical divinity, James was enraptured. It may well have been this transport of gratification that caused him to make Henry a knight. This same year brought the appointment of learned Thomas Lydiat as the new young knight's personal "Chronographer and Cosmographer." Now also the boy began to collect not merely coins and medals, as most boys do, but also *objets d'art* and pictures, and welcomed famous preachers and writers (George Chapman, dramatist and translator of Homer, among them) into his circle. Only one of his friends, Sir Walter Raleigh, could never enter the precincts of the prince's establishment. For Raleigh, by the king's command, was a prisoner in the Tower. Like his mother, Queen Anne, the boy had long been fascinated by Raleigh's splendid story and the tragedy of his misfortunes. Together, mother and son constantly pleaded with the king for Raleigh's release. To these pleas weak but obstinate James turned a deaf ear and Raleigh stayed on in the Tower.

Having made his eldest son a knight in 1609, King James created him Prince of Wales a year later. Henry was sixteen and already five feet eight inches tall. His waist was slim, his shoulders broad, his face, tanned by "outdoor sport," long and finely boned. He was auburn-haired and very handsome. Levelheaded, amiable, discerning beyond his years, highly intelligent and cultivated, he was a prince of whom the nation could well be proud, one who carried his young manhood with a dignity and gravity that "set him apart from other men."

Because there had been no Prince of Wales in England

for a hundred and one years, archives had to be searched in order to ascertain the correct procedure for the creation and for the ceremony of investing Henry with the great title. When everything had been arranged, the prince, attended by "divers young Lords and Gentlemen of special marke," came down the Thames from Richmond to London on May 30, 1610. All along the river-route fabulous displays were held in his honor and with his arrival at Whitehall Stair the thunder of cannon split the skies. From Whitehall, again in a water procession, he accompanied the king to Westminster. There came the moment when, dressed in a surcoat of purple, he knelt bareheaded before his father. The king "girded him with the sword, invested him with the rod and ring, and set the cap and coronet on his head." Later, in ceremonies that lasted two days, twenty-five young men of noble birth were made Knights of the Bath in honor of the investiture of Henry of Stirling as the tenth, and first Stuart, Prince of Wales. He was also, of course, created Duke of Cornwall and Earl of Chester. But he had already brought with him from Scotland "a garland of new titles"—Duke of Rothesay, Earl of Carrick, Baron and Knight of Renfrew, Great Steward of Scotland, and Lord of the Isles. All these titles to this day are inherited by the male heirs to the throne.

Not surprisingly, the handsome, serious-minded young Prince of Wales was swamped with adulation. Sycophants constantly, and in his hearing, eulogized his virtues and his accomplishments. Great men spoke of him as "the perfect composition of the graces of God and nature." Honest, frank, and sincere by nature (and perhaps something of a prig), flattery embarrassed Henry, often indeed stirred him to anger. A story is recorded of his once receiving a letter from a nobleman which ended "Yours before all the world." Believing that the writer had on some occasion "untruly and unfaithfully dealt with him," he deeply resented this "fulsome lip-service." Directing his treasurer, Sir Charles Cornwallis, to draft a reply, he stressed that the usual formal words of respect were not to be used, asserting angrily that "his hand should never affirm what his heart thought not."

Immediately after Henry became Prince of Wales, his household was much enlarged and, in fact, became a Court organized like that of the king. He had his own chamberlain, treasurer, comptroller, cofferer, groom of the stole, chancellor, secretary, receiver-general, and surveyor-general, and some five hundred other attendants and servants. His income from various sources, including, of course, Wales, Cornwall, and the earldom of Chester, amounted to about £25,000 annually. This increased steadily and after a few years had risen to £80,000. Unlike his father, he was very careful about money, never overspent and always "achieved a surplus of receipts over expenditure," though he bought a great many books and pictures, furnished his apartments with beauty, richness, and taste, kept a large stable, dressed elegantly, and commissioned exquisite jewels for himself. His competence in handling money matters "astonished" King James. Gradually this became part of the whole body of resentment that the king began to feel against a son so unlike him in almost every respect.

Except in scholarship, Henry in no way resembled his father. He had courage, to begin with, and had shown it even as a little boy; James was a man loaded with neurotic fears and in a perpetual fidget. Henry had a passion for "martial exercises"; his father saw himself as a man of peace. Candid Henry liked plain dealing; James was erratic and devious. James adored praise; Henry despised flatterers. Henry, even in his early teens, was very susceptible to feminine charms; James preferred young men. James could swear like a trooper; Henry believed that few things in the world were "worth an oath."

The people adored their serious, high-minded Prince of Wales, so loyal to his friends, so devoted to honor. He was to them the "expectancy and rose of the fair state." The king?

Was he at times "just a little touched in the head"? They despised his unfortunate fancy for favorites, for that silly-faced young man Robert Carr in particular. Not only had the king knighted the rogue and then made him Earl of Somerset, he had even given the creature Sir Walter Raleigh's estates while that peerless master-spirit of the age was left to languish in the Tower.

The prince, who had so much warmth in his nature, bestowing love and kindness on friends and servants, felt remote and detached from his father. During the brief years that he was Prince of Wales tension grew up between him and the king, a tension strained increasingly by James's jealousy and his curious, almost pathological fear of his eldest son. Henry, in consequence, could bring himself to show only fealty and obedience to his father, never affection. Only, however, when speaking of his beloved Sir Walter Raleigh did the prince loosen the reins of his tongue. "What man but my father would keep such a bird in a cage," he cried out in bitter censure.

The prince's popularity no longer pleased the king. The nation's and the Court's near idolatry filled him with envy and suspicion. The father who had written the *Basilikon Doron* out of love for an adored little son drew aloof from him in young manhood. What Henry did and what was done for Henry, filled the king with testy choler. He resented the prince's lack of affection for him and the fact that his daughter Elizabeth seemed, these days, to give less love to him than to "her most worthy and dearest brother." James also bitterly resented Henry's hatred of the once plain Robert Carr, now Earl of Somerset and his "sweet Robin," and was full of wrathful indignation that his son, so astonishingly careful in the management of his own funds, dared remonstrate with him, the king, concerning the state of his finances. This was a guilty ire. Poor James was forever being dragged deeper and deeper into debt by the needs and demands of his favorites.

There were other causes as well for the king's anxiety and gnawing uneasiness as he watched his son's activities with sulky disapproval. Henry, he felt, was drawing too much public attention on himself. It was obvious that "more of the nobility resorted" to the prince's court than ever went to Whitehall to do homage to their king. Above all, Henry was interfering in matters that were not his concern, "using his elbows" in the government of the realm and encroaching on the king's prerogative. Why, the boy had even suggested to England's ambassador to France that, instead of to the principal secretary, reports be sent to him! The prince, James once declared angrily, wished "to bury him alive." This conviction grew more intense when, in 1611, Henry tried to make the king appoint him president of the Privy Council.

The king's envy and suspicion of the Prince of Wales were matched, oddly enough, by the luke-warm feelings of the queen. Anne, who had created such a fuss about bringing the boy with her from Scotland in 1603, seven years later had far greater love for her second son, Charles, Duke of York, than for Henry. Charles had long since joined the family in England. Though much improved in health he was still not very strong on his legs, a misfortune about which the usually kind-hearted Henry sometimes teased the boy, "telling him that he should be a Bishop, a gown being fittest to hide his legs." The teasing often made Charles weep. But tears neither blinded his adoration nor his admiration of his brilliant, handsome elder brother. They did, however, irrigate an inferiority complex from which Charles was to suffer all his life.

The teasing of little Charles appears cruel. Yet cruelty was not in Henry's nature. He was in every sense a splendid young man. And he was pious. Three times each day he "withdrew for private devotions" and expected every member of his household also to attend prayers every day. His little Court was not only a center of culture but of good manners. He never swore and forbade swearing in his presence. All about his apartments stood small boxes into which those in his company who used bad language had to place the fines which he imposed. The money was distributed among the poor.

Henry may have been a prig. But he was, without question, an honest, sincere idealist and, in spite of the tension that existed between him and his father, an obedient son. His whole attitude in this matter is summed up in what is believed to be the last letter he ever wrote. "I choose rather to bewray the weakness of my judgement by obedience," run his words, "than that his Majesty should not find in me a willingness to do my best endeavours for the satisfying of all his commandments."

An example of Henry's obedience occurred in 1612, when the king began to plan a marriage for his heir. Two ladies were under consideration: a daughter of the Duke of Savoy and Christine, sister of Louis XIII of France. King James favored "Madame Christine." She had a dowry of fifty thousand crowns plus twenty thousand crowns more which were to be paid at a later date. The Prince of Wales would have preferred a Protestant princess of his own choice but once having, with the greatest courtesy, explained the political advantages and disadvantages of both these possible unions as they appeared to him, he concluded by saying that he left the final decision entirely to the king. The fates were to spare James the dilemma of selection.

As early as the spring of 1612 those who knew and loved the prince were worried about his health. He looked tired, had grown thin, was often in low spirits, and frequently complained of "a giddy lumpish heavinesse in his forehead." Though he was no better by June, when he was staying at Richmond, he forced himself to play endless games of tennis every day, rode out to hunt, swam in the Thames, and, on moonlit nights, went for long walks along the riverbank. Neither exercise nor life in the open air seemed to do him much good. A terrible exhaustion, which he fought with still more strenuous exertions, held him in its grasp. August brought one of the hottest summers that England had experienced in years, yet the prince in his low state insisted on riding ninety-six miles in two days, from Richmond to Belvoir, feeling it his duty to join the king on a summer progress.

Back in London in September, he exerted all his remaining strength and energy in entertaining Frederick, the Prince Palatine—a young man of whom he greatly approved—who had come to England to marry his sister Elizabeth. Though bouts of fever and violent diarrhea attacked him, he managed again and again to shake these off. Often he would lie on his bed, saying that he felt "indolent." Then he would be up again, forcing himself to play tennis with Frederick. But for all his incredible determination to keep on his feet, his illness was all too apparent. Those who saw him were horrified by his appearance, yet by some miracle of willpower he kept himself going. On October 25, emaciated and weak, he went to hear a sermon preached on the tragically prophetic text: "Man that is born of woman is of few days and full of trouble." The poor young prince was, indeed, afloat in an ocean of trouble. That afternoon, while he and Frederick were dining with his father in the king's privy chamber at Whitehall, he fell forward in a dead faint. He was carried to St. James's Palace, put to bed, and never rose from it again.

Weeks of fever and delirium followed. He was bled again and again. When he was virtually at death's door, the queen in deep distress sent a message to Sir Walter Raleigh in the Tower, begging him to send some of his famous cordial "that had saved her life." Sir Kenelm Digby, who lived from the year of Elizabeth I's death till five years after the Restoration of Charles II, described this nostrum as if it were some witch's broth, declaring that among its ingredients were viper's flesh and "mineral unicorn." But Sir Kenelm's veracity is sometimes open to doubt. Unfortunately no authentic recipe of the "great cordial" is known to exist. If, as she claimed, it saved

Queen Anne's life, it failed to do the same for her son. He died from typhoid, aged eighteen, on November 6, 1612. His last words were a question. "Where is my dear Sister?" he whispered.

Elizabeth had visited him very often, but towards the end, because of the fear of infection, she had been forbidden to enter his chamber. Little Charles, too, had sat, grief-stricken, at the bedside of his brother. But King James and Queen Anne only once called to see him. Neurotic James, terrified of death, fled for comfort to his country palace of Theobald's; the queen sought seclusion for her grief in Denmark House, the name she had bestowed on Somerset House.

In the Tower Sir Walter Raleigh's sorrow for his young friend knew no bounds. He had been engaged in writing a treatise for Henry entitled, "Of the Art of Warre by Sea." When the prince died he left it unfinished. His great *History of the World* that he had so often discussed with Henry, was now a sad memorial of his affection for a brilliant, brave young man. The first part of the work ends with a dirge for the prince. Translated from Latin it reads: "My lyre is changed into the sound of mourning; and my song into the voices of people weeping."

And the people wept, indeed. "England's soil was literally soaked in tears" for the passing of its tenth Prince of Wales, "hee that was the world's admired Lampe" and, till then, the fifth Prince of Wales to die before becoming king.

After lying in state at St. James's Palace for four weeks, Henry was buried in Westminster Abbey. Neither of his parents attended the funeral. But his dear sister Elizabeth was there; so was Frederick, the Prince Palatine, and his own small brother Charles. In the procession that took "four hours to marshal," Charles was chief mourner. He was twelve years old.

III

When Charles was born at Dunfermline in November, 1600, Henry was six. So feeble was the new infant's hold on life that a hasty baptism took place. It appeared unlikely that he would survive for more than a few days. At the time when Queen Anne, having won her battle against Mar, took Henry and Elizabeth to England, Charles was still a tiny, fragile child and had to be left behind at Dunfermline. To have taken him on such a journey, even at three years old, would have caused his death.

Not only was Charles in early childhood physically shackled. He, it seemed, was also mentally retarded. His legs were so weak that it was impossible for him to stand up on his feet, and when he should have begun to talk, he was incapable of uttering a sound. Attempts at teaching him to speak produced no result. Not surprisingly, he was "a very silent melancholy baby."

Regular bulletins about the little boy's health were sent to his parents in England by his guardian, Lord Fife. One of these brought them the comforting news that their "most noble son, Duke Charles, continues, praised be God, in good health, good courage, and lofty mind; although yet weak in body, he is beginning to speak some words. He is far better, as yet, with his mind than with his body and feet . . . . ." But even such sanguine reports did not satisfy the queen. In 1604 she sent a doctor and an apothecary to Scotland in the hope that they might hasten her son's recovery. Charles was then four; "his joints were so loose that his ankles seemed dislocated" and he could only stand with the greatest difficulty.

King James, at this stage, was all for drastic action, for encasing the boy's legs in iron to strengthen them and cutting "the spring" under the tongue to cure the impediment in his speech. Fortunately for Charles, the queen firmly refused to allow her husband's remedies to be put into practice. She insisted that the boy must be brought to England immediately and there treated with less virulent methods.

The little prince, "weak, deformed, and stammering," who by now bore a string of grand titles, for he was Duke of Albany, Marquis of Ormond, Earl of Ross, and Lord Ardmannock, arrived at Whitehall none the worse for the ordeal of his long journey. He was given into the prudent care of Lady Carey. Her kindness, understanding, and sensible treatment of the child gradually brought about a remarkable improvement in his health. Though still grave, stammering, and unable to walk with confidence, Charles was soon to show that at least there was nothing at all the matter with either his mind or his wits.

Two years after the arrival in England of his delicate younger son, King James made him a knight and Duke of York. Unable to stand properly, Charles was in no physical state to take part in the ceremony. But, "from the arms of the Earl of Nottingham," he watched the proceedings and listened to a "substitute" lordling taking the oath on his behalf.

In spite of his handicaps, Charles's education, meanwhile, had not been neglected. Ever since the age of four he had had his own "paedagogue," Thomas Murray. This perspicacious and warm-hearted man, aided by Lady Carey, worked miracles with the backward-seeming boy. Not only did Charles's health improve but he began to read and write, extraordinary achievements for a child who, until the age of four, had spoken only a few words and these with great difficulty.

But learning, it would seem, came as naturally to him as it did to his elder brother. Quite soon, he, like Henry, began writing letters to his father informing him of his progress.

One of the earliest, brief but quite charming, runs: "Sweet, sweet father, i learn to decline substantives and adjectives. Give me your blessing." This surely reads like a small boy's very own composition. But was he responsible for that letter in Latin to Henry when he was nine, and astonishingly improved in health, which says, "To enjoy your company, to ride with you, to hunt with you, will yield to me supreme pleasure. I am now reading the 'Conversations' of Erasmus, from which, I am sure, I can learn both the purity of the Latin tongue and elegance of behaviour." That sounds much more like the work of his tutor, who either dictated or wrote it himself.

Surely, however, it was again Charles, unaided, who wrote in English to his mother when she was ill with gout, saying: "I wish from my heart that I might help find a remedy to your disease; the which I must bear the most patiently, because it is the sign of a long life. But, I must for many causes be sorry; and specially because it is troublesome to you, and has deprived me of your most comfortable sight, and of many good dinners, the which I hope, by God's grace, shortly to enjoy!" No tutor *could* have written those words. They too vividly suggest the schoolboy's mind, a small boy ever ready for a tasty meal. That little Charles's inherent seriousness housed a playful merriment, a sense of fun, is engagingly unmasked as he goes on to say, "When it shall please you to give me leave to see you, it may be I shall give you some good recipe, which either shall heal you or make you laugh." He ended the letter with kisses for the "most sacred hands" of his "most worthy mistress" and signed himself with schoolboy solemnity "Your most humble and obedient Servant, Charles."

Lady Carey gave up her care of the prince when he was eleven. She had every right to feel pride in all that she had done for him. Though not yet in robust health, his weak legs had grown strong. He still, it is true, stammered, but except for excessive oversensibility, was a normal boy. During his brother's lifetime, he was kept very much in the background and the limelight that shone so brilliantly on Henry shed no beam on him. Not till he was ten did he make his first state appearance, the occasion being Henry's investiture as Prince of Wales. The brothers were extremely fond of each other, despite Henry's unkind teasing about Charles's weakling legs. That made him cry but did not make him love Henry less. Henry's splendor affected the little boy in other ways. There can be little doubt that the radiance of Henry's life, his physical perfection, and personality were a rebuke to Charles's own disabilities and that out of these and his painful sensitivity, sprang the inferiority complex that was, all his life, the essence of his character.

Charles's secluded life did not much change during the four years that followed his brother's death. But his health improved to such an extent that he began to play tennis (at which, in later years, he became adept), tentatively tackled the noble exercise of tilting, and learned to dance. The young ladies of the Court invented a new dance in his honor and called it the "Carolus Princeps," or more simply and unconventionally, the "C.P."

As future heir to the throne, Charles was now Lord High Admiral. In this capacity he frequently went to inspect ships under construction at Woolwich, where he visited his late brother's old friend, Phineas Pett, the great shipwright. Perhaps the most prominent part played by the young prince during these years occurred on the day his sister married Frederick, the Prince Palatine. The marriage was to have great significance for England, since from it sprang the House of Hanover which, a century later, came to rule Britain. Charles, thirteen at the time, is said to have looked "graceful" as he led Elizabeth to the altar.

Four years after Henry's death, at the age of sixteen, Charles was created Prince of Wales. By this time his own strength of will and courage—and the years of understanding care spent with Lady Carey and Thomas Murray—had helped him to conquer his muscular weakness. Only the impediment in his speech was with him still. Sometimes words came naturally from his lips; at others he found himself quite unable to utter a sound. Yet he was a good linguist though he could, naturally, express himself best only on paper. Not as clever as his father or his late brother, he was, nevertheless, well read. He loved music and all the fine arts and was "addicted to grave studies," including theology. King James often boasted to celebrated ecclesiastics that Charles was capable of arguing theology "with the best studied divine of you all."

The stormy November day of Charles's investiture as Prince of Wales was, unfortunately, an unhappy one for him. He was less well than he had been for some time, and the ceremony had to be performed indoors, and in private, at Whitehall. The queen, who loved Charles dearly, was not present. It was put out that she did not attend for fear of "renewing her grief for the defunct Prince" (Henry). In actual fact she was already gravely ill from the mortal disease which brought her life painfully to an end two years later. Charles adored his mother and her absence must have been a great grief to him. To crown this day of sadness for him came the awful and heartrending moment when the Bishop of Ely began to pray, not for Charles but *Henry,* Prince of Wales! All in all, the London ceremony was a dismal affair. More felicitous were the rejoicings at Ludlow. There "the love of Wales for their Sovereign Prince" was warmly expressed by the Welsh in lively celebration, "the singing of songs of gladness and hymns of praise," loud-playing bands, bonfires, and thundering cannonades.

Now Charles was the eleventh Prince of Wales but with no more liberty than in the years before his creation. He was, of course, given a household of his own. There he entertained hospitably and charmingly, showing for all his gravity true

Stuart gallantry towards ladies. Unlike his brother Henry, he was, however, disciplined and "kept on a strict rein."

Charles at this time was a very presentable, very small, auburn-haired young man. Tiny, neat, and trim of figure, he was always beautifully dressed. But by no standard was he good looking. Only his eyes were magnificent, soft brown in color and touchingly "melting." He was always charmingly courteous but remote and unapproachable, showing the world a front of unruffled calm.

The miseries and ill health of his childhood, the fact that in the light of his elder brother's brilliance he had seen himself as a useless, imperfect weakling, had made an introvert of Charles. Hiding his true personality behind a wall of reserve, he appeared cold and unbending. By temperament he needed and hungered for kindness, understanding, love, and friendship. Three people most dear to him assuaged his appetite and yearnings for these unctions: the king, to whom he was closer than Henry had ever been; his mother whom he adored; and his first really great friend, the king's latest favorite, affable, stimulating George Villiers.

Villiers of the sparkling eyes and gay, infectious laugh, had taken the place of Robert Carr, Earl of Somerset, in James's affections after "sweet Robin" fell from grace. In the year that Charles became Prince of Wales, the king raised his new favorite to the peerage; a year later he made him Earl of Buckingham and was, in time, to make him a duke. Strangely enough, Buckingham became the queen's friend, too, her "kind dog." Like the king and the Prince of Wales she called him Steenie. The little group doted on pet names. James in sentimental silliness always called Charles "Babie." The only irreverent nickname was invented by the queen. In a tantrum she often referred to her husband as "the Sow." As "the Sow's" delight in exquisitely profiled, handsome Steenie increased steadily alongside his deep affection for Charles, so did Steenie's influence on the young price. It was an influence to which Charles should never have been beholden. The only good that came out of it was the love for art that Buckingham fostered in the prince. Charles became an enthusiastic collector of Renaissance paintings. With the years his interest and passion increased and, as king, he assembled the finest collection of pictures ever seen in England. The Civil War and Cromwell's Interregnum brought about its dispersal. Many of the paintings, sold to foreign collectors, disappeared from England, never to return.

Charles should have been happier than ever before in these first years of his life as Prince of Wales. But his days were shadowed by the sorrow of his mother dying slowly and painfully at Hampton Court. He spent as much time as he could with her, often slept in a room adjoining hers, and was kneeling at her bedside when she died. The king was not present. On this occasion, however, it was not fear of seeing someone die that kept him away. He himself was ill with stone in the kidney, at Theobald's, his country palace.

After her death the queen's body was taken down the Thames to lie in state for two-and-a-half months at Denmark House. On the day of her funeral in Westminster Abbey, Charles walked alone behind the hearse. Still at Theobald's and wretchedly weak, the king spent that day on a litter lying in a field, quietly watching the deer. His legs were terribly swollen. He wondered if he would ever hunt again. Did he perhaps ever and again think of the woman who had, after all, come to be for him "a more or less comfortable though sometimes exacting companion"?

James eventually recovered and returned to London dressed in pale blue satin and with a blue and white feather in his hat, Anne out of sight and seemingly out of mind. After a while he went hunting again with his "Sweathearts," for so he now called Charles and Buckingham. He was "dere Dad" to both of them. Whenever a stag was brought down, the king immediately had its belly slit open and in this repulsive tub happily bathed his feet and legs. He firmly believed this to be "an excellent remedy to strengthen and restore the sinews."

For most of the nine years that Charles was Prince of Wales there were, naturally, negotiations for his marriage to a suitable princess. At first the advantages embodied in Henrietta Maria, the little dark-eyed sister of Louis XIII of France, attracted King James. But in due course he changed his mind in favor of a Spanish match for his son. Since both ladies were Roman Catholics neither project met with enthusiasm either from Parliament or the nation. The plan for the Spanish match had originated in Buckingham's fertile brain but from there was easily transferred to the king's. Not only, declared Steenie, was Maria, the infanta, "a likely ladie to make a prince happy," but Charles's marriage to her would strengthen and insure a useful alliance with Spain. If all went well, it was arranged that Steenie, eight years Charles's senior, would accompany "Babie" to Spain. The prince would then bring his bride back with him to England.

Though the king was filled with dread at the thought of his two "Sweathearts" crossing the dangerous ocean en route to Spain, Charles was wildly impatient to be off. For all his outward coldness, he was, like all Stuarts, deeply romantic and consequently much excited by reports of the infanta whose "face had a contour that showed her to be well-born—without one ill feature. Her figure is perfect, and some say that before she is dressed she is incomparably better than after." In his eagerness to behold this goddess he was bold enough to tell his father that "If you forbid me to go now, I will never marry at all." And so, at last, he and Steenie took their departure.

Theatrically the two young men set off, cloak-and-dagger fashion, heavily disguised with false beards, as Thomas and John Smith. They made their way to Paris where, at a

Court masque, Charles, still incognito, caught a fleeting glimpse of the young princess, Henrietta Maria, the bride his father first had in mind for him. Filled with dreamy thoughts of the allegedly fabulous infanta, his eyes took little note of the pretty French girl.

From Paris Charles and Buckingham headed for Madrid, which they reached after many exciting adventures. There a torrent of letters from King James to "My Sweet Boys and dear venturous Knights, worthy to be put into a new Romanso," swept down on them. James begged "Babie" not to spend too much money and, later, when grand festivities began to take place, "to take heed of being hurt if you run at tilts." Both young men wrote to their "Dere Dad" with great regularity, Charles giving his father a full account of what was happening and, more important, what was not happening to him in the Spanish capital with regard to his matrimonial prospects. For the infanta he had come to wed remained for a time invisible to him. First the Spanish royal family made one excuse—it was Lent and therefore not a proper time for receiving the prince—and then others. The only glimpse Charles caught of his lady-love was while sitting in a closed carriage as the royal family drove past along a prearranged route. He recognized the infanta immediately. Not only did she blush, being fully aware of his presence in the shrouded vehicle, but he spotted the blue ribbon tied round her arm, a band of identification. Though the infanta was a reluctant party to the whole affair, Charles was enchanted with his coup d'œil and Buckingham sent a report home saying that, "All he (Charles) ever yet saw is nothing to her."

Not long after this encounter the prince was invited to visit the royal family. He was warmly received; walked hand-in-hand with the king, who gave him a golden key to the palace; chatted with the queen, who presented him with gifts, among which was an "embroidered night-gowne"; but said not a word to the Infanta Maria. During the weeks that followed, despite bullfights, boar hunts, fireworks, and "showers of Spanish blessings" on his head, he was allowed to meet his lady only on the rarest occasions. Frustrated, romantic Charles once again took to watching her drive past from a closed carriage. One day he even jumped over a wall to get a peek at her while she was "gathering morning dew" near a summerhouse in the palace garden. The infanta screamed, and her attendant fell on his knees, begging Charles to be instantly gone or he would be caught and perhaps "cut to pieces."

So weeks became months and still nothing happened to further his suit, except that Buckingham's behavior grew more and more intolerable to the Spanish while the prince continued to dote on the infanta from a distance. In England, meanwhile, King James was having trouble with the pope who was urging him "to grant indulgences to his Catholic subjects." This was one thing James, fearful of the violent anti-Roman Catholicism of the majority of the people in his realm, dared not do. He was also anxious about the attempts that were being made in Spain to convert his son. Always easily frightened, he took fright now and ordered Charles to come "right speedilie away. Alas! I now repent me sore that I ever suffered you to go. I care for match nor nothing, so I may once more have you in my arms again! God grant! God grant!"

Charles, however, still cared about the match a great deal. While Buckingham had grown more and more unpopular, he, by his elegant manners and "civilised behaviour," had won high favor with the Spanish royal family, though not with the reluctant infanta. Still, he had been allowed to sit beside her in public, had even talked to her—an ambassador acting as interpreter—in the presence of the king.

Eventually a date for the marriage was actually settled, the pope having given the necessary dispensation. Then came a shattering blow. The pope died suddenly. Now a new pope would have to confirm the dispensation all over again. This was really the last straw and King James had had enough. Besides, he was not at all well and most of his subjects were growing angry at the overlong absence of their Prince of Wales. Charles must come home at once, he commanded. So Charles made ready to depart, leaving a proxy behind, in order that the marriage could be performed as soon as the new pope's dispensation arrived. Meanwhile, somewhat prematurely, the infanta took the title of Princess of Wales.

Charles arrived back in England after an absence of eight months. The nation's rejoicings were rapturous, not only because he was home again but home unaccompanied by a Spanish wife! The country was ablaze with bonfires, "108 of which were lighted between St. Paul's and London Bridge."

Bigger and better bonfires were to flare up when James, declaring to Parliament that he had been "deluded in the match," called the whole thing off. The ostensible reason was Spain's refusal to restore the Palatine, annexed some years before, to his daughter Elizabeth (now, after many vicissitudes, the exiled Queen of Bohemia) and her husband Frederick. The breaking of the "Treaty of the Match" and the recall of Charles's proxy from Madrid, brought the Spanish "Romanso" to an end.

James's delight in having his son with him again was absolute but short lived. Charles returned from Spain in 1623. Less than two years later the old king died at Theobald's. From the gates of this country palace Charles was proclaimed king. He was then twenty-five.

Charles I's tragic reign lasted twenty-four years. After a travesty of a trial ordered by the House of Commons in Westminster Hall, he was sentenced to death "by the severing of his head from his body." Gaunt but indomitable, a figure in black carrying a gold-headed cane, he walked to his martyr's death with majestic dignity. He is the only English king ever to die on the scaffold.

John Aubrey in his *Brief Lives* relates that "An Old Man

(like an Hermit) Second-sighted, tooke his leave of King James the First, when he came into England. He took little notice of Prince Henry, but addressing himself to the Duke of York (since Charles I) fell a weeping to think what misfortunes he should undergo; and that he should be one of the miserablest unhappy Princes that ever was."

One hundred and sixty-five years after his execution, the body of Charles I was exhumed in the presence of Sir Henry Halford, a royal physician to George III. The beard of the poor severed head had defied mortality and was cut up into small pieces for distribution as souvenirs. Many of these tragic relics have, over the years, been acquired by the well-known Royal Stuart Society in London, the latest as recently as 1964, by a bequest in a will.

IV

When he became king in 1625 Charles I was still a bachelor but, thanks to renewed negotiations during the summer of 1624, he was already betrothed to another Catholic lady, Henrietta Maria, daughter of Marie de Medici and sister of Louis XIII of France. She was the girl who had failed to attract his notice when, incognito, he had passed through Paris on his castle-building journey to Spain. In the June after his accession, he married Henrietta Maria. She was fifteen, a dark-complexioned, pretty, spoiled, rebellious, and obstinate little princess. Throughout the first three years of their marriage they were desperately unhappy. Very naturally, and all too frequently, Charles poured out his troubles to Steenie. He complained bitterly not only of his wife's behavior to him personally, but to the members of his Court.

A day came when Steenie took it upon himself to rebuke

the young queen. He did so in the most churlish manner and ended his scolding with the sarcastic reminder that "Queens of England have had their heads cut off before now." Needless to say this brutal caveat only made matters worse. Furious with Buckingham and more than ever resentful of his influence over the king, Henrietta Maria promptly retired from the Court with her suite and refused to have anything further to do with her husband. This wretched state of affairs continued until 1628. In August of that year, to Charles's grief, but to his queen's and his country's gratification, the great Duke of Buckingham was stabbed to death in a Portsmouth inn. From that time, it is recorded by a courtier, Charles "wholly made over all his affections to his wife . . . she has also returned such a fondness and liking for him and his person as it is much comfort to themselves as of joy to their good servants."

No better proof of the complete reconciliation between the king and queen can be given than the fact that Henrietta Maria became pregnant a few weeks after Steenie's murder. Her baby, born prematurely in May, 1629, died a few days later, having been baptized with the name of Charles. By August of this same year, the queen was pregnant again and on May 29, 1630, at St. James's Palace was delivered of a "large, swarthy, lusty son." Except for the Puritans, who kept their doors tightly shut in disapproval of the birth of a son to the king by a papist queen, the nation as a whole felt nothing but joy, expressing its jubilation with the usual lighting of bonfires and pealing of bells. A month after his birth, this baby was also christened Charles. Though declared Prince of Wales in infancy, he was never formally invested with the title.

Archbishop Laud baptized Charles as Prince of Great Britain, France, and Ireland. In England, at this time, anti-Roman Catholicism was at its peak and to many people the ceremony "smelt strongly of popery." The city fathers did not withhold their blessing for all that and gave the baby a christening present of a gold cup "a yard long," valued at £1,200, while blazing bonfires and booming cannon bore witness to a part of the nation's jubilation. Great comfort was taken in the knowledge that, as governess, the Anglican Lady Dorset was placed in charge of the baby prince's establishment at St. James's Palace. There he lived in elegance and splendor, cared for by some three hundred people, including a Welsh wet nurse, two physicians, an apothecary, a lawyer and, of course, a great number of pages, ushers, cooks, and other household staff.

That the king and queen, both of them small and slender in build, had produced so strong, large, and vigorous a baby, was a matter for satisfaction and, indeed, wonder. It was a great pity that the infant was so plain, or rather, downright ugly. But he made up for his homely looks by being good and "solemn." He rarely cried and slept most of the time. "The nurse told me," the Venetian ambassador reported, "that after his birth he never clenched his fists but always kept his hands open. From this they augur he will be a prince of great liberality." At three months the baby still behaved beautifully and "neither sucked nor wakened but once all night."

His mother doted on him, but his swarthy complexion, in which she could see no improvement as the months went by, continued to cause her anxiety. "I will send you a portrait as soon as he is a little fairer," she wrote to one of her French ladies. To the same correspondent she remarked on her small son's solemnity saying, "he is so serious in all he does that I cannot help fancying him far wiser than myself." She and her husband paid frequent visits to little Charles at St. James's Palace and were overjoyed to find him, at seven months, "continuing in blessed prosperity of health," enchanted when his swaddling clothes gave way to little cambric or white satin dresses and ravished when, having begun to walk, he was breeched and put into tiny suits cut like those of grown men.

As a baby, the little prince adored dolls, a penchant that, not withstanding future events, lends itself to no psychological probings. He loved dolls for the simple reason that the earliest in his possession were made of gum and sugar and were delicious when sucked. From dolls he graduated to more sophisticated toys—figurines in painted wood or alabaster, animals covered with real skin, lead soldiers, cannons, and hobbyhorses on wheels. These, to him, were very well in their way, but far above any of them in his favor was a quite ordinary piece of wood, "a wooden billet, without which in his arms he would never go abroad or lie down in his bed." When he outgrew his wooden billet is, regrettably, not known. What is known is the fact that his wet nurse departed when he was a year old and that her place was taken by Mrs. Christabelle Wyndham, a soldier's wife whom he dearly loved. It was probably Mrs. Wyndham, by her good nursing, who helped him to survive the clysters and purges meted out to him during his first serious illness at the age of three.

Charles, in good health, was a happy little boy and not at all lonely for the companionship of other children. His sister Mary, eighteen months his junior, was installed with him at St. James's Palace, and so, a little later, was his brother James whose blue eyes and fair beauty filled dark-complexioned Henrietta Maria with particular pride. This produced no complexes in Charles. His parents were equally fond of all their children though the king, stiff, severe, and unbending in public, found it difficult, even in their company, to relax completely. Unhappily for this loving father of "exemplary piety, the greatest sobriety, chastity and mercy," he never really felt wholly at ease with anyone except his temperamental and excitable wife. Their early quarrels long buried and forgotten, they were a devoted couple.

The king seldom allowed his children to be punished. They were certainly never spanked. On the other hand, while taking little interest in their education, he was very firm about their training in every movement of formal ceremony. In time Prince Charles was to find this exaggerated formality extremely tedious. He was much too friendly a boy to enjoy stiff punctilio. However, on his first appearance at his father's Court at the age of four, he acquitted himself admirably, "performing the stately courtesy he had been taught and for which his parents were celebrated" with consummate grace.

Charles was six years old when, St. James's Palace having virtually become the royal nursery, his little Court was moved to Richmond. There, and at the royal manor of Oatlands, he spent happy days. The king had now taken him out of "the hands of the women" (Mrs. Wyndham, Lady Dorset, and his mother) and at last his serious education began. Though he could read, write, and do sums, he had never had a tutor. This neglect was put to rights when the Earl of Newcastle became his governor and teachers were appointed to give him lessons in French and drawing.

A courteous, gallant man of unimpeachable integrity, Newcastle was a fervent monarchist. He was wise and understanding, had an original mind, many accomplishments, fascinating hobbies, and a great love for horses and horsemanship. No little prince could have wished for a kinder and more agreeable governor. Charles was immediately drawn to him and was very soon copying all Newcastle's refinements and tastes and adopting all his ideas and opinions. He did his lessons, but also learned to ride well, fence with skill, and dance beautifully.

Because the earl was an extremely abstemious man Charles, eager in imitation, strove bravely to curb a greedy schoolboy appetite—a training in the temperate use of food and drink that was to stand him in good stead later during his years of exile. By treating the boy not as a child but as a sensible young man, Newcastle won his love, admiration, and complete confidence. In the form of a letter, the earl wrote out a set of maxims specially for the little prince.

"It is fit you should have some language, though I confess I would rather you studied things than words," runs one precept in this fascinating document. Again, "I would not have you too studious,"—Charles, the schoolboy, must have grasped at this sentiment—"for too much contemplation spoils action, and virtue consists in that." Another rule counsels: "Speak well of everybody, and when you hear people speak ill of others reprehend them and say something in favour of those spoken against . . . Win people's hearts, and then you will have all they have; more you cannot have." The earl, sapient and rational himself, gave sound advice, too, against bigotry. "Beware of too much devotion, for one may be a good man but a bad king"; and on kingship itself " . . . . though you cannot put on too much King, yet even there sometimes a hat or a smile in the right place will advantage you"—advice that would have greatly advantaged that good man, Prince Charles's father.

Newcastle was the prince's tutor, guide, philosopher, and friend for three years. At the end of the first, in May, 1638, the king made his son a Knight of the Garter at a ceremony held at Windsor. This same year also brought Charles two young friends, George and Francis Villiers, to share his life at Richmond and Oatlands. Sons of his great friend Steenie, the Duke of Buckingham, the king had adopted the boys after the murder of their father. Both were older than Charles, George by two years. He was a brilliant boy who, through age and brains, gained a hold over the young prince which, weathering "fluctuations and estrangements," was to last all their lives. In contrast to Charles's sallow skin and coarse features, the Villiers boys had fair complexions and, like their dead father, were extremely good looking. But for all his ugliness, Charles carried himself gracefully, and was a charming, intelligent, lively, fearless, and immensely vital boy. He had the brightest, merriest black eyes, the friendliest of manners, was kind to all about him, and disarmingly affectionate. His servants adored him. His exuberant spirits occasionally landed him in trouble, as on the occasion when the king caught him grinning and giggling in chapel, tapped the culprit smartly on the head with the knob of his cane and scolded him roundly.

By the time Charles was eleven the quarrel between his father and Parliament had reached such a peak that civil war was now inevitable. Soon his schooldays were over, never to be seriously resumed. He was, at least theoretically, badly educated. But in the years that lay ahead the quick-witted, spirited boy learned a great deal in the hard school of life. This harsh academy opened its doors to receive him as soon as the first campaign of the war began. When fighting started, the king, fearing that the Roundheads might attempt to kidnap his sons, took the Prince of Wales and his brother James along with him, and so it came about that the boys were present at the first engagement of the war, at Edge Hill. In charge of Dr. William Harvey, the discoverer of the circulation of the blood, and at a safe distance on top of a rise, Charles and James excitedly watched the fighting from behind a hedge. Dr. Harvey, indifferent to the spectacle of war, took a medical book from his pocket and was soon so engrossed that he completely forgot where he was and why. He was rudely brought back to reality when a bullet hit the ground close to the spot where he and the young princes were seated. Much to the annoyance of twelve-year-old Charles, who had hoped to make good use of the pistol with which he was armed, Harvey instantly decided to remove the boys to a safer refuge. Charles mounted his pony and before Harvey could stop him, raced off towards the fighting. He was almost within shooting distance of a troop of Roundheads, his pistol at the ready and shouting excitedly, "I fear them not," when he was rescued, returned to Harvey and safely carried off to the village of Edgecot.

No further adventures in the field of war were to befall

Charles during the next six years, and so his mother now focused her thoughts on an advantageous marriage for her eldest son. No one, she decided, was more suitable than the rich Anne-Marie de Montpensier, La Grande Mademoiselle, cousin of Louis XIV of France. Nothing came of her efforts, but this did not prevent her from scheming for and dreaming of his union with the wealthy and famous Mademoiselle for nearly another decade. The king, early in 1645, also sought to arrange a marriage for Charles by opening negotiations with the Portuguese royal house for the hand of the plain Infanta Catherine of Braganza. These overtures were interrupted by the ill-starred course of the Civil War. Dark clouds of defeat and disaster were gathering above the Royalist heads. In the hope that the presence of the young Prince of Wales would inspire more men to enlist in the king's forces in the West country—but the boy, it was stipulated, must not "engage himself in any martial action"—a small Court was to be set up for him at Bristol. In March, 1645, three months before his fifteenth birthday, Charles said goodbye to his father and went off to his new headquarters. Though neither realized it, this was a final farewell. They never saw each other again.

Steadily and relentlessly the tide of war turned against the king, sweeping away all hope of a monarchist victory. The king, prepared, even at the cost of his life, to prevent his heir from falling into Roundhead hands, ordered Charles and his little Court to seek refuge in the Scilly Isles. So the prince took his first steps into exile.

The people of the Isles of Scilly were anxious to do all they could for "this delightful boy." There was little they could do. Food was scarce and the weather vile. The prince was often hungry and more often soaked to the skin. From this hard life he was moved to Jersey in the Channel Islands. There, too, the people were overjoyed by his presence. Because

Charles "loved to be loved," he responded warmly to their affectionate kindness. He was gay, happy, full of life, and soon began to show an eager delight in the company of pretty young women. But gradually boredom and frustration took hold of him as he came to realize that from the Channel Islands nothing could be done to help his father's cause. His stay in Jersey came to an end on June 26, 1646, when, summoned by his mother exiled in Paris, he sailed away across the narrow sea. He joined the refugee queen at the Palace of St. Germain where she was living on a pension from the French Court. The king had surrendered himself to the Scots' army a month before and, eight months later, the Scots surrendered him to the English Parliament.

Henrietta Maria all too clearly realized the gravity of her husband's plight. Only through her son Charles, she now decided, could she hope to liberate the king. Through Charles she might be able to raise money for a force, to be led by him, for the invasion of England. The fulfillment of her plans depended on Charles marrying a rich woman, on marriage to La Grande Mademoiselle, the richest woman in all Europe.

Though Mademoiselle considered the English "a heretical and half-civilised nation," the idea of being queen of England one day was not displeasing to her. Her first meeting with Charles was arranged by Henrietta Maria, diplomatically, as a chance encounter in the forest of Fontainebleau. Mademoiselle's carriage came smartly from one direction, that of the English queen, accompanied by her eldest son, from another. The arrangement worked admirably. Mademoiselle was impressed by Charles. His bright black eyes, waving hair, height, figure, graceful carriage, and beautiful manners pleased her instantly. Her nineteen-year-old heart began to flutter, her head to tingle with romantic thoughts.

Charles, looking older than his sixteen years, matured by the experiences and disillusionments of a hard life, was not impressed. Having already acquired a taste in women, his bright eyes saw La Grande Mademoiselle only as a far too tall, too heavily built, badly dressed blonde, plain in the bargain, with a nose much too big to please him. Though she was as rich as Croesus, this over-voluble coquette did not attract him in the least. That did not prevent him from being as charming and exquisitely polite to her as only a Stuart could be; but without uttering a word. He excused himself for his silence on the grounds that he knew no French, that the years of the Civil War had put his mother's mother tongue, which he had heard and spoken since a small boy, right out of his head. Since he could charm birds out of trees, he succeeded in making even his mother and his French relations swallow this highly improbable story.

In "the role of speechless admirer" he continued this dumb charade till eventually the absurd comedy petered out. La Grande Mademoiselle, wearying of his silence, flung her cap several rungs higher. There were better unions to be sought than a mere exiled Prince of Wales. She did, however, write, after he had fallen from her favor, "Could he only have spoken for himself, Heaven only knows what might have happened."

In the autumn of 1646, George Villiers, the young Duke of Buckingham, and his brother Francis, arrived in Paris to join their friend the Prince of Wales. Sophisticated George, who had "already got into all the vices and impieties of the age," led Charles, when he could slip away from his mother, into a life of wild gaiety. Young Buckingham's hold over the prince was as great as in their schoolboy days at Richmond and Oatlands. In Paris, it was he (so it is sometimes contended) who "corrupted" the prince. The two years they spent together in Paris certainly did not do the prince much good. But the days and nights did much, it must be conceded, to stimulate his taste, particularly for beauty, women, and wit.

In 1648 when the greater part of the English navy declared for the king and sailed off to Holland, Charles left Paris. He traveled to Calais and from there to Holland, where he joined the fleet. The end of the journey brought him not only reunion with his fifteen-year-old brother James, Duke of York, who had managed to escape from England disguised in woman's clothes but, during a few days spent at The Hague, a meeting with "brown, beautiful, bold, but insipid" Lucy Walter.

Lucy had originally arrived in The Hague as the mistress of Colonel Algernon Sidney. After a while he passed her on to his brother Robert who, in 1648, became groom of the prince's bedchamber. Within a few days of Charles's meeting with beautiful, brown Lucy, Robert "willingly" gave her up to his prince. By the time the prince sailed with the fleet to blockade the Thames, a venture that did nothing to save the king, Lucy now known as Mrs. Barlow, was recognized as his "public mistress." In due course she gave birth to his son James. Back in England after many vicissitudes, Charles created the boy Duke of Monmouth fourteen years later. Wild, wilful Lucy was of all Charles's mistresses, it is said, "the one he loved most—and the one he treated worst."

Charles did everything in his power to save his father, and failed. On January 30, 1649, King Charles I died on the scaffold. The news reached The Hague on February 4. William of Orange sent a chaplain to break the news to the prince. Face to face with Charles, the poor man could not bring himself to utter the awful words he had come to say and rambled on incoherently. At last he began a sentence with "Your Majesty—." He could go no further. There was a stunned silence for some moments. Then Charles burst into tears. Sobbing like a suddenly terrified child, he rushed from the room to his bedchamber. There for many hours, he remained alone.

A little more than a year after that awful day Charles, having accepted help from the Scottish Covenanters, sailed to

Scotland where, on New Year's Day, 1651, he was crowned king of Scotland at the ancient Palace of Scone. He was not quite twenty-one. A few months later he was on his way southward, over the border into England with his Scottish army, fighting a campaign to regain the whole of his lost kingdom. But events were to turn out otherwise. Help that had been promised did not materialize and at Worcester his forces were utterly defeated by Cromwell.

Charles managed to escape capture, but he was a wanted man, hunted by the Roundheads. Though notices were exhibited all over the country offering a reward for his capture and describing him as "a tall, black man, six foot two inches high," no information concerning his whereabouts was forthcoming.

Months of hardship now followed for Charles, sufferings too often overshadowed by his more romantic adventures during this period; the hiding in trees and masquerading as a servant. However, he eventually succeeded in gaining the Sussex coast. From there, in a small boat, on a dark night, he crossed the Channel to Fécamp and eight further years were spent on "travels abroad." Not till Cromwell had been dead for nearly two years and Richard Cromwell, the son who had succeeded him, was forced to abdicate, did a new Parliament vote that "according to the ancient and fundamental laws of this Kingdom, the government is, and ought to be, by King, Lords, and Commons."

On May 29, 1660, John Evelyn wrote in his diary: "This day, his Majesty, Charles the Second came to London, after a sad and long exile and calamitous suffering both of the King and Church, being seventeen years. This was also his birthday, and with a triumph of above 20,000 horse and foot, brandishing their swords, and shouting with inexpressible joy; the ways strewed with flowers, the bells ringing, the streets hung with tapestry, fountains running with wine. . . . I stood in the Strand and beheld it, and blessed God."

The Commonwealth and Protectorate under Oliver Cromwell had passed into history and England had a king again.

V

Charles II, "a prince of many virtues, and many great imperfections, debonaire, easy of access, not bloody nor cruel," a big man with a big voice, kind, courtly, full of jests, able to understand all men and a "great master of king-craft," died twenty-four years and nine months after his restoration.

"I am weary of travelling, I am resolved to go abroad no more. But when I am dead and gone, I know not what my brother will do. . . ." Charles had said to a friend a few weeks before his death. His brother James, Duke of York, to whom he had been deeply loyal all his life, was his heir. His twenty-two-year marriage to Catherine of Braganza was childless, but fourteen children by his many mistresses survived him. Of these, the one he loved best was Lucy Walter's son James, whom he had created Duke of Monmouth. Five months after his father's death the Duke of Monmouth, called by many "the Protestant prince," in retribution for leading a rebellion against his uncle, King James, lost his head on Tower Hill.

James II was the only Stuart prince devoid of that magnetic charm that inspired both devotion and loyalty. A Protestant by birth, he openly professed his adherence to the Roman Catholic faith only thirteen years before he came to the throne. By his first wife, Anne Hyde, he had two daughters: Mary, married to William of Orange, and Anne, wife of George, Prince of Denmark. Both had been brought up staunch Protestants. Shortly after the death of Anne Hyde, James married Mary of Modena, by whom he had four sons before his accession. Three were named Charles. All died in infancy.

King James resembled his brother Charles only in having fathered a large brood of illegitimate children. In almost every other respect they were utterly unlike. A man of "infinite industry," James was bigoted, despotic by instinct, and completely lacking in all the amiable qualities that so endeared Charles to the people. James's bigotry, disregard for popular feeling, and bitter persecution of nonconformists, led to his downfall after only a brief reign. The rumor that his ailing wife was, after all, again expecting a child, hastened his overthrow. The baby, if a boy, would have insured a Catholic succession and the country as a whole would have none of this.

On June 10, 1688, the queen did give birth to a son. Named James Francis Edward, the infant was almost immediately created Prince of Wales and was actually so described at his baptism on October 15. He was the thirteenth Prince of Wales to hold the title. For him, certainly, that number was an omen of misfortune.

At the birth of this baby born to adversity, a malicious story was deliberately circulated, probably by the Orange faction who wished to get rid of the Catholic king and to supplant him by his Protestant daughter Mary and her Dutch husband. According to the mendacious invention, the queen had, in fact, not given birth to a child at all. The baby was a changeling, son of a baker named Fuller, and had been smuggled into the queen's chamber in a warming pan. Since a great many prominent people, including the Lords of the Privy Council, were present at the birth, there could obviously have been no truth in the disgraceful rumor. But it gathered strength. Aware of the ever-increasing determination to be rid of him, King James attempted to allay some of the more ill-starred of his measures. It was too late. William of Orange had sailed from Holland. When he landed at Torbay he was welcomed with wild enthusiasm. James stoutly advanced against his son-in-law's forces but had to retreat when half his army deserted and joined the enemy. The situation now became so desperate for the king that he sent his wife and baby son off to France. Two days later he attempted to follow them, and was captured. But he was soon at liberty and also permitted to depart for France. At the Château of St. Germain Louis XIV allowed him to form his exiled Court. Parliament, having decided by January of the new year (1689), that James had broken "the original contract between king and people," offered the crown to his daughter Mary and her husband, William of Orange, as joint sovereigns.

At the Court of St. Germain, described by the Earl of Middleton as "the dreadfullest place in France next to the Bastille," little James Francis Edward, Prince of Wales, grew from babyhood to a boyhood "of grace, lightness, and gallant daring, which gives him special dignity and charm." In many ways he resembled his uncle, Charles II. He and Charles were blessed with magical charm to a degree far beyond that possessed by any other prince of the Stuart House. Like Charles, he was sallow complexioned, had great black eyes and dark hair, features that earned him the affectionate nickname "the little Blackbird." He was studious, pious and a devout Catholic, and was to remain so to the end of his life.

When his father died in 1701, James Francis Edward was not quite fourteen. At the gates of St. Germain, though "not an inch of Britain belonged to him," he was proclaimed king of England. The Jacobites called him James VIII of Scotland and the III of England. These were sterile titles.

By the terms of the Act of Settlement, the crown of England, after the death of Queen Anne, younger daughter of the deposed James II, was to pass to Sophia, electress of Hanover, and through her to her eldest son George. Queen Anne herself favored the claims of her young half-brother, James Francis

Edward, who, if only he had forsworn his Roman Catholic religion, might have won over most of the people of Britain. This he was never prepared to do, though there were numerous intrigues. In 1708, soon after the battle of Oudenarde, in which he fought with the French forces defeated by the great Marlborough (who had George of Hanover's son in his ranks), the twenty-year-old son of James II wrote to Queen Anne. "Surely," he declared, "you will prefer your own brother, the last male of our name, to the House of Hanover (the remotest relations we have), whose friendship there is no reason to rely on and who will leave the government to foreigners!" But there was nothing Queen Anne could do about any preference. Six years later both she and the prince's mother, Mary of Modena, seemed to be dying. Both temporarily recovered. But then the old Electress Sophia died in a chair in her summerhouse and her son George became heir to the throne of England.

When, at last, Queen Anne too died, in August, 1714, there were shouts in the streets of "No Hanover!" Louder than these, however, were the cries of a powerful faction shouting "No Popery." All necessary steps were quickly taken to secure the accession of George, elector of Hanover. He was the grandson of James I's daughter Elizabeth, who had married Frederick of the Palatine in 1612.

When the crown of England came to rest on George's head, a price of £100,000 was placed on that of James Francis Edward. Despite several attempts to regain his lost kingdom, he died, as he is best remembered, the Old Pretender. By the time of his death at the age of nearly seventy-eight, he had outlived not only his half-sister Mary and her husband, William of Orange, as well as his half-sister Queen Anne, but also two of the Hanoverian kings who had succeeded to the throne of England.

PART FIVE: HANOVERIANS

PART FIVE: HANOVERIANS

In 1701, after the death of Queen Anne's surviving child, William, the twelve-year-old Duke of Gloucester, Parliament passed an Act of Settlement. By this Act, exiled James II and his son, James Francis Edward, being Roman Catholics, were barred from ascending the throne of England. In their stead, Sophia, the Protestant electress of Hanover and granddaughter of James I, was placed next in line as successor to Queen Anne. When Sophia died fourteen years later, at the age of eighty-four, her eldest son, George Lewis, succeeded her both as elector of Hanover and heir-apparent to the British throne. He claimed both kingdoms in the same year, for, at Kensington Palace on Sunday morning, August 1, 1714, after an unbroken sequence of illnesses and recoveries, Queen Anne also died.

Casting lingering glances back at his beloved native land, the elector left Hanover for The Hague. There he embarked for England in the *Peregrine*—and "in the pocket of the

Whigs"—to preserve the Protestant succession. After being delayed by fog, he landed at Greenwich on September 18. Hailed by the proclamation that "the high and mighty Prince George, Elector of Brunswick-Lüneberg, is now, by the death of our late sovereign, of happy memory, become our only lawful and rightful liege Lord, George, by the Grace of God, King of Great Britain, France and Ireland, Defender of the Faith etc.," England's first Hanoverian king took up residence in St. James's Palace.

The new king was not entirely a stranger to London. With the idea of asking for the hand of James II's daughter Anne, the queen he now succeeded, he had paid a brief visit to the metropolis some thirty odd years before. He had departed again without regret, charmed neither by the English princess nor by England. In those thirty years London had not greatly changed. True, its population had risen to just over half a million, including, to the disgust of Dean Swift, "a race of Rakes called the Mohacks that play the devil about this Town every night." Except for little boats, London Bridge was still the only means of crossing the Thames; in Hyde Park royalty still hunted deer; and the city remained the hub of the metropolitan wheel. Wheel spokes, however, had begun to extend eastward to an industrial area, complete with slums, and westward to new squares of elegance and refinement. But in Piccadilly, Burlington House still stood surrounded by peaceful open fields and Kensington remained a faraway village famed for the salubrious air that had enticed Queen Anne's brother-in-law, Dutch King William, to rebuild Nottingham House into Kensington Palace, in the hope that the healthiness of the climate would mitigate his asthma.

George I was a heavy, solid, and singularly unattractive man. He did, however, possess a sense of duty. He was also shrewd enough to make the best of a bargain that left him the management of Hanover while England, managed by the Whigs, brought him £1,000,000 a year. But his new kingdom failed to charm him. His heart always remained where his home was—in Hanover. German to the core, he spoke no English and was too old at fifty-four, too indifferent, and too lazy to attempt to learn it. This language problem was one reason why he surrounded himself with, to him, companionable male and female Hanoverians and Germans.

The king was, on arrival in England, a species of grass widower. Many years before, in 1682 when he was twenty-one, he had married his cousin Sophia Dorothea of Celle. He treated her abominably and made her deeply unhappy. From this marriage of misery she escaped briefly into a romantic love affair with the Swedish count Philip von Königsmark. The discovery of their liaison roused George Lewis, himself a notoriously unfaithful husband, to sadistic fury. Sophia Dorothea's count was arrested, and, almost immediately afterwards, mysteriously disappeared. Rumor declared that he had been murdered and that his body was buried beneath the floor of a room in the palace. There is yet another legend which relates that, brutally assaulted but still alive, he was flung into "a red-hot oven." Sophia Dorothea, adamantly denying that she had committed adultery but admitting that she had behaved indiscreetly, was divorced by her husband, imprisoned in the austere castle of Ahlden and forcibly prevented from ever again seeing her only child, George Augustus, aged eleven. The year was 1694. She remained shut up in Ahlden until her death in 1726, thirty-two years later. During these decades George Lewis comforted himself with a selection of unlovely *bonnes amies*. And so it happened that instead of bringing a consort with him to England, he arrived with two of his graceless mistresses, the fat Frau von Kielmannsegge and the tall, thin Fräulein von Schulenberg. In due course he made the former Countess of Darlington, the latter Duchess of Kendal. English satirists nicknamed them descriptively "The Elephant" and "The Maypole."

Besides his grotesque paramours, George I's entourage

also included two personal servants, Turks named Mahomet and Mustafa. With him, too, came his son and heir by Sophia Dorothea, the now thirty-one-year-old George Augustus, who, by Act of Parliament, had been a naturalized Englishman since 1705. Queen Anne had also, a year after that, invested him with the Order of the Garter and created him Baron of Tewkesbury, Viscount Northallerton, Earl of Milfordhaven, and Duke of Cambridge—all by proxy, for George Augustus did not set foot in England until he arrived with his father.

Towards his son George I felt only one emotion, an overwhelming detestation. This may have been due to the fact that George Augustus was an ever-present reminder of the lonely prisoner of Ahlden, though Horace Walpole ascribes it to something "in the blood of the family." There is much to be said for the Walpolean theory. A virus of hostility and animosity certainly was passed on to all England's future Hanoverian kings, whose relationship with their heirs fluctuated in ferocity between intense dislike and malevolent loathing. To some degree this germ in the Hanoverian blood was inherent even in Queen Victoria.

At his first Privy Council the new king, not from any personal desire but entirely on the advice of his ministers, created his son Prince of Wales. George Augustus was not only the fourteenth, and first Hanoverian, Prince of Wales, and the first since Edward the Black Prince to have children during his father's lifetime, but also—except for that very brief spell when James II's baby son was in the country—the first Prince of Wales in England for seventy-six years.

George Augustus was born in Hanover in 1683. Deprived for ever of his mother's affection and care at the age of eleven, he grew up in charge of his grandmother, the old Electress Sophia. She supervised his education, a limited one that gave him no more than a smattering of French, history, Latin, and English. He never learned to master English completely and always spoke it with a heavy German accent. Though fond of his grandmother, the boy did not forget the prisoner in Ahlden and, when grown up and convinced of her innocence, made several attempts to see his mother. All were forcefully defeated and served only to add further fuel to his father's anger and hostility. These frustrations did not dim his cherished image of Sophia Dorothea, whose portrait he was forbidden to display. Nor did they cure him of a treasured dream that one day, when he succeeded his father, he would bring his grievously ill-used mother to England and proclaim her the dowager queen. This generous aspiration was not realized. George I outlived Sophia Dorothea by a year.

In 1705, the year when he became a naturalized Englishman, George Augustus, then twenty-two, married the sixteen-year-old Princess Caroline of Anspach, a friendly, clever, charming girl who grew into a gifted, clever, and remarkable woman. When her husband eventually became George II, her keen political insight made her the real power behind the throne. Strange as it may seem, Caroline, so much his superior in every way, was deeply devoted to her vain, irascible, shallow husband. And equally strange, he was sincerely attached to her despite a "propensity for mistresses" far greater than that of his father. Caroline was George Augustus' good genius, his staunchest partisan, and, above all, his untiring sympathizer, ever constant and understanding and the only person with whom at all times he could discuss his amours and his paramours. Even in this compliance Caroline showed herself an exceptional woman. She did not accompany her husband to England, but arrived with her three small daughters soon after he had been made Prince of Wales. Her eldest child, Frederick Lewis, was, by order of George I, left behind in Hanover, allegedly to be educated but really from a baleful desire on the part of the king to keep the boy separated from his parents. The effect this detachment produced would have delighted George I's heart had he lived to witness it.

Like George I, George Augustus was by no stretch of the imagination a glamorous personality. But he was a brave little man. He brought his justifiable reputation for courage to England, though the English already knew how gallantly he had fought at Oudenarde under the great Marlborough. For, in praise of his feats in that battle, Congreve had written a song of eulogy to the "Young Hanover brave" who

In this bloody field, I assure you,
When his warhorse was shot
He valued it not,
But fought still on foot like a fury.

Short, unprepossessing in appearance, with a high forehead, a large, well-shaped nose, and blue eyes whose loveliness belied his complete lack of any sense of humor, George Augustus was undeniably a bore, and a fussy, obstinate, peppery bore at that. Intensely conceited and self-centered, he was poorly educated, had little real intelligence and firmly believed in vampires. His main interests centered on military affairs and on his mistresses who, by and large, were far better looking than those of George I. But he himself, despite all his defects, was much more likeable than his father. Only moderately faithful as a friend and only fairly honest, since, according to Sir Robert Walpole, he did not "lie often," he made up for the half-tones in these virtues by being excessively, indeed almost devilishly, punctual. Wholly "un-English" in accent, manners, and gesture, he delighted, when he first arrived in England, to boast of the English blood in his veins and bored a great many people by telling them that he thought the English "the best, the handsomest, the best-shaped, the best-natured, and lovingest people in the world, and if anybody would make their court to him, it must be by telling him he was like an Englishman." These high-flown sentiments did not endure. In time he was to become as enamoured of Hanover as was his father, George I. The English as a whole quite liked their new Prince of Wales, though according to a letter (in the State Papers Domestic of George I), there was a plot, a year after the arrival of the Hanoverians, to "expedite both Georges"—which meant, quite simply, to murder them—and restore the Pretender.

The mutual dislike of the king and his son steadily increased in intensity after their arrival in England. There were three blatant reasons for this. To begin with, George I, with a revenue of £1,000,000 a year, stripped the Prince of Wales' allowance down to £50,000. The Commons eventually had to double this sum. Then, unlike previous English sovereigns, the king would not allow his son any hand in matters of state and refused him every chance to learn the business of statecraft. Finally, not satisfied with depriving the Prince of Wales of useful employment in state affairs, the king also refused to allow his son to practice the only profession he understood and loved, that of soldiering. To console himself, the Prince of Wales would sometimes dress himself up in the uniform he had worn at Oudenarde. Years later, when he was king, he was to find greater consolation still at Dettingen where "the French fired at His Majesty from a battery of twelve cannon, but levelled too high. . . . The Duke D'Aremberg desired him to go out of danger: he answered 'Don't tell me of danger, I'll be even with them,'" and so covered himself with glory and made history as the last English king to lead his troops into battle.

Deprived of any sort of useful employment, there was little the Prince of Wales could do except, with the help of his wife, allow himself to become popular with the Parliamentary party in opposition to the king's government and "enliven the London scene" by frequent appearances at the opera, by holding Drawingrooms and by giving musical parties, all of which the king hated. The king also hated England and the English, and longed to revisit Hanover. This was difficult in 1715 when the Jacobites rose in rebellion and James Francis Edward, the Pretender, actually landed in the North and there was street fighting even in London. However, when the rebellion was quashed and the Pretender sailed to France, the king felt that he could no longer do without Hanover. Firmly putting his foot down and commanding that George Augustus could be Guardian of the Realm but not regent in his absence, he took his departure.

Now that the king was away, the Prince and Princess of Wales were at last able to breathe freely and had a glorious time. They made progresses and set up a court at Hampton Court which was all gaiety and fun and quite different from the dull, uninterestingly vulgar ménage at St. James's Palace. In general, they both became very popular, particularly with the Opposition. The king, on his return, was furious on all these counts, and quarrels with his son reached a new peak in acrimony. Their mutual antagonism and detestation exploded violently in November, 1717, when the Princess of Wales gave birth to a second son at St. James's Palace, her first child to be born in England.

The Prince of Wales had asked his father and his uncle, the Bishop of Osnaburg, to be the baby's godfathers. To this the king agreed. On the day of the christening, however, he appeared at the Princess of Wales' bedside with the Duke of Newcastle (the Lord Chamberlain) instead of the bishop, as his co-sponsor. In a flash, choleric George Augustus, who intensely disliked Newcastle, burst into a passion of rage. Since he dared not vent his spleen on the king to his face, the almost demented prince, much to the edification of all the guests attending the christening ceremony, compromised by shaking his fist in Newcastle's, shouting "Rascal, I will find you out." To the guests' further entertainment, the king exploded into an even more towering passion than his son's. He shouted the command that the prince be immediately arrested and detained in his room. The Princess of Wales then joined the fray and refused, point blank, to allow her husband to be taken from her. Whereupon they were both confined to her chamber. And there they remained until the king, having decided that Caroline was sufficiently recovered from her lying-in, evicted his son and the princess from St. James's Palace, but kept the unfortunate newly born baby, which died within a few weeks, as well as his three little granddaughters.

So the Prince and Princess of Wales had to go house hunting. Finally they settled down in Leicester House. There, "deprived of their guard and all official marks of distinction," they set up an opposition Court to the king's. It became the rallying point for all who were opposed to the king and his government. Pleasant, gay, and dignified, and in every way a great contrast to St. James's, the small Court of the prince and princess was soon all the rage.

George I's hatred of his son, and though to a lesser degree, of "cette diablesse Madame la Princesse," was now so intense that he would receive no one at St. James's who went to Leicester House. And not only did he begin to toy with the idea of disinheriting the prince from the electoral succession of Hanover, but he actually lent a willing ear to a project for kidnapping George Augustus and putting him aboard ship, to be "carried off to any part of the world that your Majesty may be pleased to order."

The battle raged with bitter fury for three years. Eventually, with patience and diplomacy, Sir Robert Walpole managed to talk the peppery Prince of Wales into writing "a dutiful letter to his sire." This brought the prince and princess an invitation to a private reception at St. James's Palace. "Vous êtes bien-venue, Madame. Je suis ravi de vous voir ici," the old king said to his daughter-in-law. He made no effort to utter a cordial word to his son. They shook hands—and "continued to be mortal enemies."

Since they were never allowed to do anything useful, the Prince and Princess of Wales lived a happy in-between sort of life for the next seven years, drifting pleasantly between their little Court at Leicester House in London and their country house at Richmond. They were staying at Richmond when George I, on his fifth visit to Hanover during his thirteen-year reign, died suddenly at Osnaburg on a Saturday in June, 1727. Hearing the news a few days later, Sir Robert Walpole hastened off to Richmond. He arrived to find the new king and his consort incommunicado, wrapped in a summer's afternoon nap. At last George Augustus appeared "with his breeches in his hand." Still befogged with sleep, he heard the startling intelligence from Sir Robert Walpole's lips and snapped, "Dat is one big lie." But it was the truth. George Augustus had become George II.

II

The strange, sadistic streak in the character of George I that had made him insist on his grandson, Frederick Lewis, remaining behind in Hanover when the rest of George Augustus's family came to London in 1714, also made him, throughout his reign, spitefully detain the boy there. In consequence, though George II, on visits to Hanover while he was the Prince of Wales, had seen his son—and decided that he did not much care for what he saw—Caroline and the rest of her children had never once set eyes on him throughout the years. Frederick—Fritz to his family, Fred to the English people and satirists—not unnaturally grew up with a chip on his shoulder. The chip swelled into a sizable faggot when his father, on becoming George II, took a further eighteen months before summoning him to London. The summons, in any case, was a reluctant one, called forth not from affection but because the English people clamored for the presence of the new king's heir. There was another reason as well. Frederick, so the British ambassador reported, was about to make a secret marriage. This marriage to Princess Wilhelmina of Prussia, originally approved of by his grandfather was, inevitably, disapproved by George II. Frederick happened to be in love with Wilhelmina and it was with her mother's connivance that he planned the secret marriage so peremptorily sabotaged by his father, who commanded the young man's instant departure for Holland. From there Frederick sailed to England in a packet bound for Harwich and finally arrived at St. James's Palace in a hackney coach.

Frederick was seven when his grandfather inherited Queen Anne's throne and nearly twenty-two when he arrived in England to be created Prince of Wales in January, 1729. Brought up in the intellectually dull Court of Hanover, the young prince, a mixture of self-possession, vanity, and timidity, was badly educated, though he had developed some taste for music and literature. His knowledge of English was as limited as his understanding of his new role in the life of England. Years before, an exasperated tutor had written to the then Princess Caroline that her son had the manners of a "scoundrelly groom," but by the time Frederick came to join his family he could, when it pleased him, be both affable and courteous. Lord Hervey, Pope's face-painting Sporus and the new queen's friend, says the prince's "character at his first coming over, though little more respectable, seemed much more amenable than it was upon his opening himself and being better known." A less biased, though obviously more facile impression of Frederick on his arrival in England, is given by a lady who met him at Court. She saw him as "the most agreeable young man it is possible to imagine without being the least handsome" (his beautiful hair was in fact his one good feature). "His person is little," the lady continued, "but well-made and genteel. He has a liveliness in his eyes which is indescribable and the most obliging address that can be conceived. The crown of all his perfections is the great duty and regard he pays the King and Queen. . . . Pray God long to continue it!" Her pious request was not granted.

On his arrival the prince appeared, on the surface, to be in favor with his family, but this spirit of apparent unity was short-lived. The queen for some time went on making allowances for her son, but the king, who had found himself disliking the young man in Hanover, soon gave full rein to his inherited suspicion and jealousy of his heir. In no time at all he had settled Frederick into a niche of dislike and disfavor from which there was no escape. Sir Robert Walpole reported him as saying, "with an air of contempt and satisfaction: 'I think this is not a son I need be much afraid of!' "

Outside his family circle the prince steadily built up a not inconsiderable popularity, particularly among those in opposition to the king and Sir Robert Walpole's Whigs. The more antipathetic his family felt towards him, the higher he rose in favor with the king's antagonists, who, aware of the usefulness to them of this weak, vain young man, courted him assiduously and used him as a pawn in their game of "playing off the Prince against the King." By raising the question of the Prince of Wales' allowance, they adroitly stoked the fires of father-son animosity. The prince, cried the Opposition, was being disgracefully ill-used by his father who was allowing him a mere £2,000 a month plus the income from the Duchy of Cornwall, in all about £34,000. When the king was Prince of Wales, they declared, he received £100,000 a year.

George II, maddened by this hue and cry, became still more angry when Frederick asked him to settle old and heavy debts left behind in Hanover as well as a new crop reaped in England. The irascible little king worked himself into such a state that he refused to speak to his son, a breach in their relationship that was soon the talk of the town. Gossips had a field day. Countless stories, true and false, circulated from lip to ear throughout society. Even on Handel and his music, it was said, the king and the Prince of Wales acrimoniously disagreed. The king was vehemently pro which, of course, put the prince solidly on the other side. Every indication of the Prince of Wales finding acceptance among the people only served to widen the rift between father and son. When the prince was cheered in the theatre, the king was furious. Frederick certainly was at this time fairly popular with the people —because, one cynic suggested, the people "knew a great deal about the King, but little about the Prince of Wales."

Lying, it appears, was Frederick's greatest fault. "He was really childish," wrote Horace Walpole, "affectedly a protector of the arts and sciences, fond of displaying what he knew. His best quality was generosity, his worst, insincerity and indifference to truth." All in all, he was not as bad as his father had decided he was, for though, wrote Lord Hervey, there was "nothing in him to be admired, yet there seemed nothing in him to be hated." But by the time he had been in England four years, the king hated him so intensely that "whenever the Prince was in a room with the King . . . it always seemed as if the King thought the place the Prince filled a void space." The queen, still occasionally speaking up for her son, was also growing more and more averse to him, an aversion on the part of both parents that snowballed year by year. In time they came to hate their eldest son with violence greater than ever George I felt for George II when he was Prince of Wales.

Though Frederick was not, as his family came passionately to believe, bone-bad, he was undeniably inconsiderate, egocentric, and, above all, a liar. He was also, like his father and grandfather, addicted to mistresses in the true Hanoverian manner. Beauty in these—and in this he resembled his "race"—was not an essential attribute. Most of his favorites were either plain or old or both, and one was not only very unattractive and short but "very yellow." Having indulged himself from an early age in a coterie of Hanoverian favorites, he continued this occupation in England. Though it has been suggested that his penchant was bred out of boredom, women and gambling were, in fact, his two main interests.

That the prince was often bored when he first came to England is undoubtedly true. To his way of thinking his father's Court was colorless and tame. Besides, he felt very much the odd man out in the family circle. Then, too, the king would allow him no hand in matters of state nor even permit him "to go a volunteer" in the army. Not that he was imbued with heroic longings, but life in the army would have been preferable to kicking his heels at Court. So, with nothing to keep him occupied, Frederick soon began "to throw his handkerchief at this lady and that." His relationship with various women, in particular Miss Vane, by whom he had a son, made it desirable that he should, as soon as possible, be permanently tied up in marriage with a suitable and, of course, German princess.

In 1736 George II, who had long ago discarded his Anglomania, departed on one of his regular visits to Hanover. As usual, he left the queen behind as regent. Frederick, he directed, must reside with her throughout his absence, a command that, as it came from the king, the prince automatically and frequently disobeyed. The king paid so long a visit to Hanover that the nation became extremely discontented. Voicing the displeasure of all classes, notices appeared in various public places; one put up at the Royal Exchange ironically proclaimed: "It is reported that his Hanoverian Majesty designs to visit his British dominions for three months in the Spring."

However, on this occasion at least, it was not solely the pleasures of the Hanoverian Court and his Hanoverian mistress that kept the king away so long. He had other business on hand as well, involving an inspection of the Princess Augusta of Saxe-Gotha, then on a visit to Herrenhausen, as a possible candidate-bride for his detested son. Once having satisfied himself about Augusta, he sent off one of his long, affectionate, and detailed letters—detailed particularly in regard to his amatory dealings with Madame de Walmoden—to Queen Caroline, in which he requested her to inform the Prince of Wales that he must "take leave of a mistress whom he kept in so open a manner as he did Miss Vane." The queen immediately had the necessary talk, and the prince listened to her "with more willingness than compliance with her counsel" since he had already made up his mind to rid himself of Miss Vane, for a very good reason. He had recently developed a new passion—one obvious to everyone since "his nose and her ear were inseparable"—for Lady Archibald Hamilton, married, plain, and the mother of ten children. So the prince informed Miss Vane that it was desirable that she should take up residence in France or Holland for a matter of two or three years, adding, as a *coup de grâce*, that, if she obeyed, her annual income of £1,600 was assured, but if she refused not a penny would come her way. The matter was irrevocably settled by death which claimed Miss Vane and her child within a few months. Frederick, it is said, grieved deeply for his son; but not at all for Miss Vane who, at one time, had divided her favors between the prince and Lord Hervey, his mother's best friend.

In April, 1736, the king returned to England bringing the Princess Augusta of Saxe-Gotha with him. Three days later, at an evening ceremony, this very tall, gauche, and docile girl, who knew not a single word of English, was married to the Prince of Wales. He was twenty-nine, she seventeen. Feuds and squabbles respectably set aside for the time being, the entire royal family attended both the marriage service at St. James's Palace and the splendid banquet that followed, at which "nothing remarkable happened but the Prince's eating several glasses of jelly, and every time he took one turning about, laughing, and winking on some of his servants." After the dinner came the customary undressing and bedding ceremonies. Having temporarily reservoired his gall, the king did Frederick "the honor to put on his nightshift." At the same time the queen and her daughters were helping good-natured Princess Augusta to bed. Presently the king and the bridegroom joined them, and when the newly wedded couple were both in bed "everybody passed through the bedchamber to see them, where there was nothing remarkable but the Prince's nightcap, which was some inches higher than any grenadier's cap in the whole army."

Now that Frederick was suitably married, he was given a wing of St. James's Palace as a town residence, as well as a country house at Kew. For his wife's comptroller he chose Lord Bute, one of his closest friends, and as her Lady of the Robes he appointed his mistress, Lady Archibald Hamilton. To the latter appointment the queen refused to agree, but Frederick having soon enough realized that the young girl he had married, though much bigger and taller than he, was a good-natured, persuadable creature, easily enough talked her into saying that she herself desired to have Lady Archibald Hamilton about her. This affair proved strong meat for the family feud and increased the queen's growing animosity towards her son, for she had made up her mind that her daughter-in-law was nothing but an inoffensive and stupid young girl.

Augusta was not quite as stupid as the clever queen believed, and her conversation, so said Sarah, the aged Duchess of Marlborough, was certainly "much more proper and decent for a drawingroom" than the queen's. The marriage, despite Frederick's many amours, was a happy one. The prince always stoutly asserted that "the Princess was the best and most agreeable woman in the world." She bore him nine children, the last a posthumous daughter; the second, her eldest son, became George III.

Not long after the marriage of the prince and Augusta, George II again departed for Hanover, an absence which gave Frederick, aided and abetted by the Opposition, the opportunity to put up a fight for raising his allowance to £100,000. The motion for the increase was defeated in Parliament. But the prince, losing on this, made up for it on the anger that swept the country when the king continued to remain in Hanover without, apparently, any thought of returning to England. Everywhere in London derisive notices appeared advertising for the "lost or stolen King," and Frederick's stock kept creeping steadily higher.

The ever-growing popularity of the prince at last made the king pack his bags and head for England. His progress was delayed by the most frightful storms and at one time it was believed that the seas had engulfed him. Though the rumor that he had been drowned did not perturb the nation, it greatly agitated the king's daughters. They decided then and there to leave the palace "at grand gallop" if that "nauseous beast" (Frederick) succeeded. Their fears were set at rest when news came that the king was safe after all. While the sisters breathed sighs of relief, the latest scurrilous pamphlet entitled "The Lost Mutton Found: or the Royal Fly-by-Night," set the nation chuckling gleefully.

Still, even with the king back, enthusiasm for the prince continued to grow. It was further enhanced when, a fire having broken out in the Temple, he rushed off to the scene at nine o'clock at night and remained there for five hours, advising, exhorting, even helping the firemen to carry water to quench the flames. The Temple was saved and the delighted crowd that had watched the prince while he "exerted himself so much there" cried out excitedly, "Crown him! Crown him!"—a commendation that had also boomed in a theatre not many nights before.

If what the prince had done was infinitely pleasing to the people, it only added wormwood to the royal family's gall. Though there was not, as yet, an open breach between him and his parents, aversion on both sides was mounting towards a final break. It came as the result of Frederick never discussing his domestic life with his family and, therefore, until a month before the event, not telling them that the Princess of Wales was awaiting the birth of a child. The prince eventually broke the news at Hampton Court, where he and his wife were staying with his parents at the time. Their Majesties, insisting that they must be present at the birth, decreed that the baby should be born at Hampton Court. This was enough to make Frederick instantly determine that the child would be ushered into the world at St. James's Palace.

One July night during the visit, when everyone had gone to bed after an evening at cards, the Princess of Wales suddenly began to feel unwell. Frederick, realizing that the birth of her baby was imminent, hustled her into a coach and, accompanied only by Lady Archibald Hamilton and a few attendants, galloped her off towards London and St. James's Palace, crying "Courage! Courage!" as the poor girl wept and moaned in pain.

Learning of the flight a woman of the Bedchamber went to waken the queen to inform her that the Princess of Wales was in labor. "My God, my nightgown. I'll go to her this moment," cried the queen. "Your nightgown, Madam, and your coaches too: the Princess is at St. James's," her lady attendant replied. The king, conforming to the usual pattern of his behavior, flew into a passion; the queen, also as usual, said little but ordered her coaches, dressed, and in no time was ready to set off toward London in an effort to insure that no "false child" would be fobbed off on her. By the time she reached St. James's the baby, "about the bigness of a good large toothpickcase," had been brought into the world with the help of the prince and his mistress, Lady Archibald Hamilton. Eventually called Augusta, this child was destined to become the mother of Caroline of Brunswick, the unstable and impossible wife of George IV.

Frederick met the queen "in his nightgown and nightcap" in the princess's anteroom and, after dutifully kissing her hand and her cheek, described in great detail the labor and the delivery that had preceded his baby daughter's arrival. Even the strong-stomached queen could not savor this conversation and soon took her departure. Her son accompanied her downstairs, telling her that he hoped the king would honor him at the child's christening and that he would call later in the day to make his request formally and in person.

The queen then asked him to refrain from doing this as "the King was not well pleased with all this bustle you have made," a remark that was to prove the most glaring understatement of the day. Not only would the king not see Frederick but, as soon as it was possible, he had the Prince and Princess of Wales flung out of St. James's Palace in disgrace. The eviction was preluded by a letter in which he decried "the most insolent and premeditated indignities offered to me and the Queen, your mother." The prince had never, the king declared, given "the least notice to me or the Queen of the Princess's being breeding or with child till about three weeks before the time of her being brought to bed." His son's "behavior for so long has been void of duty and regard to me" that, the king wrote, he would not "suffer any part of any of my palaces to be longer the resort and refuge" of Frederick and his wife. "To this I will receive no reply," His Majesty concluded. "When you shall by consistency in your own words and actions, show you repent of your past conduct and are resolved to return to your duty, paternal affection may then, and not till then, induce me to forgive what paternal justice now obliges me to resent."

Once this letter was on its way to St. James's, the queen exclaimed with relief: "I hope in God I shall never see the monster's face again"; to which the king added, "Thank God that tomorrow the puppy will be out of my house." George II got his wish on the morrow: the queen got hers by eventually dying without ever setting eyes on her son again.

Flung out of St. James's Palace, the Prince and Princess of Wales went "into lodgings" in Albemarle Street, off Piccadilly. From there they moved to Norfolk House, lent to them by the Duke of Norfork, where their first son, George (afterwards George III), was born in June, 1738. From Norfolk House they moved to Leicester House which, as in the days when George II was Prince of Wales, once again became the headquarters of the Parliamentary Opposition. There, it is said, "between amours," Frederick used to spend hours drawing up lists of the Cabinet he would appoint when once he became king.

The king and the Prince of Wales remained for ever at daggers drawn. Each had his own Court and whoever went to Leicester House was automatically forbidden to set foot at St. James's Palace. Often the king asked the queen if Frederick could indeed be his son. Was he perchance "what in German we call a Wechselbalg (changeling)?" Regretfully she assured him that the prince was not only his son but, alas, hers too. On one occasion, the king imagining that his consort was trying to minimize their son's discourtesies, she cried out, "My dear Lord, I will give it under my hand, if you are in any fear of my relapsing, that my dear first-born is the greatest ass, the greatest liar, and the greatest *canaille*, and the greatest beast, in the whole world, and that I most heartily wish him out of it."

Frederick's sisters and brother sang the chorus in this hymn of hate. His sister Caroline not only prayed he would drop dead but declared that she grudged him every hour he lived. Frederick, on his side, did not remain silent. He did, however, come up to London from the country, when the queen was dying, saying that he wished to be near her, wished to see her. She refused. Though she spoke of him often it was "always with detestation." Forbidden to call in person, he sent members of his household to make inquiries and speak for him. But all this was no more than a token display of filial interest. When the queen was nearing her end he was heard to remark, "Well, we must have some good news soon. 'Tis impossible she can hold out long. I think I am a very good son, I wish her out of pain."

The queen's death was followed within a few years by the fall of the Walpole government. With a new government in power the king and the Prince of Wales were, allegedly, reconciled. In fact they never spoke to each other for the rest of their lives. During the next nine years the prince lived a double life, that of a country gentleman when resident out of London, and one of political intrigue at Leicester House where Bolingbroke, Pulteney, Townshend, Pitt, North, the Granvilles, the Earl of Chesterfield, the Earl of Bute, and Bubb Dodington could always be found.

In 1743, when England joined the European hostilities and George II went to lead his grenadiers to help "make kings and emperors" during the War of the Austrian Succession, and again, in 1745, when the Young Pretender, "Bonny Prince Charlie," son of James Francis Edward, landed in Scotland and swept down into England with his Jacobite force, Frederick asked to be allowed to serve in the army. The king refused his permission. He himself had a yacht stacked with English loot, all ready and set to sail to take him to Hanover if the Jacobites were successful. The anti-Prince of Wales faction declared that the king's refusal came as a relief to Frederick, that his volunteering for active service was no more than a half-hearted gesture bred not out of valor but jealousy—jealousy of his father's glory at Dettingen and later of his brother William, Duke of Cumberland, during this campaign against the Young Pretender, in which, after Culloden, William earned the title of "Billy the Butcher."

If outside his own immediate family circle Frederick's life was lived very much on a seesaw, within its limits he was extremely happy. A better-natured man and a much better father than George II, he was also, despite a collection of feminine favorites, a good husband and fond of his wife. To her, as well as to his mistresses, he wrote tributes of his affection in verse. Unlike his grandfather, George I, and his father, George II, he did not "visit the curse of hatred" on his eldest son, loved all his children and "a large and contented family grew up around him." He enjoyed his children, shared their pleasures, played rounders, push-pin and cricket on the lawn with his young sons and delighted in musical concerts at which all the older boys and girls performed.

Though often insincere, Frederick was always generous. He had many friends who, even when he borrowed money from them which he never had any intention of repaying, stuck by him. Debts he regarded as jokes. Often he boasted of how he had "nicked" Bubb Dodington, one of his oldest and closest cronies, for £6,000 in order to buy Carlton House, Pall Mall. "With all his parts," Frederick chortled with delight, "I have wheedled him out of a sum of money for the payment of which he has no security if I die, and which, God knows, he may wait long enough for if I live." An inveterate gambler, he was not always in luck either at cards or dice or betting on horses. It was he, however, who re-established the royal patronage of horseracing which had lapsed since the death of Queen Anne who, strangely, kept a stud of race horses, admittedly only "from a desire to keep alive a tradition of the Stuarts"!

Early in March, 1751, the king was ill, some thought seriously so. The Prince of Wales began to make plans about what he would do now that, it seemed likely, he was very soon to be king. But George II recovered, while Frederick, neglecting a chill, developed pleurisy. On the night of March 20 the Princess of Wales heard him call out "Je sens la mort," rushed to his bedside and found him dead.

The king, that night, was playing cards at St. James's Palace when the news of his son's death at Leicester House was brought to him. He rose from his card table, crossed the room and, leaning over Lady Yarmouth's chair, said simply, "Fritz ist tod." He spoke to Lady Yarmouth—who in the queen's lifetime, had been Madame von Walmoden, his favorite mistress in Hanover—not softly out of grief; only from relief. A thorn had been removed from his side.

Sorrow reigned at Leicester House. Augusta and her children wept; Frederick's friends mourned; his servants wore long faces in grief for the many expectancies that lay dead with their master. The next day and the next, a few solemn public voices were raised in solemn public platitudes. What, in general, the nation felt, was honestly expressed only in epigrams and satires. The most popular lampoon, while showing something in the nature of affectionate contempt for the dead prince, bespattered the rest of the royal family with vitriolic hatred. Everyone gabbled off by heart:

Here lies poor Fred, who was alive and is dead.
Had it been his father, I had much rather;
Had it been his brother, still better than another;
Had it been his sister, nobody would have missed her;
Had it been the whole generation, so much better for
the nation.
But since it is poor Fred, who was alive and is dead,
There is no more to be said.

III

George II, in spite of his dislike for his eldest son who, says Horace Walpole vindictively, resembled "the Black Prince in nothing but dying before his father," sent a kind message to the widowed, pregnant Princess Augusta. Some ten days later he called on her at Leicester House, "sat by her on a couch, embraced and wept with her." The old king suddenly fancied himself (said Horace Walpole again) in the part of "tender grandfather," and "grew so pleased with representing" himself in this role that he "soon became it in earnest."

The widowed princess was both narrow-minded and domineering. She was also shrewd. Shrewdly she took advantage of the situation. Since Frederick was dead, there was no longer any point, she decided, in carrying on the feud with her old, sick, choleric father-in-law. So, while willingly taking up the mantle that had rested on her husband's shoulders, she, at the same time, prudently reconciled herself with the king. After all, he could do a great deal for her large brood of children who were her main concern. For their sake she resolved to be pleasant to him. Secretly, she held on to certain uncompromising and inflexible reservations. One of these was a determination to bring up her son George, the new heir-apparent, in the "wholesome atmosphere" of Leicester House, and never to allow him to become contaminated by the bad influences of his grandfather's profligate Court.

George, whose full name was George William Frederick, was born on June 4, 1738, at Norfolk House, where the prince and princess took up temporary residence following their eviction from St. James's Palace. A feeble, seven-month baby, it seemed at first unlikely that he would survive. He not only survived, but soon grew strong, thanks to nourishment provided by a large, healthy wet nurse. From this time onward, through babyhood, he thrived in well-being and lived happily in the companionship of brothers and sisters whose number increased annually.

The Wales children were a harmonious family. They played cheerfully together when they were small and, growing older, learned to recite, perform on musical instruments, and act little pieces for the enjoyment of their parents and their parents' friends. At the age of seven, George, fair and pink-cheeked, together with his six-year-old brother, Edward Augustus, "passed into the hands of tutors." They were taught Latin, music, mathematics, fencing, elocution, drawing and watercolor painting; but apparently not quill-driving. Four years later George was still writing appalling English in a bad hand. The celebrated actor, James Quin, had, however, taught him to speak beautifully. In his eleventh year his grandfather, the king, presented him with the Order of the Garter. On this memorable occasion he was taken to St. James's Palace by his father. Frederick, nolens volens, "lurked behind the door" during the presentation, for the simple reason that, ostensibly reconciled to the king, His Majesty could neither bear the sight of, nor would he speak to his hated son.

When Frederick died in March, 1751, young George was not quite thirteen. A month later, his grandfather, having created him Prince of Wales, summoned him to Hampton Court for a visit. George's stay was short and unsuccessful. The king was not impressed with his grandson's "endowments," and the boy, childish for his age, was miserable away from his mother. The only person to get any pleasure from the visit was the Dowager Princess of Wales, Augusta, for she had, in any case, determined to get her son back to Leicester House as quickly as possible and, she prayed, "unspotted" by contamination with the immorality of the old king's Court.

Princess Augusta lived in a perpetual state of flutter about her eldest son, the young Prince of Wales. She was in despair because he seemed to her jejune, childish, dull, indolent, and not the least bit interested in learning. "His education has given her much pain; his book-learning she was no judge of, though she supposed it small and useless." The boy was wishy-washy. He never even flew into a temper—so unlike his grandfather who kicked his hat and wig around the room when in a rage—but only became moody and obstinate. Constantly and persistently she kept urging the reserved, rather timid boy to "be a man, George," yet at the same time, held him enclosed in the circle of her own family, firmly tied to her apron strings. She filled his mind with her narrow-minded prejudices, innate fears, and suspicions of new ideas and new ways of thought. Though critical of her son she admitted that George, often silent and morose, was "a very honest boy," good-natured and pious.

That the young prince was honest and good-natured is unquestionable; that he was sometimes silent and morose is not surprising. Princess Augusta's domineering petticoat government must have contributed in no small measure towards fertilizing the seed of neurosis that lay dormant in his character. By nature George was affectionate and amiable, a pleasant boy of simple tastes. Not intellectual, he was none the less intelligent. Inclined to be serious-minded, he was not lacking in high spirits and gaiety, but his cheerfulness was at times "tinged with gravity." Segregated from the "viciousness of young people of the times" and, as much as possible, from his grandfather's Court, he was what his mother wished him to be—"unspotted." He was also naturally and sincerely, religious. In short, he was "good" George, a reality that often annoyed the old king when the young Prince of Wales, on rare occasions, left his mother's side to reside for the briefest of intervals at Court. "George," the King grumbled angrily, "George is good for nothing except to read the Bible to his mother." George, on the other hand, was one day to say to the Earl of Bute: "The conduct of this old King, makes me ashamed of being his grandson."

After her husband's death, the Princess Augusta frequently discussed her eldest son's shortcomings with the Earl of Bute and Bubb Dodington, two old friends. Bute, in fact, was soon to gain a tremendous influence over the boy, an influence that lasted for twenty years. The prince came to hero-worship this handsome, elegant, sophisticated man, to rely on him even more than on his mother, and to regard him as his best and "dearest friend."

Whether John Stuart, third Earl of Bute, was, as generally believed at the time, the lover of tall, good-looking, and strait-laced Princess Augusta, has never been established. Appointed Groom of the Stole to the Prince of Wales, which necessitated his constant attendance at Leicester House, his association with the family was certainly very close. She considered his strong influence on her son highly beneficial and the best thing in the world for George. In her solicitude for, and care of the young prince, she found the earl a staunch ally. Their united efforts to insure that George would "be a man," satirists trenchantly labeled the reign of "the Boot and the Petticoat." The prince remained always deeply devoted to his mother, but in time Bute's influence over this emotionally unstable and mentally uncertain boy grew far stronger than hers.

In 1755, when the Prince of Wales was seventeen, the old king tried to arrange a marriage for him with a princess of Brunswick. Princess Augusta strongly objected, and won the day. George, she insisted, was far too young and much too immature for such a step. Yet there is an old story, now entirely discredited by modern scholars, which implied that the princess did not, after all, hold her son's life cupped in her hands. According to this tale, the prince had already been in love with a young Quaker girl for two years and that he had first seen pretty, brunette, demure Hannah Lightfoot (who lived with her uncle, Henry Wheeler, a linen-draper) in 1753, "on walks abroad from Leicester House."

Much attracted by her appearance, he became acquainted with her. At this point, legend relates, one of his mother's ladies-in-waiting, Elizabeth Chudleigh—who later became the notorious Duchess of Kingston—stepped in to become the mediator in arranging a curious marriage between Hannah and a young shop-assistant named Isaac Axford. Axford, so the story goes, was paid to marry Hannah at Keith's Chapel, Mayfair, on December 11, 1753, to what purpose it is difficult to understand, for when the bridal couple left the chapel several men abducted the bride in a coach and four. Hannah then disappeared. Axford never saw her again, though, it is said, she went to live at Hackney, in a house with a large garden surrounded by a very high wall. In 1759, six years later, the Prince of Wales allegedly married Hannah Lightfoot —either at Kew Church or a church in Curzon Street, or perhaps in Peckham!—and by her had three children, two boys and a girl. The eldest son went to the Cape of Good Hope in 1796 and, known as George Rex, founded the town of Knysna. George Rex, so the South African legend asserts, bore a strong resemblance to England's king, George III. He also possessed jewelry, pictures, and furniture that suggested a "strong connection with the Royal House." Descendants of George Rex still live in South Africa where, to this day, it is generally believed that he was the natural son of George, the Prince of Wales. No doubt he was George's natural son, but not by Hannah Lightfoot. Still the romantic old story lives on.

Soon after the king's abortive attempt to marry the prince to a Brunswick princess, he once again tried to rescue his grandson from the clutches of the Dowager Princess of

Wales and the Earl of Bute. This time the bait was £40,000 a year and an establishment of his own. The prince accepted the annuity but declined the residence, "on account of the mortification it would be to his mother," said Bubb Dodington, "though," he continued, "it is well known that he does not live with her either in town or country." Can this statement possibly concern the affaire Hannah Lightfoot, pretty Hannah who, as "Mrs. Axford, the Fair Quakeress," was painted by Sir Joshua Reynolds in a white satin gown? And how did Sir Joshua come to paint the runaway wife of an obscure shop-assistant? Was it to temper George's "melancholy sense of sin"—for undoubtedly the prince was pure at heart for all his "youthful longings"—that in this same year the Earl of Bute took him, incognito, to see the world, though that happened to be only Edinburgh and the Isle of Bute? This was the only time in all his long life that George was ever out of England.

Bute was not only the prince's "dearest friend," the model on whom he longed to shape his life, but his anchor, the one person in the whole world to whom he could express his deepest thoughts, his anxieties, and the inner mistrust which so often already loaded him with melancholy. At the age of twenty (1758), he wrote to the earl: "I now see plainly that I have been my greatest enemy, for had I always acted on your advice, I should now have been the direct opposite from what I am; nothing but the true love you bear me, could have led you to remain with me so long. . . . If you should now resolve to set me adrift, I could not upbraid you, but on the contrary look on it as the natural consequences of my faults. . . . If you should ever think fit to take this step, my line of action is plain; for though I act wrong perhaps in most things, yet I have too much spirit to accept the Crown and be a cypher." Though at this time two years still lay ahead before he ascended the throne, he went on to dream of abdication and retirement "to some distant region . . . there to think of the various faults I have committed that I might repent them."

The legend of Hannah Lightfoot maintains that the Prince of Wales married the little Quakeress in 1759, when he was twenty-one. But in this very year, in fact, he was deeply in love with the beautiful, fifteen-year-old Lady Sarah Lennox. "I have never had any improper thought with regard to her," he wrote to the Earl of Bute, telling him that he wanted to marry Sarah and begging for his advice. "I surrender my future into your hands," he added, "and will keep my thoughts even from the dear object of my love, grieve in silence, and never trouble you more with this unhappy tale; if I must lose my friend or my love, I will give up the latter, for I esteem your friendship above every earthly joy . . . tho' my heart should break, I shall have the happy reflexion in dying, that I have not been altogether unworthy of the best of friends, tho' unfortunate in other things." Bute's decision went against Lady Sarah Lennox and the prince dutifully submitted to the verdict. The Princess Augusta and the earl had other marriage plans for him.

On October 22, 1760, George II, "the comedian," died suddenly, like his father before him. His *valet de chambre*, bringing the old king his morning chocolate, found him lying on the floor midway between his closet and his bed. So George, Prince of Wales, aged twenty-two, a tall though not good-looking young man with protruding eyes and rather thick Hanoverian lips, but good, kind, amiable, serious-minded, honest, religious, and passionately patriotic, became King George III. "Born and educated in this country, I glory in the name of Briton," he proudly declared in his first speech to his ministers. The first *English-born* king of the House of Hanover, he was also the first never to set foot in Hanover throughout his long reign of sixty years.

England was delighted with the new sovereign. "Everyone, I think," wrote Lady Hervey, "seems to be pleased with the whole behavior of our young King, and indeed so much unaffected good nature and piety appears in all he does and says, that it cannot but endear him to all."

IV

Almost as soon as George III came to the throne he determined to get married, for marriage he considered a very "uplifting" institution. His mother and the Earl of Bute selected Charlotte Sophia, second daughter of the Duke of Mecklenburg-Strelitz, as the most suitable match for him.

Horace Walpole, who saw this princess when she arrived in England, described her as "not tall, nor a beauty, pale and thin, but looks sensible and genteel." All this she indeed was, and also infinitely sedate and respectable. But the young king, still under the spell of Lady Sarah Lennox's loveliness, "winced," it is said, when he first set eyes on his plain bride.

After a stormy passage, that had, fortunately, not discomforted her, Princess Charlotte arrived in London on September 7, 1761. The same evening she was married to the young king at St. James's Palace. George's asthmatical uncle, the Duke of Cumberland (of whom he had been mortally afraid as a child)—old "Billy the Butcher," victor of Culloden, an enormous mountain of a man with one blind eye and a limp caused by an ever-suppurating wound—gave the bride away. Beautiful black-haired Sarah Lennox was a bridesmaid. Two weeks after the marriage, the joint coronation of the king and his consort took place in "a muddle of splendour." Neither enjoyed this great and solemn occasion. The king, because of the "muddle," was in one of his melancholy moods, and the queen had a toothache.

The marriage of George III and Charlotte of Mecklenburg-Strelitz turned out extraordinarily well. They were happy together, and in living a simple, quiet life of great respectability, their many virtues made them dear to, and admired by, the ordinary people of England. The king was ever a true and faithful husband and the queen, with a deep interest in home-life and domestic matters, and none at all in politics, remained a loving wife throughout his long life, supporting him with affection and concern through many sorrows, illnesses, and, finally, madness.

This unimpeachably respectable and physically unprepossessing couple were blessed with a family of fifteen beautiful children. Their first child, christened George Augustus Frederick, was born at St. James's Palace on August 12, 1762. He was seven days old when his delighted young father created him Prince of Wales. Among the lesser gifts received by the royal infant, was "a curious Indian bow and arrows" sent by "his father's faithful subjects in New York." So lovely was this baby that crowds gathered whenever he was taken for an airing. "God bless him," voices cried, "he is a lusty, jolly young dog truly." Lusty, jolly, and beautiful, he was, within a few years, to show that he was also a small boy of singularly distinctive personality. Inoculated at four against smallpox and kept in bed, he was asked if he felt bored lying there. "Not at all," he declared. "I lie and make reflections."

Soon after his marriage, the king, deciding that palaces were not proper places in which to lead a simple domestic life and rear a family, bought a smallish, brick house standing in large grounds facing St. James's Park for £21,000 and presented it to the queen. It was called Buckingham House but everyone called it the Queen's House. Years later it became Buckingham Palace. In the Queen's House, the Prince of Wales at the age of ten, and his brother Frederick, a year younger, were given apartments of their own; there they were set to study with a board of instructors. One of these was a

Dr. Dodd, a writing-master and obviously an expert at his job, for he was later hanged for forgery.

The boys, strictly disciplined, worked at their lessons from seven in the morning till three in the afternoon, at which time they dined. Every day, and in every kind of weather, they were taken for brisk walks in the grounds. Additional exercise was provided by lessons in fencing and riding. Bright and intelligent Prince George learned Greek, Latin, and several modern languages with effortless ease. He was, too, soon riding beautifully, singing charmingly, and playing the violoncello. All this, however, was not enough to please his exacting father who, a good, kind bourgeois gentleman, had little understanding of a young boy of marked individuality and complex character. To Lord Holdernesse, the tutor the prince most adored, the king complained that his son, then aged twelve, was "evading application" and often, too, "evaded" telling the truth. For these and other misdemeanors, the boy was whipped, frequently with the king in attendance. But even before he was twelve, at the time when John Wilkes and the newspaper, the *North Briton,* were causing the king and his ministers a great deal of trouble, the little prince's high spirits proved a trial to his father. One day the king nearly exploded in a fit of apoplexy when, through the keyhole of his dressingroom, his small son, teasing because he knew it would annoy, shouted, "Wilkes and Liberty."

In the dull, staid atmosphere of his parents' homes, the prince, even in his early teens, shone like a star. Handsome, clever, radiating charm, he possessed a sparkling sense of humor, an equally sparkling facility for conversation, and a great talent for mimicry. His imitations of his old great-aunt Amelia—daughter of George II and friend of Horace Walpole —who spoke in a harsh, guttural accent, delighted and impressed all who heard him. The performance, needless to say, was never given in the presence of the king and queen. Everyone who knew the young prince was charmed by him—and spoiled him. Even dear, good Mrs. Delany, friend of the king and the queen (with whom she talked happily for hours about chenille work), found him beautiful and enchanting and lauded his agreeable manner and perfect manners, noticed by her when visiting the royal family at Windsor, or when in coaches, chaises, phaetons, and on horseback, they came en masse to breakfast with her and the Duchess of Portland at Bulstrode Park.

St. James's Palace was used by the royal family only for formal residence. *En famille,* they lived mostly either at Windsor or at Kew, where the boys, in groups according to their ages, stayed in houses on Kew Green. Each day they went to breakfast with their parents in the big house that was never big enough to accommodate the large and ever-increasing family. At Windsor, and especially at Kew, the simplest of lives was led. The king, careful and pennywise, saw to it that the strictest economy was observed—according to Horace Walpole, "the Queen's *friseur* waits on them at table" and "only four pounds of beef were allowed for their soup." Here there was neither gaiety nor *ton,* nor scandal of the kind made fashionable by society.

But there were often beatings in the king's presence when the boys misbehaved—one of them was even whipped for having an attack of asthma! In age groups, the young princes worked on their own model farms. Sometimes they played cricket together; often they danced with their sisters in the evenings; once a week, princes and princesses, in pairs, walked to Richmond with their father and mother. The royal family's way of life was a source of hilarious amusement to society; the middle classes admired its modesty and gentility, and adored them. The king's two eldest sons soon grew to hate every moment of this dull and respectable life, longed to escape from it and the whippings—and finally succeeded.

The love life of George, Prince of Wales, has been the subject of a great many books and almost as many plays. It began early and, since he had no one to fall in love with except ladies-in-waiting, that was exactly what he did. Not yet seventeen, he proposed marriage, honorably and with debonair grace, to Mary Hamilton, aged twenty-three, who attended his sisters. But by the summer of the next year he had to write and tell her that he had fallen madly in love with someone else, with Mary Robinson, the actress. "Adieu, Adieu, Adieu, TOUJOURS CHÉRE. Oh! Mrs. Robinson," he ended his letter.

The young prince first saw Mrs. Robinson in the role of Perdita in *The Winter's Tale*. Instantly enchanted, he wrote her passionate letters—again honorably offering marriage. Eventually he settled her, unwed, in an establishment in Berkeley Square. But young Florizel's ardor inevitably abated after a while and, to get him out of what his father called this "shameful scrape," the king was forced to pay £5,000 for those impassioned letters. Perdita had begun by asking a great deal more. Disappointed in the king, she never, however, forgot the prince as she knew him in those halcyon days. "The graces of his person," she wrote at the end of her short life, "the irresistible sweetness of his smile, the tenderness of his melodious and manly voice, will be remembered by me till every vision of this changing scene shall be forgotten."

The prince was in love with Perdita all through 1780, the year when, at eighteen, he made his first appearance in society, the most brilliant in England for more than a century. To the "handsomest prince in the world" this scintillating society immediately opened its arms wide. At the first grand ball of his début, "his coat was pink silk, with white cuffs, his waistcoat white silk, embroidered with various-coloured foil, and adorned with a profusion of French paste. And his hat was ornamented with two rows of steel beads, five thousand in number, with a button and a loop of the same material, and cocked in a new military style." The great hostesses of the day, the Duchess of Devonshire, Lady Melbourne, Lady Bessborough, Mrs. Crewe, vied with each other in entertaining this remarkable young prince who possessed a charm so extraordinary, so engaging, that it captivated men and women alike.

In this year of his coming-out, the question of his being given a separate establishment was raised. To such a step the king, deeply distressed by his son's extravagant way of life, refused to consent. Still allowing him only a small annuity, his father decreed that the young man must continue to live at Buckingham House—but he could, however, keep some horses of his own! Before Parliament came to the rescue and raised his allowance, the prince, in order to meet some of his debts, was forced to sell the famous stud that he built up.

For the next three years, the happiest, and certainly some of the giddiest and wildest, that this young man experienced, the Prince of Wales remained at Buckingham House. His love affairs, extravagances, and friendships—in particular his friendship with Charles James Fox and, therefore, with the Whigs—horrified the king. The intimacy with Fox was, the king held, the greatest disaster in his son's life, and he never forgave him for it. It was Fox, George III always maintained, who had led the prince astray. To this belief George Selwyn added a rider by saying that Fox had three main interests: gambling, women, and politics, in that order. The prince, he added, became Fox's close comrade in all three.

To the fact that both young men were a curious mixture of good and bad, Selwyn shut his eyes, as he did to Burke's summing up of the character of Fox, which could equally well be applied to the prince, for each, despite his faults and failings, was "a man made to be loved." In exuberance, relish for virile living, basking in the sun of a brilliant society that adored him as its leader, did the prince really behave so much worse than many of his contemporaries? But this life, and Fox's friendship, raised a barrier between him and his father that was to grow wider and higher year by year. The curse of

Hanoverian father-son animosity that had skipped George III in his relationship with his father (Frederick, Prince of Wales), now settled like a raven on the shoulders of George and his son.

On learning, in 1783, that the twenty-one-year-old Prince of Wales' debts to tradesmen alone amounted to £29,000, the king was heard to mutter miserably, "I wish I was 80 or 90 or dead." His misery was increased by the Duke of Portland's suggestion that not only should he pay the debts but grant his son an allowance of £100,000 a year. This heart-burning matter was finally settled by the prince's getting £62,000 annually, and Carlton House.

Since the death, in 1772, of the Princess Augusta, the king's mother, Carlton House had had no occupant. The prince showing little regard for the limits of his allowance, now spent lavishly on the reconstruction, decorations, furbishing, and furnishing of his first and very own establishment. "The saloon may be styled the chef d'oeuvre, and in every ornament discovers great invention," runs a description in the *European Magazine* of March, 1784. "It is hung with a figured lemon satin. . . . The range of apartments from the saloon to the ballroom, when the doors are open, formed one of the grandest spectacles that ever was beheld." The prince's taste was exquisite; to carry it into execution had cost an emperor's ransom.

With theatrical splendor and dramatic sumptuousness—and often with rowdy debauchery—he began to entertain at Carlton House. The most beautiful women, the greatest wits, and some of the most brilliant minds of the day, gathered about him. Soon Carlton House became what Leicester House had been in the reigns of George I and George II, the headquarters of those in opposition to the king and the king's government, of Fox and the Whigs. And when Fox carried his buff-and-blue colors to victory in the General Election of 1784, the prince in celebration held a spectacular fête in the garden of his home that began with breakfast and lasted till six o'clock in the evening.

The king was shocked, distressed, and angered by the behavior of his eldest son, and the Prince of Wales was left in no doubt about his father's feelings. Writing to his brother Frederick, Duke of York, in July, 1784, the prince complained bitterly about "ye very very unpleasant situation I am in at home." Apropos the king, he goes on to say: "Tho' I respect him and use him with all possible duty, deference and respect, I think his behavior is so excessively unkind yt there are moments when I can hardly ever put up with it. Sometimes not speaking to me when he sees me for three weeks together, and hardly ever at Court, speaking to people on each side of me & then missing me, and then if he does honour me with a word, 'tis either merely ' 'tis very hot or very cold' . . . with regard to the queen I cannot enough say what I feel for her, her goodness to me is such that I would bear anything to save her a moment's uneasiness. . . ." He and his brother William, Duke of Clarence, were, as William was to remind him in a letter in April, 1785, "our mother's favourites. . . ." To her he was always her "dearest son," "Mon très cher fils."

The year 1784 was to prove additionally memorable in the life of George, Prince of Wales, for two reasons: he met and fell in love with Mrs. Fitzherbert and, discovering the salubrity of Brighton, rented a house there for the summer. Because Catholic Mrs. Fitzherbert was not the kind of woman he could get on any other terms, he married her secretly a year later (December 15, 1785), a marriage that violated both the Royal Marriage Act, which stipulated that a marriage without the king's consent was illegal, and the Act of Settlement, by which marriage to a Catholic meant forfeiture of the succession to the throne.

Under the patronage of the prince and in the shadow of the oriental Pavilion that he built there for himself, Brighton which he had "invented," prospered and flourished. Paying for his secret marriage in lies, his own and those of his friends, Fox and Sheridan—knowingly or unknowingly uttered—he went on to enjoy nearly a decade of happiness with Mrs. Fitzherbert. Her influence over him was both estimable and beneficial, for she was a woman of character and intelligence.

The prince's peacock life at Brighton and Carlton House was suddenly interrupted in 1788 by the news that the king, in a "flurry of spirits," was acting strangely. Immediately the prince posted off to Windsor to be near his father. At dinner that night the poor, mentally sick king suddenly grasped his eldest son by the throat, raving wildly that George was his enemy but that his second son, the Duke of York, was his good friend. Though eventually soothed and calmed, the king's tragic "flurry of spirits" continued and it became likely that the prince would have to be made regent. This was a contingency not at all to the people's liking. The prince's vast debts and extravagances beyond the grasp of ordinary men's minds, were matters of public interest and reproach. His popularity with the masses stood at very low ebb. Happily, the king soon recovered, and the regency question could be shelved. But there could be no moratorium for the prince's debts.

Between the years 1784 and 1786 he had spent £369,977. His debts, a mere £160,000 in 1785, stood at £400,000 in 1792. Only one way out of the impasse lay open to him. If he married as the king wished, all his obligations would be settled in the bargain. But a year later he was still firmly assuring Lord Malmesbury that, "I never will marry! My resolution is taken on that subject." When another year had gone by he had, however, come to realize that a satisfactory marriage to an approved princess was the only thread that could lead him out of his financial maze. Though in June, 1794, he still addressed Mrs. Fitzherbert as "My dear love" when writing to her, and still signed himself "Ever Thine, G.P.," considerable strain had crept into their marital relationship.

Two months later he wrote and told his brother Frederick, Duke of York, of the "disagreements and misunderstandings" between him and Mrs. Fitzherbert. "In short," he continued, "we are *finally parted, but parted amicably,*" adding "*you* will not lay *the fault, whatever it may be* at my door." With almost an audible sigh of relief he went on to say, "However tout est fini entre nous, & I have obtain'd the King's consent to my marrying my own cousin Princess Caroline, the Duke of Brunswick's daughter. . . . The King told me I made him quite happy, that it was the only proper alliance, & indeed the one in all respects he should have wish'd for himself. . . . I do not say as much for the rest of the family, at least for one person" (the queen). Frederick replied that he was delighted that the prince had rid himself of Mrs. Fitzherbert's "shackles" and, he said, "As to the Princess, she is a very fine girl and in every respect in my opinion a very proper match for you." The king, during this same August, wrote to his prime minister, William Pitt, to give him the glad tidings that the Prince of Wales had severed all connection with Mrs. Fitzherbert (His Majesty knew nothing, of course, about the morganatic marriage), and said that his son was now anxious to enter "into a more creditable line of life by marriage," with the twenty-seven-year-old Princess Caroline of Brunswick.

Caroline, boosted as "a very fine girl" by the young Duke of York, had fair hair and was not bad looking. But she was, unfortunately, rather vulgar, coarse-mouthed, unbalanced, and not very clean. When she and the Prince of Wales met for the first time, one glance at her agitated his worse fears. "Harris, I am not well," he said to Lord Malmesbury, "pray get me a glass of brandy." Having gulped down his drink he hurried from the room to pour out his misery and disgust to the queen. Not long afterwards he jumped on a horse and galloped away to go "thundering past Mrs. Fitzherbert's house at Richmond."

Parliament had agreed to pay the Prince of Wales' debts, amounting to nearly three-quarters of a million pounds, when he married Caroline of Brunswick at the Chapel Royal on April 18, 1795. This stupendous fact did nothing to lift the bridegroom's awful despair at what had befallen him. He looked "like Death and full of confusion, as if he wished to hide himself from the looks of the whole world." The bride appeared "in the highest spirits . . . smiling and nodding to everyone." There is every reason to believe that, after the first night of their marriage, they never shared a bed. But exactly nine months after their wedding day a child was born to them. Christened Charlotte, she married clever, ambitious Leopold of Saxe-Coburg in 1816, died in childbirth the following year and left Prinney (the nickname invented by that extraordinary bestower of nicknames, Mr. Thomas Creevey) without a direct heir.

For a time after the baby's birth the Prince of Wales and his wife both lived at Carlton House. But they seldom met. "I would rather see toads and vipers crawling over my victuals than sit at the same table with her," he once said. At last, anxious to rid himself of his incubus, he tried to give her her marching orders by letter. "Our inclinations are not in our power, nor should either of us be held answerable to each other, because nature has not made us suitable to each other," he wrote to her, ending with the hope that they would live the rest of their lives apart, in tranquillity. The hope of tranquillity was never to be realized and for a while Caroline refused to budge from Carlton House. Eventually the queen and the prince's current mistress, Lady Jersey, made her situation so unbearable that she removed herself to a villa near Blackheath. Baby Charlotte remained in her father's keeping.

Moody, miserable, and unhappy, the prince longed to be again with his genteel Maria Fitzherbert who loved him and of whose comfort he was in sore need at this time. In spite of his treatment of her, in spite of his marriage to the Brunswick princess, and his association with Lady Jersey, Mrs. Fitzherbert's kind heart was touched by Prinney's plight. So off she wrote to her confessor in Rome to ask for guidance. Back came a reassuring answer. She was indeed the only wife of George, Prince of Wales, and he her true husband. Happily, then, Mrs. Fitzherbert was reunited with her prince. Caroline and Lady Jersey were both brushed off—as far as Caroline was concerned, only in a manner of speaking.

For the next nine years Maria shared the prince's life, much of which was spent at Brighton. There Mr. Creevey, in those days when he was still attached to Prinney, saw Mrs. Fitzherbert as "an extraordinary person, and most worthy to be beloved." But the idyll of the prince and Mrs. Fitzherbert began to fade again in 1806, when he not only fell in love with Lady Hertford but came under the Hertford Tory sway. Finding that her benign and excellent influence was steadily waning, and with her place in the prince's life sadly jeopardized, Mrs. Fitzherbert retired from the scene with dignity and grace.

War between England and France had gone on intermittently for years and reached its climacteric after the Peace of Amiens in 1802. Again and again the Prince of Wales, who had as much "bottom" (the eighteenth-century synonym for manliness, grit, and courage) as the next man, begged to be given a command. But the king refused each request. He also prevented his son from doing any useful work for the state. So Prinney was forced to drift through life. Indolence, voluptuousness, and extravagance gained on him as the years rolled by, years that brought a great deal of fun to leaven discontent, vexations, and griefs. Never-ending miseries occasioned by Caroline, the impossible royal wife whom he tried unsuccessfully to divorce, corroded his existence; jealousy of the popularity of his not easily managed, coltish daughter Charlotte, turned him into a disagreeable father. Though he gained many new favorites—chief of them, for a time, Beau Brummell, who shared his taste for exquisite snuffboxes and all the trappings of dandyism—death robbed him of old and cherished friends, among these the Duchess of Devonshire and Fox, whose funeral the king forbade him to attend.

By 1810, wit sparkling still, manners exquisite as ever, charm undiminished, the once handsomest prince in the world, two years short of his fiftieth birthday, was a fat, corpulent, middle-aged man. In the autumn of this year the death of his youngest sister, the Princess Amelia, the king's favorite child, plunged her father's tottering mind into the black abyss of insanity. Since the poor old king was hopelessly mad, Parliament passed the Regency Bill that transformed George, Prince of Wales, into the Prince Regent. His regency lasted till the death of his mad, blind, old father on January 29, 1820. Then Prinney became George IV.

For a great many decades it was the vogue to denigrate the eldest son of George III, Florizel-Prinney-Regent-King, all rolled into one. No lights nor shades were allowed to dispel the dark image. As far back as 1812, Leigh Hunt went to prison for describing the regent as a "violator of his word, a libertine . . . . a despiser of domestic ties, the companion of gamblers and demireps." Years later Thackeray took up his Victorian etching-needle and drew George IV, long since dead, as a "debauched, vulgar, profligate—a treacherous lover, perjured friend, heartless fop, soulless sot, the most Ungentlemanly First Gentleman of Europe."

Prinney was, admittedly, some of the things that were said and written about him: an unsatisfactory son, certainly; a crotchety and fickle father; and a bad husband—though no one could blame him when remembering Caroline of Brunswick. True, too, he was vain, wayward, a gambler, rake and spendthrift, lazy and unstable of character, selfish and self-centered to a degree. But there was another side to this man, "one of the cleverest and most accomplished men in Europe, full of benevolence," according to Sir William Knighton. He was, in fact, the most brilliant of all the Hanoverians. That he was lazy, cannot be denied; but he was, none the less, also able. He possessed many natural gifts and talents, loved music and literature, understood pictures and was a discerning and culti- vated art collector. True, he made and broke friendships; but he also made and kept many with men and women of genius. In a generation noted for famous talkers, he was a brilliant and witty conversationalist.

And he was kind, good-natured, and affectionate; kind- est, most loving and affectionate to his sisters in particular. They doted on him. As Prince of Wales he was always their "dearest G.P."; when he grew fat and flabby, he was still their idol, their Prince Charming (his charm fascinated great men and women throughout his life). Even when they were grieved by the sorrow he caused his father, his sisters held him dear. "Toujours présent, toujours cher, that's what you are to your poor Puss," Augusta wrote to him on his thirty- fifth birthday. Whenever the king actually said something pleasant about him, the "Sisterhood" was quick to inform him. "I pocketted for You!" was how one of them expressed her joy at hearing words of praise for him.

"If my poor prayers are granted you would never have a moment's uneasiness, and was it in my power my broad back should ease you of your affliction," Elizabeth wrote to him on a New Year's day. After his marriage with Caroline broke up, not only his brothers who, with one exception, always stood by him but, so Elizebeth wrote, the queen, too, "will do everything that lays in her power to serve you," meaning in his relationship with the king. Often, during the regency, the queen and the "Sisterhood" went to visit him at Carlton House, or stayed with him at the Pavilion in Brighton. At both places he made them happy and they enjoyed themselves because he made it his business to give them pleasure.

Edmund Burke described Prinney as "brilliant but superficial." The Duke of Wellington, seeing this remarkable man as a whole, summed him up as "the most extraordinary compound of talent, wit, buffoonery, obstinacy and good feeling —in short a medley of the most opposite qualities, with a great preponderance of good—that I ever saw in any character in my life."

Prinney, with all his faults, was a very remarkable man.

V

At three o'clock on the morning of June 26, 1830, George IV died. A miniature of Mrs. Fitzherbert, his true wife from whom he had long been parted, but the woman he had, after all, loved best, hung from a chain round his neck. Good, genteel Maria survived him by seven years. She died at Brighton in 1837.

England's new king was George IV's second brother, William, Duke of Clarence. He was sixty-five, a simple, blustering, retired old sailor living quietly at Bushey. There, at six o'clock that morning—but he was already pottering about his garden "in his old green coat and white beaver hat"—he heard the news of his accession.

Perhaps more loved than any of the Hanoverian kings, kind-hearted William IV reigned for seven years. After the death of Prinney's daughter, Charlotte, heiress to the throne of England, William, in the desperate hope of providing the nation with an heir, had married Princess Adelaide of Saxe-Meiningen. She, a most excellent wife, unfortunately "failed to provide her husband with living issue." Before his marriage, he, like most of his brothers, had had a mistress of long standing. His liaison with Dorothy Jordan, an actress had produced a great many children—politely known as the Fitz-Clarences, more often, sardonically, as "les Bâtards." None of these were in the line of succession. In 1837, on the eve of Waterloo day, he lay desperately sick and knew that he was dying. "See if you can tinker me up to last over it," the dear, simple old sailor-king said to his doctor. Whatever tinkering was done, did some good. He survived the day, but died before the next dawn at twelve minutes past two on the morning of June 20. The Archbishop of Canterbury and Lord Conyngham were at his bedside. When all was over, they immediately posted off to London, to Kensington Palace, arriving there at five o'clock. The porter, reluctant to wake the household at such an ungodly hour, kept them waiting interminably. At last they gained admittance and were shown into a room. Presently eighteen-year-old Princess Victoria of Kent appeared in the doorway in her dressing gown, a shawl thrown about her shoulders. For a moment she paused on the threshold. Lord Conyngham dropped on one knee. "Your Majesty," she heard him say. Graciously she held out her small, soft child's hand, and he kissed it.

The sixty-four-year-long reign of Queen Victoria had begun.

PART SIX: VICTORIA AND AFTER

PART SIX: VICTORIA AND AFTER

Queen Victoria, daughter of Edward, Duke of Kent, the fourth son of George III, ascended the throne as a member of the Hanoverian dynasty. Only on her marriage to Prince Albert in the Chapel Royal at St. James's Palace on February 10, 1840, did the English royal house change its name from Hanover to Saxe-Coburg-Gotha. Queen Victoria's uncles and aunts, the three sons and two daughters of George III who were still alive at this time, were the last survivors of the Hanoverian House. Deeply conscious and proud of this fact, they referred to themselves as "the old Royal Family."

The first son of the new dynasty, the House of Saxe-Coburg-Gotha, was born to the young queen and her consort on November 9, 1841. Christened Albert Edward (after his father and the queen's father, the late Duke of Kent) this son for most of his life was officially known by both these names.

His family called him Bertie. At the age of one month he was created Prince of Wales, a title he held for fifty-nine years and one month. It is, perhaps, because Albert Edward was Prince of Wales for nearly two generations in the life of man, that his image remains always that of a middle-aged, short, portly, bearded gentleman. To many people his memory recalls thoughts of their Victorian grandfathers, grandfathers who, while appearing dignified, were nevertheless *bon vivants* sporting the kind of hats made fashionable by the prince.

Yet this ancestor-evoking prince was once a baby: once he was a rather small, fair little boy, affectionate, lively, a great chatterbox bubbling over with questions, many of them awkward. In character quite unlike his handsome, reserved father, he resembled his shy mother only in having inherited her fresh and rather florid Hanoverian complexion. Anxious, indeed afraid, lest the engaging, friendly, and lovable little prince might be spoiled at Court, the Queen and Prince Albert (who, from the start, planned to channel Bertie's mind into that sea of serious thinking in which he himself was interested) were extremely strict with the boy. In every sense true Victorian parents, they were severely critical, never indulgent and always frugal in showing him affection. Though the prince consort, it is said, "loved, enjoyed and needed" his children, all of them, except his eldest daughter, were afraid of him.

The education of the small Prince of Wales began at the age of seven. The curriculum drawn up by his father, a plan whose "great object in view is to make him the most perfect man," was awe-inspiring in scope and of crushing rigor. Instead of making "a moral and intellectual paragon" of the boy, it placed so great a strain on him that he was often physically and mentally fatigued to the point of collapse. Not unnaturally this stress drove him into rages of frustration. However, at the end of the first seven of these awful years, a sparklingly stimulating event occurred. The fourteen-year-old Prince of Wales and his sister, the Princess Royal, accompanied their parents on a week's state visit to the Court of Napoleon III. Acclaimed rapturously in the French capital, the good-looking young prince enjoyed himself so much that he begged the Empress Eugénie to ask his mother for permission to remain in Paris a few days longer. Kindly the empress expressed the opinion that she was sure Queen Victoria and the Prince Consort could not do without their children in England. "Not do without us!" cried the boy prince. "Don't fancy that! They don't want us, and there are six more of us at home!"

But there was to be no reprieve. Back home he went at the end of the marvelous week, back to the dread classroom, the interminable lessons, the exhaustions of his father's plan to turn him into a model of perfection. Since it took no account of human foibles, frailties, and failings, the plan did not, indeed could not, work. In 1858 (the Prince of Wales was seventeen), his father, as much in sorrow as in anger, wrote to his recently married daughter, Victoria, the Princess Royal, in Berlin: Bertie "is indescribably lazy. I never in my life met such a thorough and cunning lazybones."

Bertie, "unlearned but unspoilt," escaped the torments of his schooldays in the following year. Now, at eighteen, he was sent up to Oxford. Though enclaved by equerries, those who got to know him then found the short, rather squat young prince with the warm and charming smile and beautiful speaking voice, delightful, naturally genial, cheerful, and good-natured. Already at this time, he was showing himself far more interested in people than in things. While still at Oxford he was sent, in 1860, on an important tour of Canada. From there, though not as Prince of Wales but as Baron Renfrew (one of his many titles) he visited the United States, charmed the president and all who met him, and planted a chestnut tree at Mount Vernon. The visit was a great success, marred only by one discordant note. Writing to the queen, a stuffy member of his entourage noted: "H.R.H. seems pleased with everything, himself included."

The trip to the New World over, the Prince of Wales returned to Oxford in an extremely happy frame of mind. Not long afterwards, however, perhaps so that it should not appear that any partiality had been shown, he passed on to Cambridge—not to live in college but some miles out of the town.

This move was to prelude a most unfortunate period in the young Prince's life, when, in the summer of this year, attached to the Grenadier Guards, he went to spend some weeks in Ireland, at the Curragh, a large military camp. For there, at the age of twenty, "he was introduced to dissipations which were new to him" (to quote his official biographer). In brief, he formed a liaison with an actress. At first the queen knew nothing of the affair. But his father did, and it filled him with a crushing distress and "terrible pain." In the end the prince consort forgave his son, but unfortunately, soon afterwards, took ill and died. By that time the queen had learned of the Curragh incident. In her overwhelming grief at her husband's death, she convinced herself that this fearful tragedy resulted directly from the anxiety and sorrow that the Prince of Wales had caused his father. The belief became an obsession that froze her feelings towards her eldest son. Nothing the kind and affectionate young man attempted to do to help her, had any effect on her. Indeed, she could now not bring herself to look at him "without a shudder," and told a member of her government: "It quite irritates me to see him in the room." And so she rid herself of his presence as soon as possible by sending him off on a trip to Palestine and the Far East.

The queen's prejudice was to continue until she was an old, old woman. The Prince of Wales, so rigorously trained for work, was never taken into her councils, never permitted an "outlet for his political interests" at home, and was never in her intimacy. She left him to make what he wished of his life, though not in silence. Yet strangely enough, his name, "Bertie," was the last word she uttered on her deathbed.

Fifteen months after his father's death the Prince of Wales married the beautiful, gay, adorable Princess Alexandra, daughter of the king of Denmark. She bore her husband six children, of whom one died in infancy. Marlborough House in London and Sandringham in Norfolk became their town and country homes. At the former, the famous Marlborough House set came into existence. The center of royal entertaining, it did not, however, become (as the residences of Princes of Wales in previous reigns) an opposition Court to that of the sovereign. This the Prince of Wales would never have allowed. His loyalty to the queen, his mother, remained unimpeachable at all times. At Marlborough House much gaiety—and horseplay—real friendliness, and kindness could be found, as well as decorum, dignity, and often good and serious conversation. Here the great Edwardian era was born.

Deprived by the queen of opportunities that would have given scope to his immense energy, the Prince of Wales devoted his zest for life to years of pleasure. He made, it is true, many mistakes; scandals, told and retold in countless books, touched his good name. Yet the "gay Guelpho," (Guelph was the name of the royal family of Hanover and Britain), was none the less a clever man of many serious interests. Wales, however, was not one of these. He had little liking for the Principality whose name he bore. A humanitarian, liberal in thought, he concerned himself with a variety of good works; with charities, for example, and the problems of housing the poor. And, not permitted to do useful work at home, traveling gained him a vast understanding of political problems abroad. By his personal contact with the rulers of the day, he may have made some contribution to the betterment of accord among nations.

From time to time his popularity in England waned; then it gained again. In the end, this Prince of Wales was both loved and admired by his mother's subjects. They grew to love him for his geniality, charm of manner, dignity, and liberality of thought and, perhaps, above all for being a patriot prince who believed in the destiny of the British people. After being England's eighteenth Prince of Wales for nearly sixty years, he ascended the throne as King Edward VII in the dawn of the twentieth century.

II

All the children of King Edward VII and Queen Alexandra were born during the years when they were Prince and Princess of Wales. Their eldest child, Albert Victor Christian Edward, known as Prince Eddie (afterwards Duke of Clarence) was born in 1864. A year later, at half-past one in the morning of June 3, 1865, a second son arrived at Marlborough House. When the Prince of Wales wrote and told his mother that he and the princess had decided on George Frederick as names for their second son, Queen Victoria replied by expressing her disapproval of George. "I cannot admire the names you propose to give the Baby," she wrote. "I had hoped for some fine old name. Frederick is, however, the best of the two, and I hope you will *call* him so. *George* only came in with the Hanoverian family. . . . Of course you will add *Albert* at the end, like your brothers, as you know we settled *long ago* that *all* dearest Papa's *male* descendants should bear *that* name, to mark *our line*, just as I wish all the girls to have Victoria after theirs." Five days later, back came a reply from the Prince of Wales to the queen. "We are sorry to hear that you don't like the names that we propose to give our little boy, but they are names we like and have decided on for some time."

The baby—"not very pretty" but "nice and plump" was Queen Victoria's verdict—was christened at St. George's Chapel, Windsor, on July 7, and given the names of George Frederick Ernest Albert. His family always called him Georgie.

Little Prince George and his brother and sisters—Victoria, Louise, and Maud—had the happiest of childhoods, spent for the most part at Sandringham, with only occasional visits to Marlborough House or Osborne in the Isle of Wight. For them life was far less formal than if their father had been king. They never had to suffer stiff court ceremony nor were they hedged around by courtiers. Not a drop of the old Hanoverian father-son animosity fell on this loving and devoted family. His enchanting, affectionate, and gay mother was the greatest influence in little Prince George's life. To him she was, and was always to remain, "darling Motherdear." At night, when they were all together *en famille*, she used to come and tuck him in bed, and in the mornings it was his greatest joy to sit and talk to her while her maid brushed her long hair. To be separated from her was an acute agony for him. For "darling Motherdear" he felt nothing but shining adoration; for his father affection tinged, however, by awe. In later years, when Prince George was grown, he and his father came to know and understand each other. Their relationship grew deep and close. "I have lost my best friend and the best of fathers," the son wrote in his diary on that day in May, 1910, when King Edward VII died.

There was love and understanding, too, between Prince Eddie and Prince George. Eddie was delicate and rather quiet; George, ever at the top of his form, brimmed over with laughter and high spirits and, like his father when a little boy, chattered and asked questions. Awed by his father, he was not at all intimidated by Queen Victoria, his grandmother. She was very fond of him and when he was eight sent him a watch, "hoping it will serve to remind you to be very punctual in everything and very exact in your duties." She was never to be disappointed in him. Twenty-one years later the very old queen still saw Georgie as "a dear boy, so anxious to do right and improve himself." He was then twenty-nine, an officer in the Royal Navy who had visited many lands in her far-flung Empire.

Prince Eddie and Prince George were seven and six, respectively, when their education began. Rising at seven each morning, they plunged into cold baths, followed these with a run round the grounds and hearty breakfasts, before settling down to lessons. With no desire to see their sons educated in aloof privacy, the Prince and Princess of Wales sent them, when they were thirteen and twelve, to *Britannia*, the training ship for naval officers at Dartmouth. There the young princes led exactly the same lives as all the other cadets. High-spirited George won great popularity. Because he was rather a small boy for his age, he was nicknamed "Sprat"; his older and taller brother was called "Herring." Both boys enormously enjoyed their two years at Dartmouth.

These were followed by three even more exciting years when, as midshipmen, they set off on a long voyage in *Bacchante*, a full-rigged sailing ship with auxiliary steam power, that took them to Australia, Japan, China, Ceylon, South Africa, South America, the West Indies, Palestine, and Egypt. Thereafter, except for short leaves ashore, Prince George was almost constantly at sea until 1892. Through the years he rose from sub-lieutenant to lieutenant, to commander and, finally, to captain. His promotion was entirely the reward merited by a first-class naval officer. In no measure was it due to his rank as the son of the Prince of Wales. "It never did me any good to be a Prince, I can tell you," he was to say, when recalling his sailor days many years later.

In 1891, during a visit by his ship to Dublin, Prince George was taken seriously ill with typhoid fever. For a while his life was in grave danger, but gradually he began to recover and, towards the year's end, was happily recuperating at Sandringham. There, on New Year's day, 1892, his brother Eddie's engagement to their cousin, Princess Mary of Teck, was announced; there, in this same January month, Prince Eddie was taken ill with influenza, developed pneumonia, and died within five days. It was a shattering blow to Prince George. He and Eddie had been close and devoted brothers.

The tragedy plunged the light-hearted, high-spirited young naval officer straight into the direct line of succession to the throne. In this sad year Queen Victoria created him Duke of York; in this same year of sorrow, sympathetic understanding drew him close to the girl, Princess Mary, who had for so brief a time been betrothed to his dead brother. Often he went to call on her at White Lodge, Richmond, and there, in the spring of 1893, he proposed to her. In giving her consent to their engagement, Queen Victoria wrote to her grandson: "Let me now say how thankful I am that this great and so long and ardently wished for event is settled." She was deeply happy for she had "so much wished for this engagement." In July, 1893, Prince George married Princess Mary who proved to be a wonderful wife and, in after years, gave him her immeasurable devotion and help in bearing the heavy burden of sovereignty.

Prince George, Duke of York, was thirty-six when Queen Victoria died in 1901 and his father became King Edward VII. This same year, after he and the Duchess of York returned from a visit to Australia, his father created him Prince of Wales. He was the first Prince of Wales to have married an English-born princess.

Prince of Wales for nearly nine years, he succeeded his father as George V, in May, 1910. The people of Britain and the British Empire did not really know much about their new king. They did, however, know that he was a man to be respected. During the twenty-six years of his reign—and some were tragic and difficult years—he not only retained the respect of all his subjects, but won their love and devotion.

It was in this reign, in the grim days of World War I, when British feelings towards Germany were at their bitterest, that King George V struck his colors in the high wind of enmity and changed the name of his royal house from Saxe-Coburg-Gotha to Windsor.

III

On a summer night in 1894, at White Lodge in Richmond Park, in the fifty-seventh year of Queen Victoria's reign, a son was born to the Duke and Duchess of York, the future King George V and Queen Mary. Seeking relief from his very natural anxiety, the young father, while waiting for the birth of his first child, sat in the library and tried to soothe his agitation by reading *Pilgrim's Progress*. Whether he was successful is open to doubt. But the tension ended at last with news that a strong, healthy baby had been born, and all was well.

That night the duke wrote in the diary which he kept for most of his life: "White Lodge, 23rd June—At 10:0 a sweet little boy was born and weighed 8 lbs. . . ." Not quite a month later the baby, baptized with water from the river Jordan, was given seven names, Edward Albert Christian George Andrew Patrick David. His great-grandmother,

Queen Victoria, presided at the ceremony and, of course, wrote about it. "The dear fine baby, wearing the Honiton lace robe (made for Vicky's christening, worn by all our children and my English grand-children) was brought in . . . . and handed to me. I then gave him to the Archbishop and received him back. . . . The child was very good. . . . When the service was over I went with Mary to the Long Gallery, where in '61 I used to sit with Dearest Albert and look through dear Mama's letters. Had tea with Mary, and afterwards we were photographed, I, holding the Baby on my lap, Bertie and Georgie standing behind me, thus making four generations." (Quoted by the Duke of Windsor in his Memoirs.)

The baby, christened with seven names, was officially known as Prince Edward. His family always called him by the last of his names, David. The first royal baby in direct succession to the throne to be born in England of English-born parents since Edward VI, son of Henry VIII and Jane Seymour, he was third in line of succession at his birth. When his father succeeded Edward VII as King George V, Prince Edward, having passed from the naval school at Osborne (where he was nicknamed "Sardine") and entered Dartmouth as a naval cadet, became heir-apparent. As the eldest son of the new sovereign he became Duke of Cornwall, a title first conferred on the Black Prince by Edward III, and on his sixteenth birthday, by Letters Patent, was created Prince of Wales by his father.

The coronation of King George V and Queen Mary took place in Westminster Abbey on June 22, 1911. Exactly three weeks later, on July 13, their eldest son, now seventeen—dressed, as he himself describes in his memoirs, in "a fantastic costume designed for the occasion, consisting of white satin breeches and a mantle and surcoat of purple velvet edged with ermine"—was invested with the title of Prince of Wales and presented to the people of Wales at Caernarvon Castle. Six hundred and twenty-seven years had passed since Plantagenet Edward I, according to legend, showed his baby son to the people of Wales at Caernarvon. No other Prince of Wales had since been so presented until George V invested his eldest son, Britain's twentieth Prince of Wales.

This prince recalls the dramatic occasion in his memoirs: "So on a sweltering day within the vast ruin of Caernarvon Castle, before some ten thousand people, with Winston Churchill, as Home Secretary, mellifluously proclaiming my titles (he told me afterwards that he rehearsed them on the golf course), my father invested me as Prince of Wales. Upon my head he put a coronet cap as token of principality, and into my hand the gold verge of government, and on my middle finger the gold ring of responsibility. Then, leading me by the hand through an archway to one of the towers of the battlements, he presented me to the people of Wales. Half fainting with heat and nervousness, I delivered the Welsh sentences that Mr. Lloyd George, standing close by in the ancient garb of Constable, had taught me."

The great and historic occasion over, the prince started his quarter of a century of immeasurable service to the nation. Journeying to every corner of the vast British Empire, and to realms beyond its borders, he became known to countless millions, who regarded him with the deepest affection. No Prince of Wales in all the long history of Great Britain had ever been so esteemed, so popular, and so loved.

On January 20, 1936, King George V died and, in his forty-second year, the Prince of Wales ascended the throne as Edward VIII. Within this same year his reign ended with his abdication. His brother Albert, Duke of York, succeeded him as George VI. At his first Accession Council the new king created his elder brother to whom he was deeply attached, H.R.H. the Duke of Windsor.

IV

A quiet, reserved, and brave man, King George VI courageously led his people through the terrible agonies of World War II. In the early years of peace, happiness came to him through the marriage of his eldest daughter and heir-presumptive, Princess Elizabeth, to Prince Philip of Greece, later created Duke of Edinburgh. He lived to share their joy in the birth of their first two children.

The eldest child of Princess Elizabeth and Prince Philip, a son, was born at Buckingham Palace on Sunday, November 14, 1948, in the twelfth year of his grandfather's reign. A month later the baby was christened by the Archbishop of Canterbuty in the music room of the palace—the bomb-damaged chapel of Buckingham Palace had then not yet been restored—and given the names of Charles Philip Arthur George. At his birth the little Prince became second in succession to the throne and bore the style of His Royal Highness. This honor does not normally belong to the children of the daughters of a sovereign, but five days before the baby was born, King George VI had proclaimed that the children of his daughter should all bear the style of Royal Highness at birth.

In the sixteenth year of his reign King George VI died peacefully in his sleep. His daughter, the Princess Elizabeth, on ascending the throne, was proclaimed Queen Elizabeth II. Her small son, Prince Charles, now became heir-apparent and, automatically—under Edward III's charter of 1337—Duke of Cornwall. He also, in the Scottish peerage, became Duke of Rothesay, Earl of Carrick, and Baron Renfrew, Lord of the

Isles, and Prince and Great Steward of Scotland. His creation as Prince of Wales was still an event of future years.

The queen and the Duke of Edinburgh determined, from the start, that all their children would be brought up as simply as possible and, as far as possible, lead normal lives, away from the limelight, without fuss or publicity. From the windows of Buckingham Palace that overlook the front courtyard and the Mall, the children, when small, were allowed to watch processions and ceremonies. Sometimes, on important occasions, they appeared on the famous palace balcony with their parents. But the greatest event in the life of little Prince Charles was the coronation of the queen. Sitting beside his grandmother, Queen Elizabeth, the queen mother, he attended the historic service in Westminster Abbey.

A governess, Miss Catherine Peebles, gave Prince Charles his first lessons. When he turned six, he began not only to visit places of interest, but to attend classes in gymnastics with other children. He had his first lessons outside the palace at a small London school in January, 1957, and in September of this year was sent as a boarder to Cheam, a preparatory school founded in 1646, that his father had attended as a boy. He remained at Cheam until 1962, and during his last year captained the Soccer XI and was a school monitor.

On July 26, 1958, when Prince Charles had been at Cheam for less than a year—and four months before his tenth birthday—his mother created him Prince of Wales. By the terms of the first creation of 1301, he at the same time assumed the title of Earl of Chester, and also became a Knight of the Garter, though his investment into this noble Order cannot take place until he is "of full years."

The announcement of the creation of Prince Charles as Prince of Wales was made at the closing ceremony of the Commonwealth and Empire Games, held in Cardiff, capital of Wales. Because of illness, the queen was unfortunately prevented from being present at the ceremony. His Royal Highness the Duke of Edinburgh introduced her recorded message, part of which ran: ". . . . I want to take this opportunity of speaking to all Welsh people, not only in this arena, but wherever they may be. The British Empire and Commonwealth Games in the Capital, together with all the activities of the Festival of Wales, have made this a memorable year for the Principality. I have therefore decided to mark it by an act which will, I hope, give as much pleasure to all Welshmen as it does to me. I intend to create my son, Charles, Prince of Wales, today. When he is grown up I will present him to you at Caernarvon. . . ."

So, as the queen promised, Britain's twenty-first Prince of Wales, like the twentieth (H.R.H. the Duke of Windsor), will one day be shown to the Welsh in his own principality. But when that presentation and the actual investiture will eventually take place, are matters which Queen Elizabeth will alone decide. It should be noted, however, that heirs-apparent are deemed of age at eighteen. Prince Charles will be eighteen on November 14, 1966.

After leaving Cheam, in the summer of 1962, when he was nearly fourteen, the Prince of Wales was sent to continue his education at Gordonstoun on the Moray Firth, where his father also had been a pupil. This famous school was originally founded at Salem, in Germany, by Dr. Kurt Hahn, but when the Nazis came into power, was transferred to Scotland. A progressive establishment, it lays emphasis not only on academic learning but on physical training and the development of initiative. On fishing, sailing, and climbing expeditions and on the cricket field, pupils meet and share adventures with the local boys. Prince Charles is treated exactly like all the other pupils, with the sole exception of his having a private detective to secure privacy from intruders. No Prince of Wales could wish for a wiser and more democratic training for his future position in life.

During school holidays the prince takes a lively interest in current affairs. He sometimes goes to the Houses of Parliament and with his sister, Princess Anne, learns something of the nation's industrial life through visits to various factories. But holidays bring much fun all round, for the prince, like all boys of his age, is fond of riding, polo, shooting, swimming, skiing, and sailing. As far back as 1954, he and his sister, during school holidays, made their first journey outside Britain. In the Royal Yacht *Britannia*, they sailed to Tobruk where they met their parents, who were on the way home from a Commonwealth tour. Since then, the prince has been abroad several times; on skiing trips with his father, on visits to relations, and, in 1964, to attend the marriage in Athens of King Constantine of Greece to Princess Anne-Marie of Denmark. On this occasion he played a part in the ceremony by helping to hold the marriage crowns over the heads of the bridal couple.

Like all notable people, Prince Charles has fan mail; his is enormous. He also receives gifts of all kinds from every corner of the Commonwealth. One from New Zealand, a small flint-lock pistol, was once given to Bonnie Prince Charlie (son of the Old Pretender and grandson of James II) by Flora Macdonald, the brave Scottish lass who helped him escape to the Isle of Skye. After Flora married, she lived for a time in North Carolina, but eventually returned to end her days in Scotland.

The young Prince of Wales is fairly tall, rather shy and, as all who know him say, extremely kind, considerate and charming. Some time in 1966 he will be ending his schooldays at Gordonstoun—where he takes a keen interest in the school's dramatic society and plays the trumpet in the school orchestra. But before that time comes he will have spent a term, as a pupil, at the Geelong Church of England Grammar School in Australia. The part of this school where the Prince began his term in February, 1966 is known as

Timbertop. Situated about one hundred miles from Melbourne, in the foothills of the Great Dividing Range, Timbertop, like Gordonstoun, places great emphasis on teaching boys self-reliance and initiative. During the week, in addition to attending formal classes, pupils also help in the school gardens and in looking after the cattle and sheep. On weekends they go into the mountains, live a tough and energetic life, explore the bush, fish, tramp for miles, and fend for themselves. Older boys at the school help the staff in the supervision of younger pupils, and Prince Charles, while continuing his own studies, will join this band of senior boys.

Prince Charles is the first member of the royal family ever to go to school in an overseas country of the Commonwealth. By making friends with young Australians at Timbertop, he will gain a knowledge of Australia that will undoubtedly prove of inestimable value to him in his future duties. He is to remain in Australia until mid-May, 1966 and then return to Gordonstoun where, soon afterwards, he will write the final examinations that will bring his schooldays to an end.

And then, on a day which Her Majesty the Queen thinks suitable, Charles, heir to the throne of the United Kingdom of Great Britain and Northern Ireland and to the leadership of the British Commonwealth of Nations, will travel to Caernarvon. There he will be invested with the coronet, the ring, and the gold rod, and presented to the people of his Principality as the twenty-first Prince of Wales.

BIBLIOGRAPHY

Akrigg, G. P. V.: Jacobean Pageant. London: Hamish
    Hamilton, 1962.
Annual Register, The: (various years)
Aubrey's Brief Lives: edited by Oliver Lawson Dick.
    London: Secker & Warburg, 1949.
Bicknell, A.: The History of Edward, Prince of Wales.
    London: J. Blew, 1776.
Birch, Thomas (compiled by): The Court of James
    the First. London: H. Coburn, 1848.
────── The Life of Henry, Prince of Wales. London:
    A. Millar, 1760.
Bowle, John: Henry VIII. London: George Allen
    & Unwin, 1964.
Bowling, W. G.: The Wild Prince Hal in Legend &
    Literature (reprinted from Washington
    University Studies, Vol. XIII), 1926.
Bryant, Arthur: The Age of Chivalry. London: Collins,
    1963.
────── The Age of Elegance (1812–22). London: Col-
    lins, 1950.
Calendar of Clarendon State Papers, Vol. 11.
Cammidge, John: The Black Prince. London: Eyre
    & Spottiswoode, 1943.
Chandos, The Herald of Sir John Chandos: Life of

the Black Prince, edited by Mildred K. Pope & Eleanor C. Lodge. Oxford: Clarendon Press, 1910.

Chapman, Hester W.: The Tragedy of Charles II in the Years 1630–1660. London: Jonathan Cape, 1964.

Chronicles of the White Rose of York (The Reign of Edward IV). London: J. Bohn, 1845.

Claremont, Francesca: Catherine of Aragon. London: R. Hale, 1939.

Cook, E. Thorton: Kings in the Making. London: John Murray, 1931.

Cornwallis, Sir Charles: The Life and Character of Henry Frederick, Prince of Wales. London: 1738.

—————— The Life & Death of Our Most Incomparable Heroique Prince, Henry of Wales. London: 1641.

Correspondence of George, Prince of Wales (1770–1812). Edited by A. Aspinal. London: Cassell, 1964.

Coulton, G. G.: Medieval Panorama. Cambridge University Press, 1940.

Cowper, Lady: Diary of Mary Countess Cowper (1714–20), edited by the Hon. C. S. Cowper. London: John Murray, 1864.

Creevey, Thomas: The Creevey Papers. Edited by The Rt. Hon. Sir Herbert Maxwell. London: John Murray, 1903.

Creighton, Louise: Life of Edward the Black Prince. London: Rivington, 1870.

Daily Telegraph . . . . . . December, 1964; January, 1965.

Dewes, Simon: Mrs. Delany. London: Rich & Cowan, 1940.

Dictionary of National Biography.

Dodge, W. P.: Piers Gaveston. London: T. F. Unwin, 1899.

Dodington, George Bubb (Baron Melcombe); Diary of. London: Wilkie & Robinson, 1809.

Doran, Dr.: The Book of the Princes of Wales. London: R. Bentley, 1860.

Dunn-Pattison, R. P.: The Black Prince. London: Methuen, 1910.

Encyclopaedia Britannica

English History Review, Vol. XLVIII, 1933: The Eccentricities of Edward II.

Evelyn, John: Diary of. London: Dent & Sons, (Everymans Library) 1936.

Falkland, 1st Viscount: The History of the most Unfortunate Prince, King Edward II. 1680.

Flood, F. S.: The Story of Prince Henry of Monmouth & Chief Justice Gascoigne. London: Longmans, Green & Co., 1886.

Francis, Grant R.: Scotland's Royal Line. London: John Murray, 1928.

Fraser, Maxwell: Wales. (The County Book Series). London: Robert Hales, 1952.

Froissart, Sir John: Chronicles of. Lord Berner's Translation. London: 1892.

Froude, J. A.: History of England. London: (Everymans Library), 1906.

Fulford, Roger: Royal Dukes. London: Duckworth, 1933.

——— George IV. London: Duckworth, 1935.

————— Hanover to Windsor. London: Batsford, 1960.

Gairdner, J.: Henry the Seventh. (From English Statesmen) 1888.

————— The Houses of Lancaster & York. London: Longmans, Green & Co., 1887.

————— Letters & Papers Illustrative of the reigns of Richard III and Henry VIII. London: Longmans, Green & Co., Longman & Roberts, 1861.

Gentleman's Magazine . . . . . . May, 1745.

Graves, Charles: Palace Extraordinary. The Story of St. James's. London: Cassell, 1963.

Green, V. H. H.: The Hanoverians. London: Edward Arnold, 1948.

Greville, Charles Cavendish Fulke: Memoirs of. (1875–87).

Grose, Francis: The Antiquarian Repertory. 1775.

Hall's Chronicles: Edited by H. Ellis. London: 1809.

Harleian Miscellany. (Selections from . . . principally regarding the English History). London: C. & G. Kearsley, 1793.

Harvey, John H.: The Plantagenets (1154–1485). London: Batsford, 1959.

Hervey, Lord: Memoirs of. Edited by Romney Sedgwick. London: Batsford, 1963.

Hervey, Lady: The Letters of Mary Lepel, Lady Hervey. London: 1821.

Holinshed's Chronicles . . . . as used in Shakespeare's Plays. Edited by Professor Allardyce & Josephine Nicoll. London: Dent & Sons.

Holinshed's Chronicles of England, Scotland & Ireland. London: Dent & Sons (Everymans Library) 1927.

Hume, Martin A. S.: Sir Walter Raleigh. London: Fisher Unwin, 1906.

Humphreys, A. R.: The Augustan World. London: Methuen, 1954.

Jacobs, E. F.: The Fifteenth Century (1399–1485). Oxford, Clarendon Press, 1961.

Jesse, J. Heneage: Memoirs of Richard III. London: 1862.
———— Memoirs of the Court of England in the Time of the Stuarts. London: 1840.
———— Memoirs of the Pretenders. London: 1845.

Johnstone, Hilda: Edward of Caernarvon (1284–1307). Manchester: 1947.

Kenyon, J. P.: The Stuarts. London: Batsford, 1958.

Kingsford, C. L.: Henry V, The Typical Medeaval Hero. London: Putnam & Sons, 1901.

KINGSFORD, C. L.: The First English Life of Henry
———— The First English Life of Henry the Fifth. (Written in 1513 by an anonymous author.) Oxford: Clarendon Press, 1911.

Lee, Sir Sidney: King Edward VII. London: Macmillan, 1925.

Lecky, W. E. H.: A History of England in the Eighteenth Century.

Life of Edward the Second: By the so-called Monk of Malmesbury (Translated by N. Denholm-Young). London: Nelson & Sons, 1957.

Lingard, John: A History of England (to the Revolution of 1688). London: Mawman, 1819/30.

Lloyd, Sir John Edward: A History of Wales. London: Longmans, Green & Co., 1948.

Luder, Alexander: Character of Henry the Fifth. London: Cadell & Davies, 1813.

Macaulay, Lord: The History of England. London: Dent & Sons (Everymans Library) 1953.

Magnus, Sir Philip: Life of Edward VII. London: John Murray, 1964.

Mattingley, Garrett: Catherine of Aragon. London: Jonathan Cape, 1942.

McCarthy, Justin & Justin Huntly: A History of the Four Georges & William IV. London: Chatto & Windus, 1901.

McKisack, May: The Fourteenth Century (1307–99). Oxford: Clarendon Press, 1959.

More, Sir Thomas: History of Richard III. London: 1513.

Moore, Dr. N.: On the Illness & Death of Henry, Prince of Wales. London: Adlard, 1882.

Morrah, Dermot (Arundel Herald Extraordinary): Letter to the *Daily Telegraph,* January 19, 1965.

Nicholson, Sir Harold: King George V. London: Constable, 1952.

Original Letters Illustrative of English History. Series 1, Vol. III. London: Harding, Triphook and Lepard, 1824.

Paston Letters, The: Edited by J. Gairdner. London: Constable, 1900.

Peck, Francis: Desiderata Curiosa. London: Thomas Evans, 1779.

Perdita (Mary Robinson): Memoirs of. London: Lister, 1784.

Petrie, Sir Charles: The Four Georges. London: Eyre & Spottiswoode, 1935.

———— The Stuarts. London: Eyre & Spottiswoode, 1958.

Powicke, Sir Maurice F.: The Thirteenth Century (1216–1307). Oxford: Clarendon Press, 1953.

—————— King Henry III & the Lord Edward. Oxford: Clarendon Press, 1947.

Queen Victoria: Letters of (1837–1861). Edited by A. C. Benson & Viscount Esher. London: John Murray, 1907.

Raleigh, Sir Walter: History of the World. 1634. London.

Ramsay, Sir James: Lancaster & York. Oxford: Clarendon Press, 1892.

Redman, Alvin: The House of Hanover. London: Alvin Redman Ltd., 1935.

Robertson, Sir Charles Grant: England Under the Hanoverians. London: Methuen, 1911.

Royal Letter Book, The: Edited by Herbert van Thal. London: Cresset Press, 1937.

Salmon, Mary: Source Book of Welsh History. London: Oxford University Press, 1927.

Selden, John: Titles of Honour. London: Printed by E. Tyler, 1672.

State Papers Domestic (various reigns).

Steeholm, Clara & Hardy: James I of England. London: Michael Joseph, 1938.

Steinberg, S. H.: (editor of) A New Dictionary of British History. London: Edward Arnold, 1963.

Stow, John: A Survey of London. London: Dent & Sons (Everymans Library), 1956.

—————— Annales or A General Chronicle of England. London: 1605.

Strickland, Agnes: Lives of the Queens of England. London: H. Colburn, 1847.

Stuart, Dorothy Margaret: The Daughters of George III. London: Macmillan, 1939.

Stubbs, W.: The Early Plantagenets. London: 1876.

Thackeray, W. M.: The Four Georges. London: Smith Elder, 1885.

Thornley, Isobel D.: England Under the Yorkists (1460–1485). London: Longmans, Green & Co., 1920.

The Times . . . . December 1964; January 1965.

Tout, T. F.: The Place of Edward II in English History. (Revised by Hilda Johnstone). Publication of the University of Manchester, 1936.

———— History of England (1216–1377). London, 1920.

Trevelyan, G. M.: England Under the Stuarts. London: Methuen, 1947.

Walpole, Horace: Memoirs of the Reign of George the Second. London: H. Coburn, 1847.

———— Journal of the Reign of George the Third. Edited by Dr. Doran. London: 1859.

———— Reminiscences. Oxford: Clarendon Press, 1924.

———— Walpoliana. Edited by J. Pinkerton. London: 1819.

Windsor, H. R. H. The Duke of: The Memoirs of—A King's Story. London: Cassell, 1951.

Wraxall, Sir Nathaniel W.: Posthumous Memoirs of His Own Time. London: R. Bentley, 1836.

Index

Raleigh, Walter, 134, 137, 140, 141
Reginald of Leygrave, 26
Renaissance, 99
Renfrew, Baron and Knight of, 135, 220, 230
Reynolds, Joshua, 198
Rhodri Mawr, 2
Rhuddlan Castle, 9, 10
Richard II. *See* Richard of Bordeaux
Richard III. *See* Richard, Duke of Gloucester
Richard, Duke of Gloucester (Richard III), 16, 17, 18, 19, 20, 24, 84, 85, 89, 90–93
  coronation of, 91, 93
  marriage of, 85, 93
  son of, 13, 93–95
  See also Edward of Middleham
Richard, Duke of York (father of Edward IV), 80–81, 91
Richard, Duke of York (son of Edward IV), 89–90, 91, 92, 94, 98
Richard of Bordeaux (Richard II), 13, 17, 57, 58, 59, 60–66, 122
  betrothals of, 62, 65
  birth of, 61,
  burial of, 77
  character of, 63–64
  conflict with Bolingbroke, 64, 66, 67, 69, 70
  coronation of, 66
  cousin of (Henry IV), 67
  death of, 21, 66
  deposition of, 66
  education of, 45
  in Ireland, 70
  marriage of, 18, 64
  relations with father, 63, 64
  relations with Henry of Monmouth, 64, 69
Richard Plantagenet (father of Edward IV), 80–81, 91
Richmond, Earls of, 90, 95, 96
Richmond, Edward of. *See* Edward Albert Christian
Richmond, England, 122, 135, 139, 140, 157, 158, 162, 179, 210, 226, 227
Rivers, Earl, 86, 87, 88, 89
Robinson, Mary, 204
Rochester, Bishop of, 86

Roses, Wars of, 19–20, 24–25, 67, 79, 80, 84, 95, 98
Ross, Earl of, 143
Rothesay, Duke of, 135, 230
Roundheads, 159, 160, 164
Royal Marriage Act, 207
Royal Stuart Society in London, 153
Royalists, 160

St. Andrew's Church, Bordeaux, 62
St. Germain, France, 161, 167
St. James Palace, 133, 140, 141, 154, 155, 157, 171, 177, 178, 180, 185, 188, 189, 192, 193, 194, 200, 201, 203, 218
  See also Charles of St. James's; George August Frederick; James Francis Edward
St. James Park, 201
St. Paul's Cathedral, London, 109, 152
St. Stephen's Chapel, Westminster, 90
Salem, Germany, 232
Salisbury, Earl of, 55, 93
Sandringham, Norfolk, 222, 224, 226
Santiago, Archbishop of, 107
Sarah, Duchess of Marlborough, 185
Savoy, Duke of, 139
Saxe-Coburg, 210
Saxe-Coburg-Gotha, 218, 227
Saxe-Gotha, 184
Saxe-Meiningen, 214
Schulenberg, Fräulein von, 172
Scilly Isles, 160
Scone, Palace of, 164
Scotland
  Edward of Westminster in, 81, 82
  Great Steward of, 135, 231
  relations with England, 30, 31, 34, 38, 39, 44, 71, 161, 163–164
  rulers from, 79
  rulers of, 128
  titles in, 135
Selwyn, George, 205
Settlement, Act of, 167, 170, 207
Seymour, Jane, 16, 79, 228
Shakespeare, 72, 73, 76
Sheen, palace of, 18, 122–123
Shore, Jane, 91
Shrewsbury, Wales, 72
Sicily and Jerusalem, king of, 79
Sidney, Algernon, 163